MIRROR MIRROR

Identity, Race and Protest in
Jamaica

MIRROR MIRROR

Identity, Race and Protest in Jamaica

Rex Nettleford

William Collins
and Sangster (Jamaica) Ltd

2nd Impression, 1972
© Rex Nettleford, 1970

ISBN 0 00 390005 3

Printed in Great Britain Collins Clear-Type Press

Contents

PREFACE

THE DECADE of the nineteen sixties will probably be in time recorded as one of the most troublous periods of Jamaica's contemporary history. The essays in this volume are some reflections on the times. They are not exhaustive of the anxiety, uncertainties or self-doubt that mark the decade but they seek to record and interpret certain important aspects of the young nation's major dilemma mirrored in the trinity of identity, race and protest.

It is hoped that these essays will stimulate discussion among Jamaicans who must find the solutions for themselves if they at all care about the future of their country as well as for the wider and more universal aspects of the human condition commonly identified with equality, self-respect and human dignity. This is not a recommendation for a young self-conscious people to engage narcissistically in a sickly contemplation of its navel. Nor is it intended to indulge typical colonial attitudes of self-hate and a perpetuation of the belief that nothing good can be achieved by us as a people. Rather, these essays imply an invitation for the Jamaican readership to turn its mind critically to its own society, and better still to do so with a sense of adventure and originality as well as with a respect for our history and the contemporary condition, even if it means a defiance of the anti-intellectual tradition which has informed the Jamaican pragmatic approach to social and political life. The adventure and originality need not be the monopoly of 'wayward' cultists, of iconoclastic young members of the educated classes, or of artists painting, writing and dancing out the so-called special experiences of the society. The established (and not so established) disciplines like history, sociology, politics, economics, anthropology and psychology are in fact indispensable aids to analysis and criticism either severally or in their diverse combinations. Yet one should hope that in the exercise 'social laws' which are hardly applicable will not be enforced without due regard for the phenomena which are the Jamaican experience.

It is part of the tradition of West Indian social analysis that what ordinary people think and do seldom form the substance

9

of one's own history or cultural perspective. The events of the sixties seem to defy this tradition. Perhaps this has been so because of the absence of an imperial master and the society's maturing concern for itself and for its present condition. The dynamic of the decade of Independence has turned on confrontations from the lowliest in the society – on the attitudes, assumptions and aspirations of the men in the street, the women in the market place, the disinherited inhabiting the slums, the alienated on the fringes of the society in addition to those of the identifiable members of the status quo, professionals, journalists, trade unionists, management personnel and of course the politicians, elected and otherwise. These assumptions, aspirations, attitudes, are by their nature difficult to quantify and measure. Yet they possess no less the force of facts. As elsewhere Jamaica suffers from the inadequacies of the scientific tradition which has offered satisfactory indicators for the gross national product and for unemployment but cannot accurately gauge the irrational intangibles which determine many aspirations and feed the moods of protest. Jamaica's economic statistical data are very respectable as tabulated: objectively they even spell progress.[1] But the underlying problems retain a cogency which renders these very statistical successes all but useless. Decision-taking about our national affairs is seldom the result of measurable aggregates and when earnest scholars attempt to bring the fruits of American behavioural science to bear on the Jamaican experience,[2] the results do not always take us very much farther along the road to understanding ourselves. This is not to discredit the beliefs which people from time to time think they have of themselves for such beliefs help to shape their reality.

Such are the beliefs which inform the trinity of identity, race and protest, three critical variables closely interacting in the social equation of contemporary Jamaica. Notions of national identity centred for a long time on the fight for self-government and the liberation of the island of Jamaica from metropolitan overlordship by way of transfer of power in the shape of progressive control of inherited political institutions by the native population. But once this phase of the 'struggle' was won, the question of national identity shifted to definitions about *who* comprised the 'native population' and, by implication, *what* constituted the 'nativeness' of the society. If the question remained in a kind of stable disequilibrium for nearly a generation, it was to emerge in all its disruptive dimensions during the sixties. And it emerged as a full assertion by the blacks who form the numerical majority but who have retained the status of a cultural minority with the added burden of economic deprivation. This is the well-known 'class/colour correlation' factor about which sociologists of the plantation society have frequently written. So it is not simply the 'masses', but the *black* masses, who are poor while those who are rich and privileged are largely of a different racial ancestry (usually Caucasian). In Jamaica, then, the obverse to the American situation may be said to be the case. For if in the contemporary United States racial tension can be said to be a prime reason why poverty has become a major issue,[3] in Jamaica *poverty* has been a major reason why race-and-colour (long thought to be dead in social considerations) has become a primary issue.

Even now some readers will object to the view that race-and-colour has been a major issue in Jamaican social life; and others while conceding the existence of a problem will prefer to label it a *class* problem rather than a race one. Depending on one's own definitions the objection could indeed be easily sustained. For terms such as 'white', 'black', 'negro', 'Chinese', etc. if used as straightforward biological descriptions would render Jamaica free from race prejudice or a race problem. Even where they are not so dispassionately used, Jamaica could boast with some justification of the virtual disappearance of discrimination on the basis of race. It would indeed be simplistic to assert that people in Jamaica are excluded from jobs or from status and recognition on the 'sole ground that they are black'. But the problem inheres in the fact that people are not black solely on grounds of their colour. Such terms as 'black' and 'white' still carry values of one sort or another tying the concept of race to a compound of variables ranging from place of origin and levels of cultural achievement to the occupations held by ancestors and the level of economic wealth and educational attainment. It makes sense, then, that much that emerged as protest against poverty in the sixties should have been expressed in terms of the call for a better life for the black man inside or outside of Jamaica. It makes further sense that the early socialism of the self-government party, the People's National Party, and the 'labourism' of the Jamaica Labour Party should be seen by many as mere *noms-de-plume* for black mass betterment. It follows then, that national identity is also seen in terms of this and anything else is easily portrayed as a betrayal, giving rise to uneasiness and to grave doubts among the black populace as to the capacity of the two-party system and related self-governing institutions to cope with the Jamaican predicament.

It would appear that as early as 1960 at least one group from among the black masses felt that neither the socialists nor the labourists had created a society which identified with the interests of the (black) masses. The most extreme reaction along these lines expressed itself in Rastafarian utopianism which was then regarded by most Jamaicans as nothing more than a bizarre aberration or at best an inverted version of an intolerable 'racialism'. The developments later in the sixties were to demonstrate how erroneous this assessment was. The essay 'African Redemption: The Rastafari and the Wider Society 1959–1969' attempts to look at this aspect through an examination of the cult's relationship with the wider society. The Rastafari were the first in the new Jamaica to question the society's identity in terms of its racial and cultural antecedents and did so on the basis of open confrontation which was to become the feature of protest everywhere during the sixties. The rejection of the Jamaican perception of itself as an extension of Europe at the expense of black roots heralded new and significant developments in the sixties which have since made Jamaica more conscious of its black masses rather than simply of its masses. Identification with Africa was to become a symbol of strategy not only for protesting millenarian cultists in search of identity and acceptance but also for a power structure seeking to contain the moods of protest and to save Jamaica from the chaos that usually attends a state of frustration and despair.[4] Where leaders at the beginning of the decade could make appeals to the multi-racial ethic, real or imagined, those at the end of the decade are called upon to identify more positively and demonstrate that the seventies at least will rid the black majority of its sense of powerlessness and hereditary degradation. Such was the relevance of the Jamaican Black Power group who, though they embraced a slogan that hardly served them well, kept up the sounds and pressure against the social ills of the society and sought redemption not in Africa but in Jamacia. For them, the society instead of being rejected, must be controlled, by the black majority. The confusion they brought into existing thought patterns forced established centres of power to define more clearly, if not to rethink their own positions. Moreover, the general concern for poverty has probably deepened more now than earlier in the sixties.

However, suggestions of racial exclusivity and claims to black 'superiority' have found effective opposition from the national commitment to non-racialism and the Jamaican dislike for racism. The essay on 'Jamaican Black Power – Notes from the Horn' (based on lectures given throughout late 1968 and early 1969) discusses some of the problems. The Black Power group in Jamaica followed consciously on the bold assertion of the black renaissance in the United States just as Rastafarian activism and the assertion of Afro-West Indian associations in 1959 and 1960 followed on the independence of Ghana and the escalation of the independence movements throughout black Africa at that time. It is interesting to observe the reactions of the national leadership to both developments at either end of the decade.

In 1960, Amy Jacques Garvey, the wife of the black visionary was reported as saying, 'as black men and women, you must stand up and claim your country, dedicate your lives to Jamaica, acquire the economic stability the 90 per cent of the population should have in relation to the 30,000 Chinese here'. The then

Opposition leader, Alexander Bustamante, denounced this as 'racialism' which he saw as 'a menace to our future'.[5] The appeal to multi-racial Jamaicanism was then invoked and a call made to the leader of Government to declare against the 'cancer of racialism'. This provoked a spirited reply from the Council on Afro-West Indian Affairs, pointing out that 'there has never been the faintest suggestion of suppressing racial movements and organisations by Jews, Syrians, Chinese, Indians, etc. in Jamaica'.[6] While itself declaring for a multi-racial Jamaica and against all forms of racial discrimination, the Council explained its objectives to raise the black Jamaican from a level of traditional servitude in a society in which he is numerically dominant. In addition, the Council saw the maximization of foreign investment in the interest of the Jamaican majority as one such means of attaining its goal. Premier Norman Manley in a statement which followed, did admit that 'equality as a socialist understands it is not fully won' though 'the doors of opportunity are opening one by one'.[7] He did, however, deplore the 'movements . . . being formed, dedicated to the destruction of the very idea of inter-racial harmony'. At the end of the decade, in 1969, it was as though nothing had changed. The protests on behalf of the black majority were mere refrains of the 1960 Rastafarian and Afro-West Indian outcries. Significantly, the responses from the leadership speaking from an orthodox position were similar in their insistence that the society is a multi-racial unit – if not in fact, then certainly with the capacity of becoming so in the foreseeable future.

There are of course validating conditions that render multi-racialism a possibility in Jamaica but these are often mistaken for the fact of harmony. Objective factors of history and the play of external forces on internal weaknesses in Jamaican society frequently thwart (and in cases even make a mockery of) the multi-racial ethic. The essay entitled 'The Melody of Europe, the Rhythm of Africa (But Every John Crow tink Him Pickney White)' attempts to discuss the problems of multi-racialism in terms of some of the inherent contradictions of the society. Here, it is important to note, the predicament ceases to be primarily that of the black Jamaican. The white Jamaican, hankering after Europe or seeking to maintain a Jamaican value-system (which recognizes the black creole but invests him with a role inferior to that of his white creole or brown counterpart) may be just as alienated as his now aware and newly assertive black compatriot. The Afro-European Jamaican, long the target of attacks from either side, may find it easy to identify with whichever racial group finds itself in the ascendance but his dilemma of a schizophrenic existence remains and becomes more acute when he indulges the mixed-blood ideal over and above the African majority. The predicament is also that of the newer Jamaicans – descendants of indentured Asians, and the still more recent fortune-seeking migrants like the Lebanese (Syrians) for they must forge for themselves pathways through the criss-cross of the Euro-African, rich-poor, black-white-brown, urban-rural, literate-illiterate contradictions in the Jamaican complex.

Who then are Jamaicans? The essay immediately following this preface addresses itself to just this question and, by way of introduction, sets the backdrop for the essays which follow it. Entitled 'National Identity and Attitudes Towards Race in Jamaica', it was first delivered as a lecture in the mid-sixties when vital Sunday morning discussions arranged by the University of the West Indies (UWI) Extra-Mural Department on social and political affairs revealed a widespread need for social self-examination among the Jamaican citizenry. The essay later appeared in the July 1965 issue of *Race*, the journal of the London Institute of Race Relations and soon after in the *Caribbean Contemporary Studies* series of Bolivar Press, Kingston. Subsequently, it was reproduced in serialized form in the *Daily Gleaner*, the Jamaican newspaper. To the editors of all three I wish to express my thanks and appreciation for their interest. My thanks, too, to colleagues at the University of the West Indies who have given useful advice from time to time in discussions on some of the views expressed in this volume – especially Drs. M. G. Smith and Roy Augier from whom I learnt a great deal while collaborating in 1960 on the short survey into the Rastafari movement. I also owe acknowledgement to those extra-mural adult groups, trade union leaders and management personnel who have provided spirited debate in lecture discussions in several sessions conducted over the years. Their experience has always contributed to the sharpening of insights on some of the topics discussed on the following pages. Actual direct sources are duly acknowledged at appropriate points in the text. My further thanks, too, to Mrs. Mildred Brooks, Mrs. Gloria Burke and Mrs. Doreen Barrow for typing manuscripts in the painstaking manner demanded of them and to Mr. S. A. Smith who helped in the correction of the drafts as well as Messrs. Michael Henry and Ferdie Sangster whose interest and encouragement throughout helped to make this volume possible.

University of the West Indies,
Kingston, Jamaica

NATIONAL IDENTITY AND ATTITUDES TO RACE IN JAMAICA

An Introduction

M.M.

B

THE NEED for roots and the attendant quest for identity are said to be natural to peoples everywhere. The phenomenon may be said to inhere in a people's desire to collate and codify their past collective experience as well as to lay foundations for the realization of future aspirations. New nations usually give large portions of their creative energy to what may be termed the 'identity problem' and the mid-twentieth century with its flux of emergent countries in Africa, Asia and the Caribbean is particularly noted for this aspect of nation-building. In Jamaica, a Caribbean country which attained independence from Great Britain in August, 1962, the search for identity has been the focus of attention for some time. It is indeed difficult to determine what exactly is meant by the term 'the Jamaican identity'.[1] It is variously expressed as 'things Jamaican' or 'the Jamaican image'.*

There are, however, ways of approaching the problem. The question 'What *are* we?' entails the desire of 'What we *want* to be'. And if what we want to be is to have any practical significance for Jamaica, there should be some concordance between the *external conception* of the island's almost two million people on the one hand, and Jamaicans' own *internal perception* of themselves as a national entity on the other.†

---

* After 307 years as a British colony, Jamaica gained her independence on August 6, 1962. A strong Jamaican nationalism had shown itself from the thirties, when labour disturbances and middle-class clamour for self-government characterized the political scene. But from the late forties there was a slight shift of emphasis to West Indianism in the plans for a Federation of the British West Indies which was actually established in 1958. Jamaica withdrew in 1961 by referendum from the Federation and decided to 'go it alone'. Since then the 'Jamaican image' has become a positive goal for different efforts in the country.

† This approach is suggested by a paper presented in the UWI Extra-Mural Sunday morning lecture series, and entitled 'Our National Identity and Behaviour Patterns' by Professor M. G. Smith of the University of California (UCLA). See Lectures on Jamaican National Identity, Radio Education Unit (REU), UWI. This essay first appeared in *Race* (Vol. VII, No. 1, July, 1965) the Journal of the Institute of Race Relations, London, and was subsequently published by Bolivar Bookshop, Kingston, Jamaica, in 1966.

This is presumably one certain way of being saved from a schizoid state of existence. The postulate seems more reasonable when one remembers that Jamaicans are a people who are constantly exposed to external influences, whose economic system traditionally depends on the caprice of other people's palates, whose values are largely imported from an alien set of experiences, and whose dreams and hopes have, at one time or another, been rooted either in a neighbouring Panama, Cuba or Costa Rica, in big brother America and sometimes in Canada, a Commonwealth cousin. Of late, they tend to be rooted in father Africa and more so in mother England.* The multi-focal nature of Jamaican life and history is often said to be the greatest obstacle to a real national identity. And the object of this essay is to relate the resulting quest to Jamaicans' attitudes towards race.

There are obvious difficulties in any such task. For one thing, data drawn from attitudes, revealed or scientifically observed, do not usually solve the problem of the transition from attitude to behaviour. For another, there is need for a

---

* This refers to the external influences on Jamaica. As a primary-producing agricultural country, the economy is dependent on the outside market. This is also true of bauxite which is shipped in its raw state or as alumina to North America. Jamaicans have also been a migrating people ever since the late nineteenth century when the first Panama Canal project was started. Between the 1880s and 1920, net emigration from Jamaica amounted to about 146,000— 46,000 went to the U.S.A., 45,000 to Panama, 22,000 to Cuba (to work in sugar), and other countries like Costa Rica (for railroad building and banana cultivation) drew some 43,000. Some 10,000 went to Britain during the Second World War for war work, while some 48,000 went to the U.S.A. in the Farm Work Scheme. The post-war period saw migration largely to Britain where nearly 200,000 Jamaican first generation now live. Emigration to Africa is the dream of some Jamaicans, who endow their sentimental attachment with religious fervour in the 'Back to Africa' movement. But West Africa has been benefited from the skills of Jamaican and other West Indian migrants who went to Nigeria, Sierra Leone and the old Gold Coast as engineers, teachers, lawyers, civil servants and missionaries. (v. Extra-Mural Sunday Seminar on 'External Relations and the Jamaican Economy', lecture entitled 'Migration—Where Do We Go Next?' by Don Mills, REU, UWI.)

social psychology of West Indian race relations. What is more, race presupposes a biological purity which is difficult to justify. This makes the concept an extremely difficult one with which to work. The fact is that claims to such biological purity are not absent from Jamaican society and these claims have traditionally served to underline, rather boldly, the social stratification, thus making the matter of race more than yeast for the dough. If one assumes that the Jamaican identity must entail a measure of national unity, though not uniformity, among all the differentiated sectors of the society, then one can pose the question of whether the phenomenon of racial consciousness or non-consciousness is an obstacle to national unity. This is the measure of the internal problem. Since race is an important determinant in people's assessment of each other in the outside world, it is of particular relevance to know if what we think of ourselves racially as a nation coincides with what others think of us in this particular. Racial attitudes, especially when they are accompanied by national or individual schizophrenia, are therefore important. The Jamaican Mental Health Association could well do a serious study of the factor of race attitudes in its records of mental illness. Paranoiac experiences sometimes turn on a patient's frustrated aspirations of being 'white'. In this context being 'white' means little more than being privilaged and rich. But the fact remains that even today one is still able to have 'whiteness' connote privilege, position, wealth and, of course, purity which is ingrained in Christian mythology. This attitude is particularly evident among many who form the large majority of the population and who happen to wear that colour of skin long associated with poverty, manual labour, low status and ignorance. The *in-betweenness* and *half-identification* resulting from these attitudes is probably one of the positively distinctive features of Caribbean communities emerging from a plantation and colonial system. It does mark us off from many of the developing countries of Asia and Africa, as can be seen in fundamental differences in attitudes to certain aspects of social and political organization.

For example, it is difficult to find the kind of logic that

would justify the renunciation of the Queen of England, as the head of the Jamaican State, in favour of a 'son of the soil'. Quite apart from the fact that any such suggestion would be confronted with letters of horror from conscientious Jamaican 'monarchists', one would have to ask who are the real sons of the Jamaican soil. Is it Sir Clifford Campbell, Sir John Mordecai, Hubert Tai Tenn Quee, Dr. Varma, Edward Seaga or Bruce Barker?* In fact they are none of them 'sons of the soil' in the sense that Tunku Abdul Rahman is of Malaya, Jomo Kenyatta is of Kenya, Nkrumah was of Ghana or Nehru of India. No Jamaican can seriously make claims to Arawak ancestry.† In a real sense, we are all of us immigrants – most of us of long-standing, but immigrants, nevertheless! We have had to work out ways and means of distributing power internally as a result of our uprootedness. Over the centuries this has been done by a certain amount of piecemeal political engineering. One significant thing about the progressive assumption of civic status is that the people receiving their share of power at the different stages of development came from groups distinguishable largely by their racial origin and were in fact so described. So, if it were the white planters and their managerial aides who first received control of representative government in the late seventeenth century,[2] it was the 'free coloureds' who next shared in the citizenship rights in 1832;[3] and although they both joined with the blacks to

---

* These are names of well-known Jamaicans of different racial origin. Sir Clifford is the Governor-General and of African stock; Sir John is a distinguished civil servant of Afro-European stock; the Tai Tenn Quees are a Chinese family and prominent in the mercantile community; Dr. Varma is an East Indian; Edward Seaga is of Syrian stock, has been Minister of Development and Welfare, and later, Minister of Finance and Planning, in the government which has been in power since independence, and Bruce Barker is of European stock who, from his letters to the press seems to disapprove of the idea of nationalism and is seen by many of his opponents as a representative of traditionalist white upper class Jamaica.

† The Arawaks are the aboriginal peoples of Jamaica.

encourage the takeover of the Constitution by white honest brokers at the Colonial Office after the chaos of 1865,[4] it was the whites and free coloureds whose wealth, influence and social position qualified them for participating in the nominated legislatures of the Crown Colony system. It was not until 1944,[5] following the disturbances of the late thirties, that the blacks who form the vast majority of the populace were given the right to share in the political cake. Despite the potential power of the black vote which followed universal adult suffrage, one still hears that the upper echelons of governments and the centres of influence do not reflect the racial composition of the country. The Queen, despite the way she looks, therefore fits into the landscape as head of state. It is fair to say that she is generally preferred to a black President, though a black representative of the Queen manages to hit a very comfortable medium. The feature makes Jamaica an autonomous Commonwealth entity resembling Canada, Australia and New Zealand inhabited by Britons overseas, more than Ghana, India, Nigeria, Malaya or Tanzania which are autochthonous entities. Jamaicans have earned the name, understandably, of 'Afro-Saxons' among some Africans at the United Nations.

Jamaica's apparently peculiar position is usually explained along lines somewhat like this: 'We are neither Africans though we are most of us black, nor are we Anglo-Saxon though some of us would have others to believe this. We are *Jamaicans*! And what does this mean? We are a mixture of races living in perfect harmony and as such provide a useful lesson to a world torn apart by race prejudice.' The harmony based on tolerance is the thing which is supposed to make Jamaicans distinct from such countries as Rhodesia, South Africa, and parts of the United States of America. In other words, Jamaica is a non-racial nation and non-racialism, besides being a distinctive feature, is an essence of the Jamaican identity. Jamaican leaders make non-racialism into an important national symbol by declaring at home and abroad that Jamaica and the West Indies are 'made up of peoples drawn from all over the world, predominantly Negro or of mixed blood, but also with large numbers of others, and nowhere in the world has more progress been made in developing a non-racial society in which also colour is not psychologically significant'.[6] This was a report of a speech made by a prominent Jamaican leader in April, 1961, to an American audience. It was, therefore, somewhat reassuring to read subsequently in a Jamaican newspaper that the Jamaican Government had admitted to the Secretary General of the United Nations that 'racial discrimination has yet to be entirely eliminated from the island'.[7] The Report was, however, soon marred by the assertion that any problem of racial discrimination still existing in Jamaica was due in part to the fact that Jamaica was a small country which received large numbers of visitors from abroad and that some 'of these visitors bring with them prejudices they acquired in societies less tolerant than Jamaica's'.[8] This betrays a somewhat smug pride in what is assumed to be tolerance and we still look outside of ourselves for the foreign bogey which should take some, if not all, of the blame. One has cause to wonder how it is that visitors find it so easy to practise discrimination when they visit Jamaica. The question could be asked whether there is a cradle ready and waiting to receive the bad seed? Or, is it that there are certain visitors who believe in the old injunction – when in Rome, do as the Romans do.

With a bit of charity one could assert that the tendency of Jamaicans to deny their own shortcomings in the matter may indeed stem from a genuine desire to free our national unity and identity of a disruptive racial differentiation. The motto is almost daily invoked in sermons – secular and religious – to make into a fact what is as yet an aspiration.* Unfortunately, it is the 'many' in the motto and not the 'one' which tends to get the emphasis. So against a background of unemployment, and disparities of economic wealth and educational opportunities, the 'many' too often connotes a differentiation according to how people look. In the minds of many Jamaicans, it is still a poor-black, a middle-class and privileged brown man,

---

* The national motto is 'Out of Many One People'.

and a rich or wealthy white man. This is the traditional colour/class correlation.[9] Chinese and East Indian Jamaicans are marginal to this structure, having come to Jamaica after the classifications were long determined in society. They tend to be assessed by the mass of Jamaicans largely on their economic position rather than on their racial origin. The peasant Indian hardly has significance outside of his membership of the lower class where he marries and still lives and has his being. Significantly, no one makes a mistake about to what section of the society the Bombay merchants and their sari-clad wives belong. The Chinese have grown in stature since the early days when terms like 'Madam' and 'John' expressed attitudes of disrespect or even contempt for the men and women in what has always proved to be a self-contained and restrained minority group. They, the Chinese, chose to stay out of the society as long as they could and now enter it at the top on the basis of their wealth and education. When the commercial banks yielded to pressure to employ Jamaicans of colour the Chinese were among the first to be used to break tradition. They provided a gradual and smooth transition for the more recent developments in those very commercial banks.

Yet both the Indians and the Chinese intermarried, or rather cohabited, with the blacks quite extensively to produce a new group of Jamaicans numbering some thirty-six thousand.[10] This new development bolstered an attitude long evident among the middle-class people of mixed African and European blood. This attitude is expressed in the idealization of mixed blood. As an integrating force in the national life of Brazil this phenomenon has reputedly helped that country to find and project an identity generally accepted at home and abroad. Indeed, it can probably be said that the objective norm in the minds of many Jamaicans (both black and coloured) who choose beauty queens is the hybrid or the miscegenated person.* The trouble with this solution to our race differentia-

---

* Beauty contests are held frequently for the selection of 'queens' from all sections of the community. Traditionally 'Miss Jamaica'

tion problems is that if the hybrid is the norm, then the vast majority of pure blacks must be the aberration. It therefore invests the mixed-blood idealization with a middle-class unction which is unacceptable to the lower-class blacks. The implications are also a source of great irritation to a growing body of middle-class black opinion which insists that, despite the virtues of a mixed-blood ideal in Jamaica, it is the 'African' which is the constant in the racial complex and all other racial strains are variables among the majority of the people.

The 1960 census bears this out by padding the categories into which people are placed. These are African, European, East Indian, Chinese or Japanese, Syrian, Afro-European, Afro-East Indian, Afro-Chinese, and Other (meaning, no doubt, odd admixtures).[11] The prefatory remarks in the provisional report give something of a clue to our racial attitudes. For it declares that it is the 'intention that the first five categories should contain persons who appeared to be racially pure and the following three, various mixtures'. This betrays a certain sensitivity to universally accepted norms which classify races into Caucasoids, Mongoloids and Negroids, usually in that order. But the Jamaican classification betrays also a sensitivity to the realities of the local situation. It not only puts the Negroid group first, it gives a detailed breakdown of groups of persons who in the wider world would be termed simply 'coloured'. The preface further informs us that enumerators were 'instructed to include in the "African" group persons of pure African descent, that is those who were classified as "black" in 1943'.[12] This is a clear indication of the growing refinement in attitudes since the term 'black' had

tended to be either near-white or with coffee-coloured European features and straight ('good') hair. This fact sparked off controversy in the Press from time to time until in 1955 the island's evening newspaper—*The Star*—sponsored a 'Ten Types One People' contest giving the titles to Jamaican women who span the colour spectrum from 'Ebony' (black) through 'Mahogany' (coloured), 'Lotus' and 'Satinwood' (Chinese and East Indian), and 'Pomegranate' (Mediterranean type, Syrian-Jewish), to 'Appleblossom' (Caucasian). The event received wide international Press coverage.

long been considered an epithet of opprobrium in the country and not suitable for use in official circles. It had in a sense changed places with the term 'African' which once meant 'primitive' and 'uncivilized' in the vocabulary of Jamaicans.* The enumerators were also instructed to include in the term 'European' persons usually listed as English, French, Spanish, German etc. Could this mean that attitudes which once marked off the English as a privileged group among whites had changed? It certainly makes for easier census-taking, if nothing else. The same cannot be said, however, of the group that used to be classified 'coloured' in previous censuses. The Jamaican census restricts the term to Afro-European though the outside world would include Afro-Asians as well. Small wonder, then, that the resultant large areas of doubt as to people's descriptions of themselves led the census organizers to omit the racial classification of Jamaicans from the final census reports.

This does not, however, prevent racially conscious black Jamaicans from keeping their eyes glued to the census figures. For although the blacks cannot claim prior discovery of Jamaica (the Jews were here before) nor effective occupation (the economy is still said to be in the hands of the white and half-white groups) they make strong claims for more influence on the basis of their numbers. For of every 100 Jamaicans, 76.8 are of pure African descent, 0.8 are pure European or White, 1.7 are East Indian, 0.6 are Chinese, 0.1 are Syrian, 14.6 are Afro-European, 1.7 are Afro-East Indian, 0.6 are Afro-Chinese and other mixtures add up to 3.1.[14] If we add together all the persons of obvious African descent (pure or mixed) we get some ninety-one persons out of every hundred with the 'tarbrush'. It is this obvious fact which apparently leads to the external conception of Jamaica as a *coloured country* – a conception which does not coincide with the current internal perception which is one described usually in

---

* The Rastafarians had long before declared a preference for the term 'black' to describe themselves though they used it interchangeably with the term 'African'.

terms of *multi-racialism*. Now this implies a number of things. It gives to the hybrid groups a positive racial quality which in terms of external classifications they should not have. There is nothing necessarily wrong with the claim, however, since it further implies a robust and even healthy refusal on the part of some Jamaicans to bow to the rather arbitrary and crude classification of human beings into coloured and white. Such Jamaicans prefer to see the world in terms of greys and 'in-between colours', each shade and hue deserving of its own individual identity. This, taken to its logical conclusion, produces in practice a denial of that half of the racial ancestry which is regarded as inferior and a corresponding exaltation of the other half which happens to be respectable in the sight of the world at this particular time. This comes out in many Jamaicans' attitudes towards Great Britain and the white world in general and to the black world and emergent Africa in particular.

The historical antecedents of slavery, the plantation system, and colonialism which are responsible for this, are too well known for detailed recapitulation. But the conscious choice by some Jamaicans and the projection by those Jamaicans of civilized 'whitedom' over primitive 'blackdom' result from the firmly rooted attitudes of a plantation society of a perfect pyramid with white masters at the apex and black labour at the base. The free coloured buffer between the two extremities developed out of widespread miscegenation and formed a natural middle class. This middle class became the target as well as the expression of all the pressures and psychological problems of a society that depended for its rationale in the long run on theories and attitudes of superiority on the part of a white governing and ruling class over an inferior black labouring group. The free coloureds had to pay for their African taint by suffering indignities in the early stages but they were later to benefit from their European blood-stain through the acquisition of wealth and inheritances and from culture through exposure to tolerably good education both in Jamaica and in England. As the pure white population dwindled, the free coloureds became the heirs to the European position and power and regarded themselves as the rightful sons of the Jamaican soil since they, of all groups in Jamaica, were the ones that came directly out of the peculiar circumstances and conditions of early Jamaican society. After all, the argument seemed to go, the blacks can look to Africa, the whites to England, the Chinese to Formosa or Hong Kong, the Indian to India and the Syrians to Lebanon. But they, the coloureds (*mulatos*), must look to Jamaica.* This 15 per cent of Afro-Europeans form the core of the middle class and persist in attitudes which bolster the motto, reprimand the Rastas for turning the clock back, and indulge in a strange love-hate relationship with the whites of both local and expatriate vintage who threaten their claim to the inheritance from Britain. They regard themselves as the true heirs to the governing class despite their small numbers if only because they were the first to display a capacity to assimilate completely the ideals of the masters. They could be as good as, if not better than, the whites. John Hearne in his essay on 'The European Heritage' discusses this group's striving towards the European image – an effort which was further aided by the system of boarding and grammar schools in which some 'five generations of this new brown ruling middle class learned by rote all the attitudes, patterns of behaviour and values taught to English contemporaries.'[16] These are the people who dominate the trading classes and exert influence in the taking of decisions of national moment.

---

* The problem is succinctly expressed in a Trinidadian calypso which carries the following refrain:

> 'You can send the Indians to India,
> And the Negroes back to Africa,
> But will somebody please tell me,
> Where they sending poor me, poor me?
> I'm neither one nor the other—
> Six of one, half a dozen of the other,
> If they serious 'bout sending back people in tru—
> They're going to have to split me in two.'

'The Mighty *Dougla*' (*Dougla* in Trinidad vernacular means an Afro-Indian).

The assertion by Rastafari cultists* that since 1938 there has been a series of 'brown-man governments' therefore makes sense in the light of Jamaican history.[17] And the further assertion that these people are really white in attitude is merely another way of describing what the sociologists call the 'white bias' in a society with a population of which 76 per cent is black. The incongruity has led Jamaican commentators to declare that Jamaica will never know what she really is until she accepts the fact that she is a *black country* and projects a black personality. This is a counter-claim to the unspoken but eloquent claim by the brown middle classes that the Jamaican image should root itself in that group of Jamaicans to which they belong since they are the very embodiment of the tensions set up by the counterpoint relationships in the twin heritage from Europe and Africa. A well-known Jamaican journalist and political commentator once said that 'the most obvious bar to integration of our society is the white bias that assaults and degrades the sense of self-respect of the vast majority of the Jamaican people. If everything worthwhile is to be associated with white – goodness, beauty, even God – and if the society as a whole accepts these standards without question, then you are condemning the non-white groups in our society to a permanent and perpetual inferiority since they are inexorably outside the pale of whiteness.'[18]

This plea for a fundamental change will have to be seen in a wider context. The Jamaican's conception of his own racial rank is going to be determined partly by the conception of racial segmentation in the world at large. It is significant that with the rise of black Africa, greater confidence has developed

---

* The 'Rastafari' are a Jamaican millenarian cult whose doctrines of social rejection postulate a promised land in Africa in general (and Ethiopia in particular) where their earthly deliverer and leader Haile Selassie lives. They see repatriation as an ultimate necessity since there is no hope for them in Jamaica from which they are alienated. (See M. G. Smith, Roy Augier and Rex Nettleford, *The Rastafari in Kingston, Jamaica*, ISER, UCWI, Mona, Jamaica, 1960.)

among the black people of the society. And many a black middle-class professional need no longer carry around with him a protective hostility to the group he has left behind. He can even marry a black woman of class and thus save her from life-long spinsterhood in the confines of the teaching, social welfare or nursing professions which Professor Fernando Henriques once observed to be havens of black unmarryable spinsters.[19] Many Afro-Europeans of the middle class are even now discovering the beauty of the blacks among them and there are now several places in the sun for Jamaican young women of all shades through the fetish of the beauty contest. These have even received Ministerial blessing. Such harmless terms as 'bad hair' and 'good hair', meaning African kink and European straight respectively, are still being used and one can still hazard the guess that certain mothers will prefer a white Glasgow carpenter to a Jamaican flag-black civil servant for their daughter.* The latter alternative might just mean hardships for everybody concerned. In 1964, the *Daily Gleaner*, Jamaica's only daily newspaper, could carry without fear of contradiction a leader, the first paragraph of which read: 'Many people in Jamaica still boast that they have never entertained a negroid person in their homes. They do not say it openly but that is their boast nevertheless. Every change in our society that has enabled the people really to live like the nation's motto is pain and distress and "disaster" to them'.[20] A letter to the editor published subsequently commented on the inconsistency between the view and what is often proclaimed as the island's attainment of racial harmony.[21]

If we look at the expressed attitudes of people on the Jamaican Government's plans to make a national hero out of the late Marcus Garvey, we find the anxieties and emotionalism that

---

* 'Flag-black' alludes to the symbolism behind the colours in the Jamaican flag, which are green, gold and black. The black symbolizes 'hardships' and this was criticized as a further example of Jamaican attitudes to that colour. Significantly, the argument sometimes ran, the black in the Trinidad flag symbolizes strength.

exist among many Jamaicans on the matter of race.* It is more than coincidental that it should be a white Jamaican who took the trouble to chronicle the misdemeanours which Garvey reputedly committed during his lifetime.[22] One could indeed have predicted the sharpness of the replies in the Press. They all expressed people's belief in the importance of African consciousness in Jamaican development. Here is a typical argument against the fuss that was made over Garvey: it is in a letter to the *Daily Gleaner*: 'Certainly, transporting of Negroes from America to Africa does not in the least affect the welfare of Jamaica. To my way of thinking we do not have in Jamaica any Negroes, Chinese, Syrians or English; we have Jamaicans and certainly if we are to spend thousands of pounds on a monument to honour someone, let it be spent to honour a Jamaican who has contributed tangibly to the development of the nation.'[23] This was doubtless written with the best intentions, but this may well be mistaking a wish for the facts!

---

* Marcus Garvey is to some African and American negro leaders the greatest 'black prophet and visionary' since negro emancipation. His 'Back-to-Africa' movement won enormous support from some six million American negroes in the early 1920s, and his advocacy of the dignity of the black man and his rightful place in the world made him a *bête noir* to European rulers at the time. His Universal Negro Improvement Association (UNIA) was designed as a 'social, friendly, humanitarian, charitable, educational, institutional, constructive and expansive society' founded for the general uplift of the negro all over the world. He was convinced that given the time, opportunity and self-confidence, the negro could equal the whites in all the latter's intellectual, cultural and technological attainments. He even set up a provisional Government of Africa complete with himself as President and a court of titled men and women. Bad business management put paid to the scheme. His involvement in Jamaican local government politics was not successful and he went to England, where he died in 1940. His remains were brought back to Jamaica in 1965 and placed in a shrine as Jamaica's first National Hero. (See G. Padmore, *Pan Africanism or Communism*, London, Dobson, 1956, pp. 22 ff.; Marcus Garvey, *Philosophy and Opinions*; *Declaration of Aims of the U.N.I.A.* at the Convention, August 1, 1920; Amy Jacques Garvey, *Garvey and Garveyism*, Kingston, 1963; D. Cronon, *Black Moses*, University of Wisconsin Press, 1955.)

There are indeed all the racial groups which the writers claimed not to exist. There are people 'negro' enough to feel a sense of personal affront when reports of discriminatory acts against a black American college student are reported in the local press. There can hardly be any difficulties of identification. There are people 'Syrian' enough to want to return to Lebanon for a spouse. The bond among the Chinese of Jamaica may be said to be a racial Chinese one and not a sophisticated *Jamaican* one. And there are 'English' or white people who are English or white enough to want to help out people who look like themselves when it comes to the matter of a job. Whether this kind of differentiation is strong enough to rend the society apart is doubtful outside the framework of purely private individual relationships. But this is where the shoe pinches, and a localized pain can affect the entire body. The scores of letters from middle-class citizens clearly indicated further that Garvey's championing of the dignity and self-respect of the black man is a very tangible contribution to the development of a nation which is 91 per cent of African descent.

Yet for all Garvey's work, one might say that attitudes among the black-skinned masses still exist which betray a self-contempt and a lack of self-confidence. Herein lies the greatest danger to attempts at finding an identity in terms of race. For a people who do not believe in themselves cannot hope to have others believing in them. The insecurities of this important racial grouping persist with a vengeance. A poor peasant is indeed glad to have her children rise above the peasantry, marry brown, and forget the roots. A bright young university graduate must suffer praise for a barely tolerably competent speech because of no other reason than he 'use the white people dem word good good'. People like the Rastafari and their neighbours in West Kingston are still convinced that there is some dark conspiracy to keep 'black people down' and although Millard Johnson's coarse *negritude** was rejected

---

* Millard Johnson, a Jamaican barrister, attempted to base his campaign on racism by invoking the name of Garvey during the 1962 (April) General Elections. His People's Progressive Party (PPP)

the leadership of two bona fide political parties are sometimes identified with the brown middle-class. A maid insists that she would never work 'for black people'; and well she might not, for the bad treatment meted out to servants by coloured and black middle-class housewives is usually a topic for conversation among some visitors to the island. A watchman in a private compound coldly informs a black-skinned university student that he cannot proceed on the compound for the authorities have instructed him (the watchman) not to let 'any black people pass there after six o'clock'. A black doctor goes into stores in Kingston and fails to receive the civil attention due to every citizen until he pulls rank and invokes his status. A worker in an industrial plant finds it impossible to have any interest in the plant because 'there's no hope for the black man' and he resents the black supervisor in authority. The black supervisor in turn abuses his unaccustomed power in dealing with his own and toadies to the white boss. A young black woman destroys a photographic print of herself because it is printed too black; and an older black woman insists that she is giving her vote to a white candidate 'for no black man can help me in this yah country these days'. The examples just cited are based on actual occurrences and betray an interesting ambivalence on the part of these people in their attitudes to race. They also betray a signal lack of self-confidence.

This happens to coincide with coloured and near-white Jamaican group-attitudes towards the blacks. So when a black-skinned official replaces the white official at the old colonial governor's mansion some middle-class verandahs sigh sighs of disapproval and even apprehension. The Afro-European middle classes seem to be fighting on two fronts. For they are beginning to experience competition from a growing group of newer white expatriates who are felt to be without caste since they speak with the wrong accents and betray no sensitivity

polled 12,616 votes with no seats while the People's National Party (PNP) now in opposition polled 279,771 votes and the ruling party, the Jamaica Labour Party (JLP) polled 288,130 votes out of a total of 580,517 votes cast (i.e. 72.88 per cent of registered voters).

for the finer things.[24] The trouble is that these people come in and take their traditional place of privilege in the white bias structure. They drink in the right bars and hotels and even get into the right kind of brawls. The coloured middle class resent their pretensions and even object to their own children 'picking up cockney intonations from certain expatriate children'.* It might very well turn out that the coloured middle class will be the ones to find greatest satisfaction in the new act designed to limit the employment of expatriates.† The resentment of the Jamaican blacks to this group of people and indeed to white visitors in places like hotels may very well be an extension of their dislike for the Jamaican high browns who have long been the symbols of wealth, influence and privilege in the society.

The important thing about all this is that the black-skinned Jamaican senses that he must compete on the same ground as his brown, Chinese and white compatriots. In many a case he has to work twice as hard because of the handicap of being years at the base of the social pyramid. Psychologically, he does not possess such a strong racial memory of great cultural achievements as these European, Chinese and Indian compatriots. The Africans, of all the groups which came to the New World, came as individuals and not as part of a group which maintained identity through some great religion, or activity through age-old recognizable customs. The obvious answer for the African or black Jamaican is to sink his racial consciousness in the wider, greater aspirations to acquire education and other means of making himself economically viable. Of course, if he sees no chance of doing this he is bound to fall back on the religion of race which is the one thing which he will feel makes him distinctive and which is aided and

---

* The view of a coloured Jamaican housewife in an interview with the author.
† The Foreign Nationals and Commonwealth Citizens (Employment) Act, commonly called the Work Permits Act, came into force in Jamaica on April 1, 1965, limiting the employment of aliens only to those jobs which cannot be suitably filled by Jamaicans.

abetted by the rise of black Africa and the increased stature of the black man in the world at large.

It could indeed be argued that there is nothing necessarily wrong with stratification based on racial consciousness *per se*. But there is everything wrong with racial stratification which has no compensatory responsibilities to complement it. In other words, each racial group must be assured of such things as adequate educational opportunities, of accessibility to rewards for efforts and of an environment which provides incentives to even greater efforts. Only with these will there follow an accelerated social mobility, which is yet another compensatory responsibility. Such compensatory responsibilities do indeed exist in Jamaica and this is frequently the cause of the hyperbolic expressions of the virtue of racial harmony in Jamaica, but in fact they are extremely limited. However, where attempts might be made to plough more money and planning into the black groups, as the Malayan people did among the Malays, there is fear that accusations will be made that blacks are being favoured at the expense of other racial groups in the society – colour prejudice in reverse. And this is so even if politicians are able to justify their actions with the democratic argument of the greatest good for the greatest number.

The truth of the matter is that while in Malaya the Malays are the accepted indigenous sons of the soil and the foundation of the Malayan image, in Jamaica the blacks are not regarded as the desirable symbol for national identity. The fact is that we are still enslaved in the social structure born of the plantation system in which things African, including African traits, have been devalued and primacy is still given to European values in the scheme of things. The developments of the twentieth century are putting pressures on the structure but most people seem to prefer to remain with the known evil rather than accept the uncertain good. As I have said elsewhere, the parboiled state of our national identity will continue to be just this until adjustments are made in the society in bold economic and social terms.[25] People who look like Africans will then no longer have evidence to support their much-repeated claim that their poverty, destitution and loss of hope is somehow organically linked with the fact that they are of a certain ethnic origin in a country controlled by people of another ethnic origin who think themselves superior.

AFRICAN REDEMPTION

The Rastafari and the Wider
Society* 1959-69

JAMAICA'S multi-racial nationalism which officially under-
pins and seeks to definitively prescribe the nation's groping
identity met its fiercest and most positive antagonism from
the black activist Rastafari movement, particularly in the late
fifties and the first half of the nineteen sixties. 'It is for the
mind genuinely seeking a solution for the problem they (the
society) have caused, to rid their conscience of hypocrisy and
take a new view of the situation and realize that the only
Jamaican is the one who originated here, for example the
extinct Arawaks and the immediate [sic] mulatto . . . Remember
there is no negro from "negroland", neither [are] Jamaicans
from Africa . . . Indeed the Rastafarian is he who never will
relinquish the fact that he is an African'.[1] To the Rastafarians
who are black Jamaicans, multi-racial Jamaica becomes the
Babylon which holds them in the captivity of a protracted
diaspora. Here there is no pleasure of exile, only oppression
and suffering at the hands of imperialist Europeans and 'their
derivatives' (meaning the Jamaican brown men and privileged
evolved black members of the middle classes). There is, too,
among the oppressed blacks a deepening of the conviction that
the Return is imminent, that redemption and freedom for the
true (black) Israelites is in the land of their forefathers – Africa
in general and Ethiopia in particular. The Promised Land of
Ethiopia awaits the Return (Repatriation) of the 'children of
the seed of Israel' and the ruler Haile Selassie fulfils in the
twentieth century the prophecy that a 'king would arise out of
Jesse's root' as 'God Almighty for his people and a liberator
to all the oppressed of the earth'. The oppressed of the earth are
all black people 'whose forcible displacement (i.e. slavery) from
their original habitat Ethiopia until this day, has caused the

---

* Footnote for Half-title, page 39:
The notion of the wider society is suggested by the two extreme
positions taken by the Rastafarians (the 'captive Israelites') and
representatives of the status quo ('Babylon' to the Rastafari, in effect
Government, private citizens, the police, sections of the Press etc.)
in the confrontation that took place in the late fifties and early
sixties. That these positions were far from irreconcilable is one of the
points made by this essay.

41

slaves [*sic*] to be resentful and at times revengeful of the cause of their enforced exile and ultimate privation'.[2]

The Rastafarian twin concepts of African Redemption (Repatriation to Ethiopia) and the divinity of the most revered ruler in Africa – Haile Selassie I, King of Kings, the Conquering Lion of Judah (and to the Rastafarians the Christ Re-Incarnate) – have marked the Rastafari movement off, ever since its inception in 1930, from the increasing and varied Jamaican manifestations of black awareness and of consciousness of the African heritage in Jamaican life. These twin doctrines inform and support such other doctrinal phenomena as the pre-eminence of Marcus Mosiah Garvey in the pantheon of black prophets and harbingers of the Black Redemption. They also support a basic tenet that Black is good (as it is beautiful) and White is wicked. This tenet would seek to effect a complete reversal of the equally extreme white oriented value system which has dominated Jamaican society. Yet the strongly Judaeo-Christian antecedents of the Rastafarian belief system have forced the most militant into accommodations with the wider society it challenges, always leaving room for dialogue (even if not always pleasant) between both systems.

It is this dynamic relationship between Rastafarianism and the supporters of the Jamaican status quo, particularly after the UWI study of 1960, that concerns us here. This dynamic has partially saved the movement from the fate of quietism and passivity which Worsley in his study of millenarian cults observes to be a feature of such movements.[3] The activism of the Rastafarians cannot then be said to be totally unfulfilled, though over the decade only a few of the unmistakable adherents have actually 'repatriated' to Ethiopia. Further, the Emperor Haile Selassie has denied his divinity, but with little effect on the movement's key tenet since the divine revelation cannot be gainsaid even by the Omnipotent Selassie himself, according to Rasta doctrine. Perhaps their capacity to accommodate to the non-fulfilment of the prophecy is to be explained in part by what the Jamaican sociologist Orlando Patterson said of the movement some years ago. His view was that the 'overwhelming desire of the members to change their position in the order of the social system (rather than the system itself), so as to be accepted by it, is expressed in and displaced through the medium of group fantasy'.[4]

Three years before there were enough declarations of Rasta belief by Rastafarians themselves to lead one to agree substantially with this view. But one could not agree with Vittorio Lanternari who saw the Rastafari movement in Jamaica merely as a 'typically escapist movement, rather than a revolutionary force'.[5] Probably the conclusion derives from the fact that his chapter on the Jamaican cult is informed largely by the pre-1956 studies by Professor George Simpson which suggest that the Rastafari movement was merely a variant of the wider revivalist cults concentrated in the depressed area of Western Kingston and much of Simpson's evidence at the time amply supported the view.[6] But by 1960 the situation had changed, as the University study team was to discover. The Rastafari they studied were a far more complex group of people – some indeed committed to a political and military struggle, others revivalist in orientation and in origin, some quietist but all deeply involved with the poverty and deprivation that was their climate of prime concern.[7] Although the Red Hills incidents arising out of an armed conflict with young black militants from New York invited this assessment of the Rastafarian movement, they proved to be *revolutionary* not in the sense of a Guevarian overthrow of the status quo, but by their identification of basic incongruities in the colonial and inherited power structure, by their bold assertive call for a change in the situation and even by the offer of a solution in a psychology of withdrawal and in a doctrine of social rejection, which they seek to give practical expression through repatriation to the 'ancestral home of the blacks'. The wider society was particularly critical of this Rastafarian tenet since it formed a threat to the fundamental idea of 'a nation of Jamaica for Jamaicans.' Yet objective factors of heavy migration to the United Kingdom at the time by many Jamaicans seeking their fortune, as well as the habitual looking to England by privileged

43

Jamaicans (white Rastas as the journalist Frank Hill once called the upper classes) for example and inspiration, made the Rastafarians into rather conventional Jamaicans in their other-directedness. What they did was to substitute Ethiopia for the United Kingdom, the United States and all those other places to which Jamaicans have migrated since the late 19th century. Some even eschewed a physical Return while settling for Africa as a 'spiritual home' in the way that England seemed to have been for many brown and white Jamaicans, Lebanon for the Jamaican Syrians, and what China (under the Kuomintang) had been for the Jamaican Chinese.

It is this 'Jamaicanness' of the Rastafarian movement that gave a certain justification to some of the recommendations made in the 1960 University Report advocating rehabilitation without incurring the wrath of the movement as a whole. The building of low-rent houses in greater number and the intro-duction of self-help co-operative building, the extension into slum areas occupied by squatters of such facilities as light, water, sewage disposal and garbage collection, the establish-ment of civic centres in Kingston with facilities for technical classes, youth clubs, child clinics, an invitation to establish a branch of the Ethiopian Orthodox Church in Western Kingston and the extension to leading members of the movement press and radio facilities.[8] All these implied a belief by the study team in the adherents' capacities to be rehabilitated into the wider society. This met with approval from the majority of the Rastafari brethren though 'rehabilitation' was rejected out of hand by the Niabinghi militants, many of whom were to be found in the group called 'the Church Triumphant'. They were interested, declared one of their spokesmen up to late 1963, only in 'going back home' to Ethiopia.

The first and second recommendations in the Report had enjoined the Jamaican Government to send a mission to Africa for the 'emigration of Jamaicans', that 'some Rastafari brethren should form part of this mission', and that operations for this should be started immediately. It was these two recommenda-tions which invited strong criticism from the wider society at large; and understandingly so, for these recommendations turned on those very tenets of the Rastafarian doctrine which posed fundamental threats to Jamaicanism. First there is the implied allegiance to a foreign (albeit friendly) Head of State. Secondly, the emphasis on Africa brought uneasiness to a country which had never regarded itself as black. Thirdly, the adoption of the Rastafarian faith was to the orthodox Jamaican Christians blasphemous and anti-Christian. Rastafarian brethren on the other hand have been known to conform to standard modes of dress, even shedding their locks to facilitate job-seeking. But such concessions do not automatically result in the renunciation of fundamental beliefs about repatriation and the divinity of Haile Selassie. Outward conformity by the 'brethren' with some of the mores of the wider society has often won them support from the members of the society which they reject, but it has sometimes misled people into dismissing the entire belief-system as pseudo-drama and poetry of dubious merit with a future in the Apocalypse but not in the reality of the experience of the day. This further serves to underestimate the 'revolutionary' feature of the movement in its part-conscious challenge of some of the society's basic value-assumptions. Orlando Patterson in defining a millenarian cult sees the Rastafarian movement as 'outlet' rather than an agent 'for revolutionary social action'.[9]

Yet Rastafarianism in the years that followed the Report may be said to serve as such an agent in the sense of Firth's view that cults like the Jamaican Rastafari are *'creative* attempts of the people to reform their own institutions, to meet new demands or to withstand new pressures'.[10] In this the wider society's reactions and attitudes to the cult is of major significance. Such reactions and attitudes were to make outcasts of the members of the Rastafari movement but not of the entire belief system. The years that followed 1960 witnessed continued confrontation with the wider society provoking persecution of the brethren, hardening of positions on both sides, violence, grudging recognition and a truce between the police and the cultists. The chiliastic myth involving the human

45

appearance of the Messiah was even encouraged by the organized State visit of Haile Selassie to Jamaica in 1966 – presenting difficulties, doctrinal and ideological, which are yet to be resolved by the movement as such.

Yet the role of the Rastafarian movement has been a dynamic one in the wider society of which it is really a part. Many of the ideas and much of the mood of this group have seemingly passed on to the younger generation at large. What would have been regarded as peculiarly Rastafarian in 1959–60 was to be assimilated ten years later into the mainstream of thought on black power and majority control. Many of the views have since developed a cogency partly because they were to come from persons who had passed through the established educational institutions of the country and could no longer be seriously dismissed as the escapist indulgencies of an economically worthless and lunatic fringe. As early as 1963 a Rasta spokesman was heard to say 'we know that as every turn of the night light unto day and every turn of the day light unto night . . . a potential Rastafarian is born . . . in the colleges and universities and the schools of this country for it means that men are thinking within radical terms and cannot take imperialism as a way out or a goal . . . the Rasta man stands to receive all those who find that within the faith of our conception [*sic*] there is life for all'.[11] By the late sixties there was much more widespread embrace of Rastafarian attitudes, ideals and even practices among bona fide members of the wider society. The symbolic expressions of long and carefully unkempt hair and the wearing of bright garb believed to be 'African', the open defiance of 'the unjust law' against the smoking of ganja which is still prohibited by the rules of the wider society but remains the holy and wisdom-giving weed to the Rastafarians, the unashamed commitment to Africa and a yearning for knowledge of the African past, the conscious reference to the self as *black man* rather than as *negro*, the unfaltering expressions of wrath against an oppressive and what the Rastafarians regarded as a 'continuing colonial society', the campaign against police brutality suffered by the poor presumably because of their poverty and the mal-administration of justice, the expressed hatred for the humiliating 'white bias' in the society though not necessarily for white people, the deprecation of the agonizing logic of a history of black slavery and white domination – all the above were to be appropriated by many Jamaicans during the 1960s in a growing awareness of the need to define their existence or by those who, according to one Rastafarian, had been 'liberated from the obscurity of themselves'.

Social Context

Certain independent factors turning on the social context of the country facilitated the survival of the movement in Jamaica as well as the accommodation of Rastafarianism by the wider society. Like millenarian cults elsewhere the Rastafari phenomenon marked the 'critical moment at which tensions and differences have reached a climax'.[12] In the late fifties these tensions and differences took the form of social and economic disinheritance and the progressive disillusionment among the dispossessed with the Jamaican colonial government and the political parties. A decade later brought substantially little change in this direction – the widening gap between rich and poor and the attendant deepening of class differences, the failure of political leaders to find effective answers in the wake of independence, the disinheritance following on increasing foreign ownership of key resources, all served to give the Rastafarian 'rumblings' a rationality and a continued centrality to the quest for identity and for economic security among the black majority. Despite a record of economic and constitutional progress since 1938, in 1959 when the Rastafari burgeoned into prominence Jamaican society persisted in its deeply stratified structure based on a high correlation between class and colour, with the black representing the vast majority of the population, conspicuously precipitated at the base. It is true that the stratification resists any simplistic explanation and often

47

serves to confuse many an analyst of Jamaican social relations. But this very difficulty in turn encourages the propaganda proportions of the claim usually made for a harmonious multi-racial society. And Jamaican nationalism has long rooted itself in this assumption.

However, by 1960 there were those Jamaicans who felt that they were not part of the 'harmony'. Unionized labour had procured for workers increased wages and conditions of work superior to those in 1938, but there was clear evidence that the black poor, of all the groups in Jamaica, had benefited least from the efforts of the regimes that governed Jamaica between 1944 and 1960. The white and brown upper and middle classes seemed to be the major beneficiaries of the progress. The evidence was clear to the Rastafari in the lucrative positions which accrued to the Creole elite, i.e. the middle classes, of which the government bureaucracy formed a sizable fraction. Successive salary revisions, new houses, motor cars were the barometers of the new benefits which flowed in directions away from the black lower classes. Inequalities were further underlined in the mal-administration of justice and the indiscretions of the police. There was educational reform in 1957 procuring for scions of the middle classes more school places in the educational system but social mobility seemed almost as limited in 1960 as in 1937. In any case, even if conditions grew better for many, the upward vault-like movement of the society left the black lower classes in the same relationship as before with the brown middle classes and the white upper classes. Emigration provided one outlet for those who desired status but many were kept at a virtual standstill by increasing unemployment and underemployment which paralleled the growth in population. The mushrooming of middle class housing schemes (Mona Heights, Red Hills, Harbour View) whetted the appetite of the poor blacks in the slums. They who had benefited least from change therefore viewed the development since the thirties as a betrayal. The hope for widespread reform had swept to power in 1955 the People's National Party whose declared commitment to socialism seemed at the time as a better alternative to the loose pragmatism demonstrated by the Jamaica Labour Party which managed power for ten years previously. But by 1960, widespread social change seemed to have taken second place to constitutional advance and involvement in a West Indian federation. Concern for meaningful reform seemed smothered by the smug declarations of multi-racial harmony, impressive growth rate and an exemplary Civil Service – all of which meant little to the poor.

The heaviest concentration of these alienated and unemployed poor was to be found in West Kingston and among these were the largest number of Rastafarians. Official estimates were from 15,000 to 20,000 for the City of Kingston. Other estimates were as high as 70,000.* The University study team found at the time that the slum belts were occupied by populations which were either declared adherents of the Rastafarian faith or at least sympathetic to it. Many of these people were 'squatters' on the land, to which they had no legal right and were therefore eligible for eviction by bulldozing at any time. Inadequate shelter and lack of such communal facilities as sewage disposal, water, light and roads were exacerbated by the absence of Government assistance and by overcrowding by new recruits from the country. The new recruits were said to come largely from the 20,000 annual rural migrants to Kingston. When the Report was written, slum areas as Back o' Wall and Kingston Pen were fully occupied though slum clearance and re-settlement programmes had been carried out in 1947, 1949 – 50 and 1953.† The University Study in 1960 found that 'crowded into these ghettoes, unemployed without Poor Relief or Government assistance and lacking any contact with upper and middle classes who preach Jamaica's prosperity, these slum

---

* Especially by Mr. Horace Gordon of the Jamaica Social Welfare Commission who conducted a survey in 1959 in West Kingston and was instrumental in setting up the administrative framework for the University study in 1960.

† At an earlier period, in the late 1930s, Governor Sir Edward Denham cleared Smith village and built Denham Town in its stead.

dwellers turn in on themselves, quarrelling with one another, sharing misfortune and kindnesses with enclosed solidary groups whose bases are usually religion or kinship. As the urban population grows by recruitment from the depressed areas, new arrivals are absorbed into these communities and come to share their institutions, values and attitudes as well as their humiliating experiences . . . the cost of living goes up and so, perhaps, does the rate of unemployment . . . the tolerance of the unemployed declines over time and goodwill is consumed'.[13]

This remains as apt a description of the late sixties as it was of the late fifties and the situation continues to offer a choice between purposelessness and protest. The Rastafari doctrine provided at an earlier date a vital purpose; the phenomenon of rude-boy and the rise of Black Power seem to have done so during the later period.

A decade after the University Report critics of the status quo were still deprecating the perennial problems of unemployment (estimated at anywhere between 15 and 20 per cent) and the persistence of deprivation among the majority of the urban population. In 1969 a report by a Canadian professor of economics responded to the situation with the advice many Jamaicans had long given themselves, namely the need to 'bridge the gap between the modern and the traditional [sectors of the economy] before the frightening vacuum in the cultural environment of much of the nation's youth is filled with forces destructive of the entire society'.[14] The colonial tradition of foreign expert guidance aside, the Chamber of Commerce which commissioned this report hardly needed a new voice on the old subject. Ever since the Rastafarian rumblings of the late fifties, it has been repeated that the country is standing with a lighted match over a powder keg and the dynamic interplay between those who held political power and the deprived Rastafarians who questioned the legitimacy and the use of that power, resulted from the knowledge that all was far from well in the society at large. Rastafarian, rude-boy, Black Power advocate, each represents at different points in the troublous decade of the sixties active responses to a milieu of social and economic disinheritance. As late as 1967 the Jamaican government sponsored a survey into housing conditions in Trench Town which could be regarded as one of the better-off districts in the slum-belt, but which continued to receive rural migrants into the city of Kingston. It was the view of a commentator that 'the facilities available to the householders . . . leave a great deal to be desired judging by any reasonable standard of civilized living'.[15] The survey further revealed as unemployed some 29 per cent of the heads of households, with 13 per cent of those who had worked, working for only six months or less during the previous twelve months. The commentator added 'the human disorganisation, the anxiety, frustration, bitterness and human deterioration which must accompany such unemployment, experienced in surroundings which give such little hope for improvement, needs no emphasis'.[16] The Rastafarians had been this emphasis itself and it was against this backdrop that they articulated their social protests and acted out their confrontation with the wider society.

The Trench Town survey revealed an interesting fact which is germane to an understanding of the Rastafari movement: the vast majority of the household heads interviewed said they wished to remain in the area.* The Rastafari cry to leave the Babylon of Jamaica for their ancestral home Ethiopia has itself betrayed a similar ambivalence once described as a 'total involvement in the society and a passionate need to be accepted by it, expressed in terms of a denial of any wish to be accepted'.[17] It is in this schizophrenic area of relationship that the parry and thrust between Rastafarian cult and wider society is played out. This serves to throw further light on the significance of the Rastafarian movement in Jamaica, especially after 1960. Certain areas of the cult's belief-system proved most sensitive. Many of these were attacked by the wider society in public

* cf. Edward Seaga's Tivoli Garden's scheme – transforming the slums into comfortable habitats with modern facilities but leaving the inhabitants in the neighbourhood with which they are familiar.

comments on the study team's report. But there were others which formed the basis of a continuing tension, tacit and overt, between Rastafarian doctrine and the ideals of the wider society from which they wanted to escape but from which they simultaneously sought acceptance.

The interplay between the religious – revolutionary ethic of the Rastafarians and the combative orthodoxy of the wider society may be seen in (*a*) the public's attitude to the 1960 University Report; (*b*) the Rastafarian view of Ethiopia (Africa) as home vis-a-vis the cultivated ideal of *Jamaicanism* – a conflict which entailed, inter alia, the divergent notions of the prescription on the one hand of a society that is functionally black and the actual perspective on the other of a multi-racial Jamaican nationalism; (*c*) the doctrine of repatriation versus the notion of rehabilitation; (*d*) the cultists' claim to basic individual rights versus the prevailing commitment to con-stituted law and order (and this embraced decided views on violence by the wider society and the status of ganja or mari-juana under the law, as well as the right to be oneself, including the freedom to worship Haile Selassie as God – the Christ Re-Incarnate); (*e*) the rationalization by the unemployed and unemployable that to work in Babylon is corrupting for the true Israelites versus the vestigial beliefs by the wider society in the theory of natural indolence and in the puritanical ideal of work for work's sake which is dominant in the belief-system, if not in the actual practice, of the wider society. These notions, however conflicting, proved extremely capable of mutual accommodation (even if not of total resolve) so that by the end of the decade Rastafarianism was as much assimilated by the wider society as the wider society was to be deeply influenced by it.

The Public and the 1960 University Report

The Report on the Rastafari Movement was the result of the rapid survey by a team of researchers from the then University

College of the West Indies. The object was to collect information on the doctrines, history, organization and needs of the Rastafari movement in Kingston and to publish a brief account of these conditions. The steady deterioration since 1954 of relations between the Rastafari 'brethren' on the one hand and the police (and by implication the wider society) on the other was marked by increasing arrests of the brethren for the possession of ganja as well as a continuing verbal confrontation between the cultists and the officers of the Crown. The riots of May 7, 1959, added to the backdrop of discontent and general dissatisfaction against which the study team made some recommendations with a view to finding practical solutions for the problems. It was these recommendations which were to be the target of attack and general comment by the wider society.

The Rastafari brethren whose letters had prompted the study in the first place were on the whole satisfied with the outcome. Even if they were not pleased with all the findings in the Report they seemed gratified with the developments in the wider society. For the first time, their cause was being publicly aired. The first two recommendations suggesting a Back-to-Africa mission to investigate the possibilities of repatriation and on which Rastafarians should be represented was seen as a practical approach to one of the most central needs of the movement. The Government of the day, on receiving the Report, intimated its intentions of implementing this recommendation and this gave the Rastafari much hope. Some members of the wider society accused the Rastafari of using the new-found recognition as an excuse for licence and reported attacks by cultists on policemen drew a stern rebuke from the Premier who warned that the Report and the resulting plan by Government to send a mission to Africa was 'no licence to do what they like'.[18] A report in the newspaper had charged Rastafari brethren with forcing the police at Denham Town station to set a prisoner free. This renewed defiance by many Rastafarian brethren was blamed on the Report while the Rastafarian groups seized every opportunity to organize or be organized into public forums and radio panels in order to explain themselves to the wider society.

The Report itself received wide distribution and the influential *Daily Gleaner* carried thirteen instalments of the document.[19] It also carried a cartoon which correctly gauged prevailing attitudes among the wider society towards the movement and indeed to the Report. The cartoon showed a Rastaman as a patient. The doctor, sketched in the likeness of the University's Principal and labelled *UCWI*, is examining the patient. Premier Norman Manley stands apprehensively over the bed behind the doctor. A very relaxed nurse, labelled *public*, stands on the other side. The caption beneath reads:

DOCTOR: He needs a change.
NURSE: He needs a purgative.[20]

The commendable capacity to laugh at oneself notwithstanding, the humour merely provided the veneer for the underlying lack of social conscience among the more fortunate classes in Jamaica and for the prevailing belief that the Rastafari were stupid, irrational and unlawful Jamaicans. The Report was to attempt what a *Gleaner* editorial admitted nine years after, namely to draw 'a line between the believers and the fakers – those who worshipped truly and pretenders who dabbled in dungle crime'.[21] The Report had in fact said 'some brethren are addicted to ganja, others abhor it. Some are criminals, others are not. Some wear beards, others wear plaited locks of uncut hair. Others wear neither beards nor locks. Some brethren seem to live in camps, most live dispersed throughout the city. Most of the brethren are unemployed, many of these for several years . . . Many brethren are willing to take employment providing they are not required to shave their hair and beard . . . Other brethren reject the idea of wage employment but are quite in favour of co-operative Rastafari group production'.[22]

This wide range of beliefs, practices, appearance and differences of doctrinal emphasis did not, however, prevent the wider society from persisting in the blanket denunciation of all cultists as criminal, lazy, irrationally emotional, hopelessly mad and dangerously violent. A letter from a renowned Jamaican scholar and Roman Catholic cleric questioned the entire academic basis of the Report.[23] A reply from one member of the study team sought to clarify the confusion on the very matters relating to the specific task of identifying who the Rastafarian was.[24] The Report had claimed that far from being an isolated dissident, the Rastafarian was a Jamaican responding to the inadequacies of a society which he felt gave him little hope. The clerical critic had earlier insisted that the 'Rastafarian Movement was a difficult one to handle since it was *purely emotional*'[25] [my emphasis]. The doubts about the soundness of the Report had been anticipated by an editorial on August 17, 1960, in the *Daily Gleaner*. The writer suggested that the exercise of the Report was pointless since it read, inter alia, with 'an almost universal failure to make sense of what it seeks to signify'.[26] Yet the very same editorial conceded that there was a net gain in respect of this 'thorough documentation which now becomes part of the island's history; and also the resultant awareness among the cultists, who at any rate can no longer say that notice has not been taken of them'. Such ambivalence was typical. Not many lines later the writer chided the 'recorders of the Report' for their subtle acquiescence to 'the notion that there should be thousands of people who should think it right that the community owes them compliance but that they in return owe none to the community'. The editorial further expressed the view that a recital of facts and figures was not adequate. Appraisal, it said, in social, psycho-analytical and religious terms was mandatory. This in fact was not the intention of the Report. As M. G. Smith later pointed out, the team was concerned with concentrating the public's attention on the essentials of the analysis. The social context of the movement was deliberately omitted, for example. The judge likewise sums up evidence without repeating the entire proceedings as Smith rightly pointed out.[27] The doctrines were actually stated in a separate chapter of the Report making it into an invaluable primary source for all readers who wish to analyse and draw conclusions for themselves. This it was felt would free the team of charges of bias towards the underdog.

As it turned out the charge of whitewashing the Rastafarians was nevertheless levelled by correspondents to the press and the University was to earn the reputation of being a sanctuary for and sympathizer of such dissidents in the society. The later call by a feature writer for a more adult and 'serious study' so as to find the causes – 'historical, psychological and economic' – and so that the problem could be tackled from 'the stand of sound knowledge',[28] was clearly designed to discredit the Report. But this line of cant merely betrayed an uneasiness about the developments and the legitimacy which the Report seemed to be then gleaning for the Rastafarian movement. The 'sound knowledge' called for was in fact readily available in the many studies of Jamaican society before 1960 and since. But many of these were either not taken seriously or not known to the power elites in the privileged sectors of the society. Problems of plantation society and the vestigial traces of oppression among the black masses were sufficiently documented to provide the movement with contextual relevance. But the Rastafarians were at the time victims of the prevailing view that they were little more than a menace to the middle classes and the State power – a lunatic fringe to be pressed into conformity or left to the mercy of the Dangerous Drugs Law and the Law relating to Vagrancy. The reference to mental illness was predictable. The study team interviewed several Rastafari brethren who had been patients in the island's mental hospital and at the time of the study there were several hospitalized at Bellevue. The early leaders were either taken to gaol on sedition or to the asylum for lunacy. In fact, many brethren at the time accused the police of committing them without any clear clinical diagnostic evidence to the mental asylum whenever they 'spoke for their rights'. So from very early the wider society associated Rastafarianism with madness. The process of becoming a Rastafarian is still regarded by the wider society as one of mental deterioration and the more recent embrace of the creed by young educated high school and University graduates is seen as an urgent matter for the psychiatrist.

The Report was nine years later to furnish the necessary background for a 'psychological study' of group beliefs and social stress among the Rastafari.[29] This paper could hardly be considered definitive in the field but it examined briefly the Rastafarian beliefs, or rather 'knowledge', in the light of the 'delusional system' in Transcultural Psychiatry. The author posed a question which the general public after nine years of exposure to the 'problem' was by now ready to receive. In speculating about the mental health of the brethren as compared with their slum neighbours, he underlined what he termed 'the dilemma inherent in the mental health concept, [viz] is it healthier to live in peace and assurance subtended upon a delusion, or is it healthier to live in despair but open to the realities of the existence'. Public opinion expressed in criticisms of the Report nine years earlier would have supported the latter proposition, even if it meant 'rehabilitating' the Rastafarians around to it.*

The Report was to inform many subsequent studies and accounts[30] despite the earlier reservations expressed by some people from the wider community who had accused the study team of cynicism, irresponsibility and even bad faith. What actually happened was that the Report had broken new ground in its serious approach to the Rastafari and had begun to explode the popular myth that the Rastafarians were a group of criminals and lunatics.[31] More immediately it proved to be a palliative in what was in 1960 a very explosive situation. The Government of the day was obviously relieved. Its leader declared his appreciation, despite the spate of the letters of

---

* This paper was presented at a meeting of the Caribbean Psychiatric and American Psychiatric Associations in May, 1969. The venue was in Ocho Rios about 60 miles from Kingston. A group of Rastafarians led by Mortimo Planno, one of the key brethren in the 1960 period, invited themselves to the session, were allowed in and contributed to the discussions led by Dr. Vera Rubin of the Institute for the Study of Man, New York and one Dr. Ari Kiev.

public outrage at the sympathetic tone of the Report: 'I regard the Report as a distinctive contribution to our knowledge and understanding of this difficult matter. I think it is an excellent example of how the University College of the West Indies can contribute to the life of the community and the solution of its problems'.[32] It took the wider society some time to reconcile itself to the idea of official recognition of the Rastafari and after 1960 the mutual hostility was to manifest itself on various issues.

The Rastafari and Jamaicanism

Rastafarian beliefs affected the wider society in respect of their implied 'anti-Jamaicanism'. Even when the Government conceded the point of a Mission to Africa to investigate possibilities of movement of people from Jamaica, it was made clear that this was part of a wider policy on *migration*. Rastafarians were Jamaicans, it was insisted. The *Gleaner* in the safety of its position as formulator and articulator of the formidable Jamaican middle class opinion, was not willing to countenance any blatant lack of patriotism. 'The cultists are no less repugnant to the notion of helping to build a *Jamaica for all Jamaicans*, they are no less wedded to the notion that there is a Zion in Africa . . . they are no more agreeable to share the common lot with their fellow-Jamaicans . . .'[33] The inference was that the Report was not going to help change these fundamentally reprehensible views in the Rastafarian belief system. The Report was blamed for not offering any co-operation from the separatist elements to help the million and more Jamaicans in their pledge to build a better Jamaica. The doctrine of social rejection by the Rastas was here deemed as a threat to the security of the fledgling nation which had committed itself since 1944 to building up a harmonious society from its transplanted diversity. To many, the Rastafarians were retrogressive and their cause was seen as political separatism, a betrayal of the movement towards self-government and a disrespect for the carefully nurtured Jamaican nationalism –

a nationalism which was to take the country out of the West Indies Federation a mere one year later. The *Gleaner* editorial betrayed an understandable concern for the future locus and distribution of the power which was in the process of being transferred from Great Britain. The *Gleaner* had itself been very instrumental in articulating to its readership the objectives of the exercise of transfer since 1944. It was therefore important to many that this power should be transferred to legitimate hands. News in the Jamaican press of developments in revolutionary Cuba in 1959 could not have been salutary at the time and anything that threatened the status quo and the course of contemporary history would be held suspect. The Rastafari were accused of introducing something alien and destructive into Jamaican life. The invocation of the 'national good' invited responses from the Rastafari brethren who insisted (and still do) that they had been left behind, through no fault of their own, on the road set by historical events in Jamaica and so did not count themselves among the beneficiaries of the progress. Logically then, they could hardly be expected to make the sacrifices which the wider society demanded (and still do) of them. 'Jamaica can offer a future to those of goodwill who wish to help Jamaica. Let the Rastas think of their duty to Jamaica,' exhorted the *Daily Gleaner* in a later editorial.[34] An Afro-Jamaican enthusiast responded – 'Africa is the legitimate, moral and righteous home of all Negroes and now that the time is coming for all to assemble under their own vine and fig tree, we feel it our duty to arouse every Negro to a consciousness of himself.'[35] The Rastafari (then as now) remain vulnerable on this matter of patriotism. The abhorrence of black nationalism was rooted in a belief that this was bad for *Jamaican* nationalism. The idea of repatriation was seen to be antagonistic to the nationalism of the status quo though the notion of migrating is not deemed incompatible. The 'dropping-out' of the society is regarded as a betrayal of the ideals of Jamaican unity in diversity, and assertive language for change is seen as a major threat to the proverbial 'stability of the country'.

In 1960 Monsignor Wilson's adverse criticism of the Report was timely since it came in the middle of the trial of Claudius Henry who was charged with treason felony and that is an unpatriotic thing. Henry, though disowned by a great many Rastafarians, shared many Rastafari beliefs seeing himself as a prophet come to redeem the blacks into Africa and styling himself 'Repairer of the Breach'. Everything at the time seemed to point to his conviction. A crime against the security of the State was everybody's business and so new interest was aroused by the Wilson statement against the Report. The Rastafarian allegiance to the country of their birth was therefore demanded by the wider society. The Rastafari brethren did not always prove intransigent. The mass arrest of Rastafarians after the 1963 Coral Gardens incident in Montego Bay forced out of a leading Rastafarian a public plea for restraint in the wider society's reactions to his 'brethren' who he said were 'also citizens of this multi-racial island'.[36] Such an admission betrays a shift of position from the classic social rejection doctrine to identification with the established power structure.

It, however, remained central to the formal Rastafarian belief system, that Ethiopia was 'home' and that the brethren are 'strangers' in Jamaica. The coming of independence in 1962 only served to intensify the activist Rastafarian belief that Jamaican nationalism had no relevance to their existence. 'Jamaica today is independent', writes the self-styled 'Interpreter' of Rastafari doctrine in 1963, 'yet English customs and laws and English instructions still leads us. The white queen still rules. The black Governor General is but her representative, how much voice do we have in saying what laws will pass at Gordon House?* As far as I am concerned, politics was not the black man's lot but the white man's plot'.[37] This clearly anticipates the questions asked in the late sixties about who really controls the society – questions which have become the concern not merely of Rastafarians and their descendants, the rudies and the black power militants, but for many of the

---

* The seat of Parliament – Duke Street, Kingston.

wider society including members of the power structure itself. But the Rastafarian 'Interpreter' had more to say in 1963: 'The black man in this country and throughout the West has united with the heads of Government in helping to build a better Jamaica, but we the black majority who has helped plow the soil, planted the vineyard and gather the fruits thereof, we are not the benefactors. Those who benefit are the protectors. They share the crops, they boss the work and own the shares . . . the majority of Jamaicans are black – why then are not the black supreme here. We want no promises we want fulfilment now. Three hundred years of slavery in the Western World – What for? Jamaica's independence means a well without water, a treasury without money'.[38] Behind the self-conscious and sonorous rhetoric there were gems of truth about Jamaican history and society which brought instinctive responses of defence from the caretakers of the status quo in the wider society. Such ideas are no longer regarded as bizarre or unrealistic though a too vigorous expression of them still puts the heirs of political power on a defensive almost approaching panic. There is even greater understanding today of the early Rastafarian view that the entrenched two-party system (which they say produces 'brown man government') is bankrupt and that institutions which are pillars of Jamaican nationalism are oblivious to the needs of the cultist and, by extension, of black people.

The wider society's conception of a harmoniously multi-racial and stable nationalism is challenged fundamentally by the Rastafari. The movement was objectively to inform the wider society of the inherent incongruities of the Jamaican social system in which the poor grew poorer and the rich more prosperous. By the late sixties these incongruities were to become the stock-in-trade of many commentators on the social system including those who ten years before would have regarded the stating of these as intolerable if not subversive. Such was the backdrop of this greater understanding of Rastafarian doubts about the virtues of Jamaican nationalism, when the Government of the day started to encourage visits to

Jamaica by African dignitaries culminating with the historic visit by the Emperor Haile Selassie himself. The Jamaican missions to Africa (see below) had started the two-way traffic between that continent and Jamaica. It could not be that such visits were intended to condone Rastafarian anti-Jamaicanism. Rather, they were regarded by some people as a necessary exposure to combat the frustration born of ignorance and even to cure the Rasta desire for Africa by an overdose. Throughout the early and middle sixties the Rastafari, however, stayed firm in their beliefs about the mythical goods that Africa had with her. Not even as skilful a politician as Okpara (then Premier of the Eastern Region of Federal Nigeria) could convince the Rastafari brethren that Jamaica was home. His offer of congratulations on Jamaica's winning of independence was not well received by his audience of Rastafarians and his exhortation for them to 'play their part as citizens' in Jamaica which 'now belongs to the black man' was answered with cries of 'Africa for the Africans at home and abroad'.[39] The Press and radio made reports of Okpara's call for discipline among the Rastafari which he was indeed forced to repeat throughout his much interrupted speech. The Rastafarian 'Interpreter' countered with the view that the 'white controlled' news media had overstated the injunction in their reports and had suppressed Okpara's more important statements about black consciousness and the reasonableness of the Rastas' desire to 'return' to Africa.[40]

The visit by Haile Selassie in 1966 pointed up the weaknesses of the Jamaican nationalism. 'Thousands of Jamaicans for whatever reason, were in a frenzy over an alien leader around whom they had woven legends' wrote someone for an editorial in the *Sunday Gleaner* in October, 1969. 'Perhaps for the first time many were seeing Royalty embodied in the unaccustomed hues of Mother Africa, making it easy to establish kinship and identification'.[41] (Selassie brought in his entourage two members of his family – H.R.H. Imabet Sofiya Desta, a granddaughter and H.H. Prince Mikael, a grandson). Clearly the lesson was not lost on the hierarchies of both political parties which have alternately governed Jamaica since 1944. Their leaders have made a point of visiting Ethiopia and other countries of Africa with understandable hope of approval from among the black-conscious masses in Jamaica.

It had been predicted before the Royal visit in 1966 that the natural enthusiasm of the mass of Jamaicans 'may well break out into boisterous cheers'.[42] It did and the news media caught the spirit of the event with such headlines as 'Wild welcome for Negus . . .', 'Airport overwhelmed with rampant crowd', 'Savage joys swamps Palisodoes formalities' and 'Multitude surges, surrounds plane.'[43] The *Gleaner's* Political Reporter pointedly commented that there never had been in the 'whole history of Jamaica such a spontaneous, heartwarming and sincere welcome to any person, whether visiting Monarch, visiting VIP or returning leader of a Jamaican party . . .'[44] In effect Selassie, a foreign Head of State, was receiving from a sizable segment of the Jamaican population the unprecedented spontaneous enthusiasm that rightly belonged to Jamaican leaders who would normally be regarded as the embodiment of Jamaican nationalism. Not all Jamaicans approved of the display; some termed the even wilder display of loyalty at a reception given in the National Stadium as hooliganism but judging from the reports in the Press, there was a reluctance to condemn the Rastafari and related black nationalist groups for the expressions of affection; and the Rastas' 'capture' of ceremonies as well as their participation in the several official functions were all sympathetically reported. As the weekly *Public Opinion* stated 'The Rastafarians rubbed shoulders with the greats of the society and can no longer be regarded as outcasts'.[45] But that very acceptance by the wider society into the 'Establishment' as it were, carried with it implicit contradictions, both for the Rastas and for the wider society. One view was that by being accepted the Rastafarians had 'lost the dynamic of protest . . . From now on the Rastafarian reformer has to play by the same ground rules as the Establishment legislator'.[46] The problem for the wider society ('the many-branched tree of the Jamaican Establishment' as a columnist called it) would have to work out new modes of relationship with this new 'respectable force'.

In fact, it was to prove less difficult than was feared. Both Rastas and the wider society were quite ready for such accommodation. The Rastafarian anti-Jamaicanism was less intractable than their critics would admit: the belief system could be cut underground if certain needs were met. Deference to the cultists by the wider society was certainly one such need and ever since the University Report much of this had been done. Books had been written about them, researchers from foreign universities had sought them out constantly. Missions to Africa had invested their claims with some legitimacy, the Government was itself displaying much interest in Africa and the press and radio had carried regular and increasing reports on Africa. All this also helped to prepare the middle classes for the Rastafarian 'victory' on the visit of Selassie. Marcus Garvey, father of Jamaican black nationalism had been made a National Hero. Jamaica was said to be getting 'blacker' in its attitudes even if this were more metaphor than fact. One month after the Royal visit a member of the Jamaican Senate gave notice of a Motion that the Jamaican Constitution be amended to make the Emperor of Ethiopia H.I.M. Haile Selassie, the King of Jamaica in place of Queen Elizabeth II of the United Kingdom. He justified his motion on the grounds of racial ties between Jamaicans and the Emperor and the fact that the people of Jamaica had shown greater affection for His Imperial Majesty than for 'our alien Queen'.[47] The shortcomings of Jamaican nationalism were therefore still a matter for comment after the Emperor's visit.

But Rasta day had not come, after all, despite the rubbing of shoulders with the greats of society. As late as 1969 the General Manager of the Government radio station could bring to a close the one year old weekly broadcasts by two groups of Rastafarians, known as the 'Disciples of the Great King' and the 'Sons of Negus Churchical Hosts' on grounds of the un-Jamaican nature of their content. The broadcasts ('Speak Love' and 'The Lion of Judah Time') proclaimed Rastafari

(Haile Selassie I) to be God, the Returned Messiah, asserted that Jesus was not white, swore allegiance to the Emperor of Ethiopia and threatened destruction if there is no Repatriation, with prophetic biblical support from Isaiah, chapter 48, verse 20. The contents prompted the General Manager's letter which stated that 'specifically the JBC is not prepared to accept for broadcast any programme (i) which states or implies that His Majesty Haile Selassie is God (ii) which we believe could adversely affect racial harmony (iii) which, in our opinion, could be regarded as seditious or disruptive of law and order and the peace of the land and (iv) which in our view is manifestly contrary to public policy as enshrined in our national motto "Out of Many One People" '.[48] The letter reflected views which belong in temper to the early sixties, yet the decision by the radio station met with no voice of protest from either the Rastafarians or those in the wider society concerned with human rights. Meanwhile the alienation from a nationalism which is claimed as inadequate finds its continuing expression in the doctrine of Repatriation.

Repatriation or Rehabilitation

Repatriation in so far as it maintains a centrality in the belief system remains a focus in Rastafarian relationship with the wider society which still expects rehabilitation rather than flight. The inherent ambivalence of the millenarian ideal also served to convince many that greater opportunities and tolerance would knock 'the nonsense' from their heads. But as late as October 1969 the society was still being forced to take the Rastafarian call for Repatriation seriously. The Jamaican mass media beamed reports on the visit of both Prime Minister and Leader of Opposition to Ethiopia and more importantly to Shashamane, two hundred miles from Addis Ababa, where some twenty Rastafari brethren (including women and children) are resident.[49] They were occupying land which was the gift of Haile Selassie to 'the black people of the West' and to be administered by the Ethiopian World Federation Inc.[50] The most recent migrants or repatriates had left Jamaica in early September under the sponsorship of the Jamaican EWF whose fund-raising committee had raised the fares. Although the EWF spokesman spoke the language of 'repatriation' of members to Africa, 'the homeland of their ancestors', the efforts at raising funds through an Ethiopian Settlement Fund[51] to effect the Return reveals an important difference between members (who are not all Rastafarian *per se*) and hard-core 'brethren' who feel that their involuntary enslavement and migration from Africa warrants them a free return. In classic Rastafarian doctrine, the twenty million pounds sterling voted by the British Parliament in 1834 to compensate slave owners for the liberation of their chattel is said to have been intended for the blacks. The historical discrepancy notwithstanding, this is regarded as a strong argument 'based on facts of history' and was used by the militant core of the movement in the late fifties.

There are appeals other than to history. The redemption dynamic according to Rastafari doctrine is rooted in the Bible. The Scattering, the Exile, the Return are all recorded and prophesied in the Old Testament. Each year brings hopes of the 'millenium' when fulfilment will be realized in 'repatriation' to the black man's vine and fig tree, Ethiopia. In 1960 the brethren of the Church Triumphant of Jah Rastafari concentrated their energies on preaching about Repatriation. Their foremost spokesman identified a 'true Rasta' by the intensity of his belief in the divinity of Haile Selassie and in Repatriation to the land He ruled. 'We readily, violently, internally denounce the word "rehabilitation"' said the Rastafarian spokesman.[52] Yet another had this to say, 'We must repatriate back on the shore of Zion where we shall be steady and in wants no more. There is no question of bearing the costs since "our parents and foreparents have done sufficient work to compensate any passage or any financial incurrence repatriation might [im]pose upon any Government today'.[53] The strength of the belief had evoked from the University study team the recommendation that a mission should be sent to Africa to investigate possibilities of migration. Opinion as expressed by the wider society in letters to the press, radio commentaries and interviews was unanimous in its denunciation of the recommendation as nonsensical, a waste of public funds and 'unrealistic in the light of needs of the African continent'.[54] This reflected views which were prevalent in the society from the time of Garvey who preached Back to Africa. The Jamaican folkpoet Louise Bennett in 1947 had caught the attitude in:[55]

> 'Go a foreign, seek yuh fortune
> But noh tell nobody sey
> Yuh dah-go fe seek you homelan
> For a right deh so yuh deh.'

In other words, while there may be some point in migrating to seek one's fortune, migrating in search of roots is hardly sensible since Jamaica is home 'oonoo all bawn dung a Bun Grung/OOnoo all is Jamaican' (i.e. You were all born in Burnt Ground, you are all *Jamaicans*). This feeling that the Rastafari cult is too Jamaican a phenomenon to want to exist elsewhere is a common one in Jamaica. Patterson analysed the psychology of Rastafarian withdrawal in this light and the influential Political Reporter declared that even if plans for 'migration' succeeded, the Rastafari would not be the ones going.[56] Migration to Africa has had less success than anticipated and Rastafari brethren are among those who have participated in the modest beginning. The twenty who reside in Ethiopia are now plagued with problems of land tenure and difficulties of settling in but the Emperor has given assurances of plans to resettle them.[57] With the Jamaican Government's declared plan to establish an Embassy in Addis Ababa, a base for positive developments may itself be assured for further migration to Ethiopia.

This would be a continuation of a policy initiated in 1960 when the Government of the day implemented the University Report's recommendation against the expressed opinion of other members of the wider society. There was no concession on the matter of 'repatriation' for Rastafarians were considered to be *Jamaicans*. Moreover, the majority of the recommendations turned on rehabilitation within the Jamaican society. But Premier Norman Manley could justify his Back-to-Africa mission on (i) his government's commitment to migration as a matter of policy and (ii) Government's traditional role in helping to find out 'as far as possible what countries will accept migrants, what sort of persons will be allowed to enter as migrants, and under what conditions they will be allowed to enter'.[58] The Government was in 1960, therefore, prepared to accept the same responsibilities of facilitating migration to Africa as it had done with regard to migration to such countries as the United States and the United Kingdom. The Rastafari brethren were aware of the dilemma presented by the new situation but they were too flattered to reject the offer and in any case the opportunity of a Return for some at no expense (which would itself be a fact of prophecy) could not be treated lightly. Some three Rastafari brethren were indeed included on this Back-to-Africa Mission in addition to others representing various groups of an African-connexion persuasion.* Not surprisingly a Minority Report was submitted by the participating brethren who felt that the Majority Report did not paint an accurate enough picture of what transpired. Both Reports had in fact registered with satisfaction the cordial and friendly reception the delegation received from the Heads of State and other officials of the countries visited. Both attested to the emotional involvement of African officials with the idea of their 'brothers overseas' wanting to return home. But it was the Majority Report which realistically recorded the concern expressed by Africans with problems of assimilation since

---

* The unofficial Mission to Africa visited 5 African States and held discussions with Heads of State about 'their migration policies and the possible movement of persons from this island to settle in those countries'. Countries visited were Ethiopia (1 week), Nigeria (2 weeks), Ghana (1 week), Liberia (6 days), Sierra Leone (1 week), with two days in New York and one week in London.

'centuries of exposure to western ideas and customs must tend to modify Jamaicans into a way of life dissimilar to the African'. The Minority Report, however, affirmed unequivocally that 'the African Governments were willing to co-operate in resettling people of African descent within their ancestral borders' [*sic*]. The Majority Report introduced a note of caution in informing of a proposal by some Africans that an 'advance goodwill corps from both sides, Jamaica and the African States, should be sent into the countries of source and destination, to study and to teach'.[59]

Repatriation, the Rastafarians were to discover, was a more complex affair than they had anticipated. The African countries wanted skilled personnel, as several Jamaicans back in Jamaica had warned.* The Rastafari brethren, however, persisted in the belief that all Africa, and particularly Ethiopia, was ready to receive them. Skill did not mean a University degree, declared one cultist two years after the unofficial mission had visited. The continued cry for Repatriation throughout 1961 prompted the appointment by Government of a Working Party 'to undertake an immediate appraisal of all the factors which will be involved' in the migration and settlement of Jamaicans in five African countries of Ethiopia, Nigeria, Liberia, Ghana and Sierra Leone which were visited by the unofficial Back-to-Africa Mission. Section 7 of the Working Party's interim report dealt with 'Repatriation'. The Working Party had interviewed the three Rastafarian members of the Mission to Africa who signed the Minority Report. They outlined their doctrinal position on Repatriation and 'constantly referred' to their cause being taken up in the United Nations. The Working Party took the view of the wider society. 'It is clear', read the interim report, 'that a distinction must be made between repatriation in a cultural and sociological sense and the technical-legal implication of repatriation. *Those who argue*

---

* *e.g.* Archdeacon Lennon who was a missionary in Africa for 37 years. He warned in a lecture to the Afro-West Indian society that there was room for professional people in Africa but none for 'louts and laziness'. *Daily Gleaner*, August 26, p. 18.

*for repatriation are in fact Jamaican nationals in a legal sense
and possess no citizenship rights in any other country* . . . The
Working Party recognizes that this matter of repatriation does
not fall within the terms of reference as such'[50] (my emphasis].
The Working Party, however, admitted that to ignore the
Rastafarian claims in any plan for migration could result in the
creation of 'a very serious problem', and so in the summary
recommendations it was included that 'emotional and sentimental motivations for migration should be borne in mind'.[61]
It was clear that in official circles Repatriation had to be seen in
the wider perspective of migration which was of 'no little
importance to Jamaica'.[62] Africa was merely regarded as a new
outlet for Jamaica's surplus population.

The Jamaican Government implemented one of the major
recommendations of the Working Party and appointed a
technical Mission which visited Nigeria, Ghana and Ethiopia
between January and April, 1962, to investigate the 'technical
problems involved in any plan for the movement of persons
from Jamaica to any of the nations of Africa'. This Mission,
led by R. A. Foreman who had been Chairman of the Working
Party, was to act as follow-up to the earlier Mission but it
widened its scope to explore as well the possibilities of long
term cultural and trade relations.* The 1962 Technical Mission
found that the West African countries were concerned primarily
with attracting professional and skilled Jamaicans but the
Government of Ethiopia appeared willing to make lands
available to selected Jamaican farmers who were prepared to
live on the land and accept Ethiopian citizenship. The Mission
attributed this attitude to Ethiopia's desire to make full use of

---

* The author was a member of this Mission along with Messrs.
D. O. Mills of the Planning Unit, Mr. Wesley Miller, Trade
Administrator and Mr. R. Aston Foreman, Commissioner of Lands
as leader of the Mission. The Mission's Report was never published
since Governments changed following on a General Election on
April 10, 1962. The Jamaica Labour Party which took over plunged
into preparations for Independence and African migration lost its
public focus.

its lands and for improving techniques as well as its recognition of the feelings that many Jamaicans have towards the Emperor and Ethiopia itself. The Mission visited Shashamane where the Royal donation of land is situated. A West Indian couple (Mr. and Mrs. James Piper) were the sole occupants and they worked some 50 acres of the available 600 acres of fertile, level land. They were fully assimilated into the community around Shashamane but they admitted to members of the Mission their wish to see early settlement of the remainder of the land by Jamaicans and other West Indians who were willing to migrate to Ethiopia.* The 1962 Technical Mission finally submitted to the Ethiopian Court proposals for settlement of Jamaicans in Ethiopia. These, it was intended, were to form the basis of firm proposals to be made by the Mission to the Jamaican Government. The Jamaican Government changed within a week of the Mission's return and the matter was shelved, seemingly for the rest of the decade.[63]

There was in fact a sequel to the early action programme of investigation. It involved three enterprising Rastafarians – Filmore Alvaranga, Douglas Mack (both from the first Mission) and Samuel Clayton – who voluntarily formed themselves into a delegation and made a fifteen-month tour of Ethiopia, Nigeria, Kenya and Ghana to seek help with the repatriation of 'brethren' to Africa. They first visited New York and picketed the United Nations. On their return in March, 1965, little attention was paid them: the nation was preoccupied with the issue of the newly proposed Jamaican Works Permit Law and the implications for the regional University. A report by the travelling brethren two weeks later, however, revealed that the delegation had presented the Emperor Haile

---

* The Pipers were to be at the centre of a land tenure dispute with Rastafarians who later migrated to Shashamane, forcing out of the Emperor a decision to settle the Rastafarians elsewhere after intervention by the visiting Jamaican Prime Minister Hugh Shearer and representations made prior to this by influential Jamaicans working in Addis Ababa. See *Daily Gleaner*, October 17, 1969, front page report – Prime Minister's return.

Selassie with a petition on behalf of 'ten thousand Rastas'.[64]
The delegation had in fact collected thousands of names
indicating addresses and skills from persons all over the island.
This exercise itself betrayed an understanding on the part of
some of the movement's leading members of the practical
considerations relating to repatriation. Examination of one
sample list of names reveals a wide range of skills and occupations with 'builders', 'drivers', 'masons', 'mechanics', 'painters',
'plumbers' and 'fishermen' claiming the largest numbers.
Many simply wrote 'skilled' beside their names and 'housewives'
were well represented. Also represented on this list were a
draughtsman, an accountant, a custom-broker, a radio tech-
nician, a telephone linesman, a tractor operator, a stenotypist
and some welders. This was the first attempt to determine the
skill and occupation potential of the movement.

The widespread attachment to Ethiopia is difficult to assess
with any accuracy in Jamaica but the scenes of enthusiasm and
joy on the visit of Haile Selassie were a revealing, if surprising,
measure of the extent and depth of feeling Jamaicans have for
Africa, Ethiopia and the Emperor. One cannot conclude from
this that all such Jamaicans would wish to migrate to Ethiopia
nor that the Emperor would throw open his country indiscriminately to his worshippers. But the members of the Rasta
delegation still recall with delight the hospitality meted out to
them by the Emperor who gave them ready and frequent
audience and bore the cost of their six-month stay in his
country. Although the three brethren likened their visit to
that of the biblical three Wise Men on a visit to the King of
Kings in the East, their report revealed a unique realism and
they recommended to the Jamaican Government early communication with the Government of Ethiopia so that the
resettlement of the thousands of Jamaicans who had a 'burning
desire' to go to Ethiopia could be effected. They saw themselves as the legitimate 'ambassadors for the Back-to-Africa
Movements', and pledged themselves to 'centralize our movement into a Registered Organization'. But though this was
done, official policy flagged. It is to be doubted, too, whether

the Ethiopian World Federation which is historically the trustee of the Emperor's gift of land, would wish authority and legitimacy to pass into the hands of the three brethren. Nor would other contenders for 'leadership' in the Rastafari movement accept these three brethren as official intermediaries between themselves and the 'divine Selassie'.

The wider society was to be free of having to contemplate Rastafarian desires and the Government of the day must have sighed relief that rational organization was giving place to elusive fissiparity. Not only could the movement be better controlled, cultists could be easier rehabilitated if not assimilated. It seemed that from then on, rehabilitation of the Rastafari brethren in Jamaica would supersede considerations of repatriation to Africa. Even when a leading Rastafarian in 1969 maintained the language of repatriation in a letter to the press, he found no difficulty in simultaneously declaring 'we will not try to even unbalance the harmony of the people who are at peace. We need opportunities to develop our skills and economy this day'.[65] It may be that the coming of Haile Selassie contributed to the waning ardour of the desire for physical Return. But up to late 1965 a seven-man deputation from the 'Ethiopian African National Congress' met the Minister of External Affairs to seek Government aid to be 'repatriated to Africa'.[66]

The notion of 'rehabilitation' as outlined in the 1960 University Report (Recommendations 4, 5, 6, 7) was based on a recognition that social problems among the Rastafari were common to all people living in the depressed areas of the city. In fact, proposals for building low-rent houses, encouraging self-help co-operatives as well as for slum clearance and civic centres were to become the commonplace ingredients of work programmes of several welfare groups and service clubs which were later to operate in West Kingston. Whether the cultists have benefited from schemes of social welfare in the area is a matter for present conjecture and future study. As non-political persons, they could hardly have been the beneficiaries of improvements brought about by party functionaries in the areas affected. Some do hold the view that benefits of economic development in depressed areas such as West Kingston have not touched the Rastafarians and the decrease in numbers in that zone of the city must be explained not in terms of assimilation but by the fact of dislocation, both voluntary and by force, into other areas of the city and even into some rural districts. East Kingston now houses a greater number of Rasta camps than in 1960 when the UWI survey was done.

Since 1965 Eastern Kingston has also housed the headquarters of one of the most effective agents of rehabilitation. It is the Rasta Brethren Repatriation Association which was registered on May 26, 1965, and which has been administered by the three Rastafari brethren who comprised the independent delegation to Africa in 1963–65. The Association listed as its purposes (i) the promotion of Repatriation to Africa of its members (ii) teaching of 'spiritual and religious knowledge of the Solomonic Dynasty . . . perpetuated in lineage to Emperor Haile Selassie I of Ethiopia, King of Kings (iii) promotion of African history, culture and languages (iv) assistance for the development of Africa (v) promotion of 'the general welfare of our members' (vi) providing health benefits for members in need (vii) raising of funds to carry out its programmes.[67] While (i) – (iii) reflect the African redemption ethic, (iv) – (vii) betray some willingness to accommodate themselves to the Jamaican society; and this is what has been done in large measure. In 1969, prominent members of the association were engaged in jobs as electricians, masons, millwrights, 'contractors', leather craftsmen and professional musicians. The association had a modest haulage business, having invested in a truck, and five members were completing two-bedroom cottages all built on a co-operative basis with each member contributing his skill voluntarily and free of cost. They had laid down roots in Babylon but still hoped for physical return to Ethiopia. One spokesman of the group said that it was necessary that 'the brethren see an example of what can be done with the little that we have in this land'. He was himself pursuing a course of study at the Jamaican College of Arts,

Science and Technology. The Rastafari Brethren Repatriation Association is merely one example of the many ways in which Rastafari brethren have adjusted to the wider society, working in fishing co-operatives, in small farming, at such crafts as upholstering and shoemaking, at carving and at hawking and peddling.

In 1959 the movement was amorphous and structurally ill-defined. But the inclusion of the brethren in the Back-to-Africa mission forced on them some form of institutionalization to facilitate participation in the planning of the tour and to determine the basis of choice of representatives. The pending visit of Haile Selassie quickened the process somewhat and in 1966 there were recognizable groups. The United Front (Locksmen*) with headquarters at 76 King Street, was led by Brother Campbell. The Church Triumphant of Jah Rastafari (Locksmen) with headquarters at 99 Redemption Avenue was led by Ras Shadrac and Ras Daniel Heartman (the latter being an artist with works hanging in the University, the Institute of Jamaica and many private homes, the former with a plot of ground on University lands from which he was subsequently evicted). The Rastafari Movement (Locksmen) had its headquarters at 1000 Marcus Garvey Drive, which has since been cleared for port facilities, and was led by Br. Sam Brown, who contested a seat in the 1962 General Elections and lost. The Ambassadors of Negus Group (non-locks) was the alias for the Rastafari Brethren Repatriation Association already mentioned above. The Ethiopian Orthodox Church (once Locksmen but non-locks in 1966) was led by Brothers Dennis Chin

---

* 'The most obvious source of division and dispute among the brethren is the treatment of the hair. The brethren fall into three categories: the Locksmen, whose hair is matted and plaited and never cut, neither their beards; the Beardmen, who wear their hair and beards but may trim them occasionally and do not plait the hair, but keep it clean. Both these groups wear moustaches. Thirdly there is the Baldhead or "cleanfaced" man who is not obviously distinguishable from the ordinary Jamaican except by some article such as the yellow, green and red pompom or scarf.' *The Rastafari Movement, Kingston, Jamaica.* ISER, 1960, Chapter IV.

and Buckley with headquarters in Georges Land and the Ethiopian National Congress had its headquarters in West Kingston.

There persisted, however, the individuals who held allegiance only to the cult as a whole and to no particular group under any particular leader. Mortimo Planno, who was a member of the 1961 unofficial Mission, was one such person. His 'yard' in West Kingston was the scene throughout the early sixties of many educational programmes in which Amharic and African History were taught. He was to emerge at the time of Selassie's visit when he was called to address the surging enthusiastic crowd around the Emperor's aeroplane, requesting them to allow the Emperor to land. The voices of constituted authority had failed to have any effect. He has since, however, returned to a state of quiet, living at ostensible peace with the wider society. Then there is Ras Dizzy who belonged to the militant core in the early sixties. He is the self-appointed 'interpreter' of the movement. He writes prolifically in Rasta argot about the social and economic ills of the country as seen through the eyes of the cult. He is also a self-taught painter who organizes side-walk exhibitions and draws heavily on the middle classes for support.

While Repatriation remains a formal commitment in the belief system of these groups and individuals, they have found ways of participating in the wider society without any apparent psychological problem attendant on their having to compromise their position. Rehabilitation may be seen in forms of outward conformity, some brethren even shedding their locks to facilitate employment. Accommodation with the wider society has also shown itself in such activities as the performing arts in which Rastafari brethren have participated, whether in the annual Festivals or in a play chronicling the triumphs of a National Hero,* or as drummers in various variety concerts promoted and attended by members of the wider society. There are

---

* 'Ballad of a Rebellion', written by Sylvia Wynter Carew and sponsored by the Government. The part of Paul Bogle, the national hero, was played on stage by a Rastafarian.

several painters besides Heartman and Dizzy among the Rastafari brethren who find a ready market among middle class connoisseurs, thus establishing a vital contact based on mutual respect (and needs) between themselves and wider society. The Rastafarian who contested the 1962 General Election betrayed a willingness and desire to participate in the normal power processes of the country despite the doctrine of Exile.

The facility with which the Rastafarians have found community with the wider society can be explained in terms of the many values they share with the lower classes who nurture an anger against deprivation but do not abate it, as the Rastas do, with a doctrine of social rejection. Such values are most explicit in the realm of religious worship and much of Rastafarianism before the middle fifties was as George Simpson suggested a variant of the Revivalism which is rampant in the depressed urban areas. Although regarded by the wider society as an aberration, the Rastafari movement could easily be tolerated by a society that has grown up in a strong tradition of religiosity. The missionaries under and after slavery, the Great Revival of 1860s and the upsurge of Zionism and Pocomania, the memory of Bedward, the spiritual leader, and the secular counterparts of 'prophets' in politicians like Garvey, J. A. G. Smith and Bustamante, all provided a psychological frame of reference for the Rastafarians and the wider society. The Jamaican environment of want had always thrown up the cry for deliverers including the British Crown at the time when Crown Colony Government was imposed and the Rastafarian could be seen as yet another variant of the recurring phenomenon in Jamaican life.

A closer look at the Rastafarian practices reveals that much in their way of life is in any case based on a moral code akin to that of the 'subculture'.[68] Like the revivalists they condemn deceitfulness, stealing, lying, evil thinking, fornication, and covetousness and like them they suffer lapses from the mores, though many Rastafarians would claim greater commitment to their beliefs than they feel other cultists could to theirs. Such taboos as are found among revivalists are also to be found among Rastafarians, e.g. the non-eating of pork, or of any sea-food with shell or scaleless fishes. Nor will a Rastaman lie beside a woman during her menstruation period. Fasting, praying, the singing of hymns, the reading of the Scriptures are common to both groups in their confrontation with the short-comings of the world (Babylon to the Rastafari) and the Rastafarian withdrawal by Repatriation may be seen as a parallel to the revivalist's hope for life in the next world. There is the difference that while some younger politicians particularly since the early sixties have managed to politicize the revivalists, the Rastafarians have held firmly to the view that involvement in the political processes of Babylon is sinful and detrimental to their preparation for the life in Ethiopia. This position serves to reinforce the status quo and induces some tolerance on its part in its dealings with the Rastafari brethren, and this in turn facilitates, paradoxically enough, the 'rehabilitation' of the Rastafarians into the wider society. The fact that the Rastafari had shared religious values with many others in the subculture should not, however, serve to deprive the Rastafari movement of its own personality and the challenges it presented to the wider society. And if the wider society has assimilated the Rastafarians that society has also been profoundly in-fluenced by the Rastafari movement. By the middle sixties the influence was particularly evident among the young and though cynics still attribute much of this to the factor of ganja, there is clear evidence of more profound influences on the life of both those emerging from the poor and those who still form the sediment at the base.

Rastafari and Law and Order

The Rastafarian doctrinal position on *ganja*, the Wisdom Weed, maintains the movement's constant contact with the civil power – the police. Although there is less urgency about these relations recently than there was ten years ago, developments in Jamaica since 1960 still put the Rastafarians in constant conflict with the law of the land, and raise wider problems of law and order which the ex-colonial milieu invokes with indignation and rigour. The Rastafarian position on ganja is itself not altogether unambiguous, as the 1960 study team discovered. There were brethren who would not use the herb, except for its proven curative qualities. There were others who felt that the weed was merely used by outsiders to exploit the Rastafarian situation.[69] Yet to the vast majority of Rastafarians ganja had deep religious significance according to Genesis 8, Psalm 18, and Revelation 22. The wider society have always had other ideas, however. Public debate on the drug had long revealed that general opinion saw it as a harmful narcotic, which disrupts mental stability. To the police, ganja is a dangerous drug and all users a danger to the established social order.

Yet there have always been sympathizers in the wider society who saw the Rastafarian use of ganja not only as a sacrament of ritual but as a necessary agent of escape, 'transporting (Rastafarian) devotees away from the awful reality [of poverty, near starvation and depression] into a hypnotic land of milk and honey. It also helps to keep them from feeling hungry. There are very few fat Rastas'.[70] This view was expressed in 1963 at a time when public concern about ganja had reached proportions of panic in the country. It was Holy Thursday, 1963, when a group of Rastafari ('bearded men' according to the reports) attacked a gas station at Coral Gardens, ten miles from Montego Bay, the internationally famous tourist resort. They killed the lone attendant, set the building afire, advanced on a nearby motel, killed a guest (a Jamaican), then fled to the nearby hills and attacked an overseer's house. On the arrival of the police a gun skirmish ensued with passers-by participating. In the end eight persons were killed, including two policemen and three Rastafari brethren. Three cultists were subsequently held for murder but within twenty-four hours some one hundred and fifty Rastafarians were arrested following raids by the police in some four parishes and confronted with charges ranging from vagrancy, unlawful possession, being a suspected person, being in possession of dangerous drugs, to being in possession of dangerous weapons. [71]

The Coral Gardens incident confirmed in the public's mind the old connexion between Rastafarianism and ganja, which had supporting evidence, as well as between ganja and crime with violence, which is more debatable. On this last matter, the debate still continues as to whether ganja begets crime and violence. In 1963 a Jamaican psychiatrist considered to be an authority on the subject was to testify in the murder case against the indicted Rastafarians that in his opinion ganja was not a drug that created addiction nor did it induce diminished responsibility or lead to violence, except possibly in persons who are already psychotic. [72] He seemed to have confirmed what many Rastafarians themselves usually claimed that its general effect is to create euphoria or general well-being and forgetfulness of troubles, or else it sends the subject to sleep. Paradoxically, this evidence by Dr. Williams, witness for the prosecution, on the non-violent, non-addictive features of ganja, was used by the trial judge to guide the jury to its decision. The three accused men were condemned to die. Dr. Coley, an expert medical witness for the defence, gave the opposite view – that ganja did affect the mind towards violence, so that a man who commits murder under its influence is not really morally responsible though he might know what he is doing. The Rastafarians may have lost three men but they won for their cause expert testimony favourable to their oft-repeated claim that they are non-violent whether under the influence of ganja or not. [73] A lawyer who was a known sympathizer of the Rastafarians contributed to the debate by emphasizing to the press that there had been no conviction in the courts in which any crime had been put down to ganja smoking up to 1963. [74] The wider society was therefore exposed to a variety of views on the subject. The Rastafarians got some support in their view that they were not the major users of the drug since they could hardly afford to purchase the costly goods. The yet unsubstantiated rumours that ganja-growing was big business involving respected citizens and even members of the constabulary did not bring to the Rastafari any sympathy from the wider society. The Rastafarians therefore saw themselves as suffering the fate of heavy fines and inevitable imprisonment that usually befalls the poorest sections of the society.

The war on ganja and the 'war' on Rastafarians became one and the same thing. The Minister of Home Affairs announced in the House of Representatives the Government's plans to launch a campaign to eradicate ganja – a helicopter was to be provided for the police force, monetary rewards were to be offered for information concerning the weed and leading to the arrest and conviction of persons trafficking in the drug, a committee of Cabinet Ministers (all with legal training) was named to study the existing Dangerous Drugs Law with a view to amendment for greater efficiency and Government was to embark on a full-scale publicity campaign to enlist public support in 'stamping out this menace'.[75] On the same day the clergyman delivering the eulogy at the funeral of one of the policemen slain in the Coral Gardens skirmish was reported as urging legislation against the Rastafarians whom he described as 'a band of vicious people whose doctrine and activities could not suit this or any other government'.[76] Meanwhile Prime Minister Bustamante gave grave warning of his intention to effect radical changes in the existing Dangerous Drug Law which he found to be inadequate. He was particularly concerned about the good reputation of the country with an eye no doubt on the tourist trade and with a concern for the bad image the incident might have given to his country which was projected abroad as stable, peaceful and harmonious.[77] 'Wherever ganja is grown, whether on the hills, on the plains, in the forests, on platforms between trees or in pots, I intend to see that there is no resting place for those evildoers until this country is rid of the menace', he declared. This was endorsed by the *Daily Gleaner* which averred in an editorial that 'most [sic] crimes of violence in Jamaica, as in India, British Guiana, Trinidad and other places can be traced directly to the use of ganja'.[79] Such statements were readily received by the gullible wider society which was already firm in the belief that ganja-smoking Rastafarians were violent. The Rastafarians acted as though the Armageddon between themselves and the wider society had come and the weekly newspaper, *Public Opinion*, saw the confrontation as a war not only between 'economic classes but also a struggle between conflicting cultures'.[80] The newspaper saw the war against ganja merely as a deepening of the struggle. 'The true Rastafarian abhors violence and does not deviate from the dogma of peace and love irrespective of racial differences' wrote a leading Rastafarian,[81] but this did not prevent the Parliament passing the historic and far-reaching Amendments to the Dangerous Drugs Law 1 of 1951. Increased penalties, high fines and mandatory sentences were significant features of the new law and it gave the public a feeling of tranquillity and Government an ease of conscience.

While few would wish to dishonour the international conventions on the traffic in dangerous drugs to which Jamaica is subject, many have long questioned the wisdom of the stringency of the law as it operates in Jamaica. By the late sixties, the debate on ganja had assumed new dimensions, particularly with the emergence of hippies in North America and Europe and the unconcealed and much reported use of the marijuana by the young as well as by international celebrities. A digest of views by West Indian and Anglo-American experts vaguely concurred on the harmfulness of *cannabis sativa* (the botanical name for marijuana). But there were as many reservations as to the true knowledge of its long-term effects on users or whether the penalties meted out for smoking and possession were not offensive to logic and commonsense.[82] At least one opinion emphasized the need for research and the Jamaican Government announced plans to cultivate its own crop of ganja for research while still pledged to full-scale eradication of private fields wherever found. One such exercise resulted in the conviction of a cultivator who appealed against his sentence. The Jamaican Court of Appeal was to decide by a majority verdict (one Justice dissenting) that the word 'ganja' in section

2 of Cap 90 means the pistillate or female plant of the genus *cannabis sativa* and does not include the staminate or male plant.[83] The technicality of terminology had opened a new chapter (and new difficulties) for the wider society. The Rastafari brethren made no public comment, probably knowing that the new developments could never end the debate on a law which committed Jamaica to international agreements. Not long after the verdict by the Court of Appeal, a judge was to offer his opinion that the Dangerous Drugs Law could never seriously make a distinction between the pistillate and the staminate plant in ganja, and hoped that the Judges of Appeal would find cause to change their view on the matter. To him 'ganja' was ganja.[84] To many in the wider society it is still the inducement to violence and those who use it are still considered violent.

Such was the view held of the Rastafari in 1963. Their cause after the Coral Gardens incident was not helped mainly for two reasons – firstly the disproportionate excitement displayed over the event by sections of the mass media and secondly the role that ganja was made to play in the search by police and public for a motivation for the Rastafarian rampage. The radio stations referred to the event as an 'uprising' and though the Government was quick to rebuke the news media for exaggeration, a combined police-military operation was nevertheless mustered and an emergency visit made by the Prime Minister, two Cabinet Members, one Chief of Staff and the Commissioner of Police. A pathological fear of violence from maybe genuine revolutionaries could be the only rational reason given for what was best described as an 'overkill' on the part of the Government of the day. Perhaps the memories of the Reverend Claudius Henry died hard and no chances were going to be taken by Government in its newly-won Independence.

Claudius Henry, the self-styled 'God's Annointed, Annointed Prophet and Repairer of the Breach' had issued to thousands of the faithful, membership tickets for his Africa Reform Church at one shilling per head and had promised a return

trip to Africa on October 5, 1959.* Charged with fraud and
disturbing the peace he was bound over to be of good behaviour
and to keep the peace. But within six months he was again in
the news. Police raids on his premises at 78 Rosalie Avenue,
Kingston, had revealed the existence of detonators, 'a shot-gun,
a .32 calibre, 18 sticks of dynamite, a large quantity of machetes
sharpened on both sides, swords, batons, conch shells filled
with cement, a club and a spear'.[85] This discovery was to lead
to the arrest of Henry and fourteen of his followers, charged
with breaches of the Firearms Law, the Gunpowder and
Explosives Law, the Dangerous Drugs Law and most serious
of all, the Treason Felony Law. This last law had not been
invoked for nearly one hundred years. In this, Claudius Henry
was making history of a sort but his arrest merely confirmed in
the minds of the wider society that people who preached Back-
to-Africa were violent. The charge against the accused was
clear enough. 'Before or after December 5, 1959, with other
persons unknown they did feloniously intend to incite insurrec-
tion against the Government of the island in order to intimidate
and overawe the Governor, Legislative Council and House of
Representatives and such felonious incitement did feloniously
express by divers overt acts.' Such overt acts, as the preliminary
and Circuit Court trials revealed, turned *inter alia* on the
possession of the weapons found at Henry's home as well as
reported statements by the Rev. Henry threatening bloodshed

---

* The ticket read 'pioneering Israel's Scattered Children of African
Origin back home to Africa, this year 1959, deadline date October
5, this new Government is God's Righteous Kingdom of Everlasting
Peace on Earth, "Creation's Second Birth". Holder of this Certificate is requested to visit the Headquarters of 78 Rosalie Avenue
off Waltham Park Road, August 1, 1959, for our Emancipation
Jubilee commencing 9.00 a.m. sharp. Please preserve this Certificate
for removal. No passport will be necessary for those returning
home to Africa. Bring this Certificate with you on August 1st for
"Identification". We are sincerely "The Seventh Emmanuel's
Brethren" gathering Israel's Scattered Children for removal, with
our Leader, God's Appointed and Anointed Prophet, Rev. Henry
R.B. (Repairer of the Breach).'

and the evidence of a letter addressed to Fidel Castro soliciting the Cuban revolutionary's advice.[86]

Bail was refused the accused at the end of the preliminary hearing and it was while Henry was still in gaol that news of the Red Hills incident broke. On June 21, 1960, a confrontation between a raiding party of police and military who uncovered a Rastafari arms cache in Red Hills and 'desperadoes with rapid-fire guns' resulted in the fatal shooting of two infantry-men and the hijacking of a van by a gang of five men, 'some bearded' according to a newspaper report, who escaped into Sligoville near Spanish Town, the old capital. The Premier called on the public to help and immediately gave to the incident national importance.[87] The Rastafari were believed to be the instigators behind this. But the *Daily Gleaner* in a conscious effort to calm the mood of the wider society offered the view that the miscreants of Red Hills were foreign to the local movement of cultists. It appealed to the 'largely friendly . . . elements which comprise the large majority of cultist groups' to show 'their oneness with the community at large and *their disapproval of any philosophy of violence*'[88] [my emphasis]. Here was an attempt to exonerate the Rastafarian cult as such from any implication in the acts of the desperadoes, though the editorial expressed the prevailing view that Rastafarianism was a letting down of the side and an undermining of the hoped-for harmony in a society on the make. By June 22, the situation was much clearer. It was reported that some coloured Americans or Jamaicans long resident in the United States and led by Claudius Henry's son had come to enlist the support of Rastafarians in a 'definite plan to foment disorder'. By June 25, the Minister for Home Affairs (William Sievright) was also clearing the name of the Rastafarians as a group, referring to the recent deputation by a group of United Rases requesting settlement in Jamaica on terms similar to those afforded the Maroons.*

---

* The Maroons were originally the freed slaves of the Spaniards who fled to the hills at the time of the English occupation in 1655, providing a haven for future runaway slaves and developing into a

Then on the following day three Rastafarians were found
dead in a grave in Red Hills. They were all members of
Henry's African Reform Church and were apparently shot in
the head as the post-mortems revealed. The theory gained
credence that they were executed on orders by the Americans
who had usurped leadership from them. This gave further
suspicion to the notion of a carefully planned revolution
involving a well ordered and disciplined unit of guerillas with
a properly worked out code of behaviour, etc. This could
hardly have been fully the case since the four Americans were
taken into custody on June 27 having been found off-guard,
asleep. The search for the men narrowed down to five by the
end of the month while the four captured were all charged
with the murder of the infantrymen and three with the murder
on June 15 of the three Rastafari brethren. The manhunt
continued throughout the following week, giving rise to
Rastafarian accusation of police brutality and growing distrust
among the public of the entire cult. In St. Thomas one Rastafarian was charged with the unlawful possession of a police
cap.[89]

The Methodists' decision to embark on a programme of
rehabilitation of the Rastafari and their appointment of a
deaconess (Sister Julia) on a full-time basis for the purpose
was one of the few compassionate exceptions in the general
public outcry against violence and, by extension, against the
Rastafari.[90] Then in a historic session of the House of Repre-

source of harassment for the English colonists who by the 1730s were
outnumbered ten to one (in favour of the black slaves). The
Maroons were to be pacified with a treaty concluded in 1739 between
the English and Cudjoe, the leader of the Leeward Maroons in the
Cockpit country. The treaty offered jurisdiction over some acreage
of land in return for promises to deliver up in future all runaway
slaves and to assist in suppressing other parties of Maroons who
refused to make a similar treaty. This, according to the historian
Philip Wright, made it possible for Quao, the Windward leader,
to sign a similar treaty later in 1739 (See 'War and Peace with the
Maroons 1730–1739' article by Philip Wright in *Caribbean Quarterly*,
Vol. 16, No. 1, 1970, and *The Fighting Maroons*, by Carey Robinson,
Collins-Sangster, 1969).

sentatives on July 27, 1960, the Detention Powers Bill was passed, amended to be on the Statute Books for one year. It provided for the detention of a suspected person for one time only. The Jamaica Labour Party Opposition argued against it as an infringement of individual rights but the People's National Party's Minister of Home Affairs justified the bill on the grounds of clear and present danger to public security. The member for Southwestern St. Andrew (Clem Tavares, JLP) asserted that the absence of internal revolution made the bill superfluous, that the Gunpowder and Firearm Laws were sufficient to cope with Henry's Church at Rosalie Avenue, that the provision of appeal to the Minister was a case of Caesar appealing to Caesar and that the problem was not one of security but of sociology, of which 'the Rastafari movement formed a fractional part'.[91] The PNP leader admitted the unpalatable nature of the bill but insisted that it was necessary for reasons of security. The events had to be seen, he said, as a threat to the legitimate power. Early in the debate, Premier Manley stressed that the bill was intended for the master minds from New York who were reportedly behind the insurrectionist movement in Jamaica. The assurance implied that the Rastafari movement as such would not be oppressed, an assurance later sought by the Deputy Leader of the Opposition (Donald Sangster). In the debate in the Legislative Council on July 29, Edward Seaga (JLP) blamed the events of the period on the unhealthy relationship between the police and the masses and the inability of the island's economy to provide sufficient advance for the masses.* He saw some point in Government making a positive statement on Rastafarians migrating to Africa and accused the Government of the day of mismanagement of the current dangers in the society which he admitted to exist.

It was against this background that many Rastafari brethren

---

* Nearly ten years later the same reasons were given by critics of the JLP government in which Mr. Seaga has held the positions of Minister of Development and Welfare and Minister of Finance and Planning.

approached the University to do a study to show the wider society what the movement was about. 'Among those that are Rastafarians, there are many who are honest, religious, decent and peace-loving and whose only desire is to inherit a home in . . . the land of the Lion of Judah' wrote a Back-to-Africa advocate.[92] Such were the true believers who abhorred violence and lived by the injunctions of 'peace and love' claimed many of the brethren. The Ethiopian World Federation which sympathized with the movement, dissociated itself from any acts of violence, plots etc., and a Commissioner of the United Negro Improvement Association (Garvey's organization) made it clear that the UNIA did not tolerate such 'unJamaican and undemocratic activities'.[93] Yet despite such declarations and the publication of the University Report, the trial judge passing sentence some months later on Henry and his fourteen church members described the Rastafari doctrine as '*a wicked doctrine* which had been allowed to take a hold of the poor, illiterate people of this country'[94] [my emphasis].

In his final address Counsel for the Defence tried hard to minimize the significance of the Henry affair. The burden of his submission was that the charge of treason felony and the proportions of a Circuit trial far exceeded the enormity of Henry's misdemeanours. The approach by Government, he said, betrayed an over-reaction to a 'few sticks of dynamite' in the hands of 'fishermen, a country preacher [and] carpenters'. He compared the Henry trials to the trial of the Seven Tailors of Tooley Street. Defence Counsel could hardly have won the Crown Prosecutor's patience by further asserting that 'the accused have exerted a political influence and have scored a political victory for what they seek – the governmental approach of people of African origin returning to Africa'.[95] The Crown Prosecutor denied to Henry any claims comparable to say a 'George William Gordon, a J. A. G. Smith or a Garvey'.*

* George William Gordon, the 19th century Jamaican patriot and Marcus Garvey the black visionary are 'National Heroes'; J. A. G. (Jag) Smith was a prominent lawyer and legislator who flourished between 1919 and 1940 in Jamaican public life.

He described their religious doctrines as 'fantastic stupidity' and reminded the jury of the country's responsibility to stamp out 'organized violence'.[96] A wide cross-section of the Rastafari brethren were eager to extricate themselves from any charge or suspicion of organized violence and to be free of the disadvantages imposed upon them by the increasing deterioration of relations with the police. Nor would they have wanted a leader whose Defence Counsel had described him, albeit in a last plea for mercy, as 'a racial and religious fanatic, a man of little judgement and logic and a very naive character'. The description, paradoxically, might well have been made of Garvey by his detractors at less propitious times in that visionary's turbulent career.

Other factors emerged from the Henry affair in respect of attitudes to law and order. The Rastafarian cry for religious freedom and the right to worship Haile Selassie as their God, is not always heeded with charity by the wider society which is marked by its religious orthodoxy. Henry's Counsel had emphasized the right of a citizen to hold political views which may be unpopular with the status quo as long as these did not lead to political conduct designed to overthrow a duly elected government by violence. Such pleas for fundamental rights were to remain a feature of the Rastafari movement throughout the sixties.[97] During the late sixties the wider society had joined in emphasizing the need for Government to operate with such rights in mind. Jamaica's sponsorship of 1968 as Human Rights Year at the United Nations focused some attention on the question and invited expressions of doubt as to whether Jamaica had been scrupulous in her observance of such rights, which are written into her Constitution. The traditional voices of protest in the society were to be joined in the issue by the Jamaica Council for Human Rights deprecating the raids carried out by the police and military in 1968 on Claudius Henry, who since his release from prison had formed himself into a religious organization known as the New Creation Peacemakers' Association, with branches at Kemp's Hill, Clarendon, Kingston and elsewhere.[98]

Work, Youth and the Rastafari

Laziness was early associated with the Rastafari in the minds of the wider society. Many of the cultists had projected a 'theory' of work which amounted to refusal to work for the oppressors in Babylon. Even though this made sense in the logic of a doctrine of Exile, practice rarely followed theory and as the University Report pointed out, the attitudes of Rastafarians to work paralleled closely the attitude of the wider population in a situation of chronic unemployment and underemployment. 'Much of the psychology of the brethren is the psychology of the unemployed in any part of the world, and is similar in its essentials to that of the unemployed working class in Europe or the United States during the 1930s'.[99]

Shiftlessness, loss of hope, demoralization and the lapse into an attitude that regards work (unavailable as it is) as unnecessary, characterize the postures of many persons caught up in the intolerable situation. Such was the case with many of the brethren interviewed in 1960. Yet there were others who believed in work, though they admitted a preference for self-employment over living 'in slavery' under the 'Babylonian' captors. The University Report also recognized a majority group of 'average disposition'.

The University Report further observed that the movement is rooted in unemployment: 'If the supply of jobs in Kingston were to catch up with the demand for jobs, a hard core of religious belief would remain but the movement would cease to have mass significance'. The supply of jobs did not catch up with the demand in the decade of the sixties. The Five Year Independence Plan for 1963–1968 admitted that 'unemployment is clearly the major social and economic problem in Jamaica' and emphasized the 'serious difficulties facing school-leavers in regard to obtaining employment'. Surveys carried out in 1957 and 1960 revealed some 18 per cent (or 120,000) of the labour force to be unemployed and though the authors of the Plan were careful to emphasize that the survey of 1957 was conducted at a time when employment was affected by low seasonal activity in sugar, tourism and other industries, the figure was phenomenal enough to present the entire society with serious social problems. The 1960 survey showed an improvement in the unemployment figures but the 82,000 recorded as unemployed was arrived at when the sugar industry was at its peak of employment capacity in April of that year. The factor of migration was also believed to have contributed to the low figure.

At the end of the decade the number of unemployed had increased substantially, however. In 1969 the much publicized Doxey Report was confirming what everybody said they already knew – 'the unemployment position is growing worse'.[100] The migration of labour from the rural to the urban areas and particularly to metropolitan Kingston, the growth in population and the blocking of outlets for emigration (particularly to the United Kingdom) are the reasons given. Where emigration opportunities presented themselves, as to the United States of America, such opportunities were for skilled workers, thus leaving the mass of unskilled labour untapped. The 1968 Economic Survey gives at best an uncertain estimate of the work force as being 750,000.[101]

With a three to four per cent annual increase in the labour force the percentage of unemployed is sometimes estimated as high as 20 per cent. Though admitting the crudity of the data and estimates resulting, Doxey offers the view that 'the economy will need to generate between 200,000 and 300,000 new jobs in the next five years'. The absence of accurate data merely intensifies the problem and the guess that the number of young recruits to the Jamaican labour force may be larger than the national average invests our subject under review with a special relevance. *'There is'*, says Doxey, *'the alarming probability that many young persons will pass through the greater part of their lives having never been regularly employed'*[102] [his emphasis]. This is not a new phenomenon in Jamaican life. Many of the Rastafarian brethren interviewed in 1960 had had just this kind of experience and continue to have it after ten years of alleged prosperity in the wider society. 'It shows', according to a *Gleaner* Editorial,[103] 'that in spite of all the development which has taken place during this decade, the number of unemployed continues to rise. Neither the heavy investment in the bauxite and alumina sectors, nor the hundreds of new manufacturing industries which have been established have been able to solve the unemployment situation'.* George Cumper, the UWI economics professor, in an earlier comment on the 1960 census had observed, quite rightly, that 'the unemployment data grossly underestimate the incidence of poverty – namely, the fact that many jobs are paid so low that even regular employment does not guarantee an income sufficient for the needs of a large family'.[104] This explains in part the approach by many young people to work. Many decide to remain unemployed or simply to 'scuffle' rather than work for a 'starvation' wage. The prosperous in discussing such people invariably fall back on the theory of natural indolence and it is Cumper who again suggests that this approach is 'often a device by which those who are prosperous protect themselves from the painful business of thinking seriously about those who are not'.[105]

The wider society has proposed remedies for these ills. A reduction of the birthrate, estimated at 2 per cent annual increase between 1950 and 1957, readily recommends itself and the Government has given full support to a family planning programme.[106] Some members of the wider society see this as a long-term solution. The Rastafarians reject it completely on doctrinal grounds. They see birth control as a 'plot to kill off black people'. They see it as murder and a contravention of the Old Testament prophecy 'the seeds of Israel must be numberless'. Officials of the St. James Family Planning

---

* *The Star* carried an editorial the day before on the subject pointing out that the group of companies introduced by the Jamaica Industrial Development Corporation employed an average of 20 persons. To absorb the unemployed (est. 107,000–214,000) somewhere between 5,250 and 10,700 new factories of the JIDC type would have to be established 'assuming that they have or can acquire the necessary skills'. *Star*, October 23, 1969.

Association were given the Rastafarian views on the matter in a meeting held in Montego Bay in early 1968. A spokesman for the cult was reported as saying that 'no Rastafarian will allow his queen (wife) to be mingled with or interfered with by a physician'. When the doctor present outlined the different methods of birth control there was the typical Rastafarian comment from the audience: 'They want to turn our queens into graveyards'.[107] Earthquakes, nuclear war and other catastrophes would take care of the excess population, he said. The Rastafarians were concerned with the present, not the future and the best way of solving the unemployment problem would be to give people like the Rastafarians more land to work so as to provide Jamaica with more food.

To encourage people to work the land is also a remedy frequently cited by spokesmen of the wider society. But the realities of an accelerated urbanization and the disinclination of the rural youths to spend their lives in back-breaking work for subsistence-level wages, constantly thwart all efforts to make agriculture appealing. There is no evidence that all Rastafarians who claim to want to work the land in Ethiopia would wish to do likewise in Jamaica though the demand for free land for squatting and for subsistence farming is constantly made by many of the brethren.

Migration is yet another remedy that has long formed a part of Jamaican government policy. There are those[108] who think that Jamaica had a 'moral right' to send away its surplus population and the Rastafarians, for other reasons, concur with special reference to their repatriation to Ethiopia. The unemployment problem being what it is at the end of the sixties, the Government of the day seems to be re-activating the policy of migration to Africa which received serious consideration between 1960 and 1962. In 1969 the yearning after a millennium is probably no less intense on the part of the listless unemployed but the millennium redemption is now seen, particularly by the young, as possible in the context of a more just and equable society in Jamaica!

The young (many of them unemployed, unemployable or

underpaid) have always been attracted to the Rastafarian cult. In 1960 many of the militant and most articulate spokesmen of the movement were in their mid or late twenties. In 1964 the average age of a sample group of 497 Rastafarians domiciled in the Corporate area and four rural parishes was 27. The persistence of the intolerable social conditions which breed Rastafarianism and other cult-groups made it easy for the deprived and alienated young to align themselves with the established cultists passing their time away in euphoric escape by the smoking of ganja and in bitter contemplation of the inherent injustice of a social system which threatened to keep the black Jamaican forever at the base of society. This last point was to strengthen the adherence of educated middle class youths, who despite the benefits of education, adequate shelter and opportunities for advancement in the wider society, have embraced Rastafarian creed and habit in their own quest for identity and social reconstruction. The speech pattern of Rastafari brethren is evident among many of these middle class youths who have lifted the black nationalist tenets of Rastafarianism wholesale from the Rastafari creed and invoke it in the name of 'Jah Rastafari'. 'Unity is the only solution to these problems, now that we are conscious [i.e. of ourselves as black men who have been deprived and wronged] *through the blessing of Jah Rastafari*' reads an article entitled 'Things must come to bump' (a head) in the first issue of 'Youth Move', a student newsletter issued by high school students.[109] It is clear from other articles in this newsletter that these young advocates had no commitment to Repatriation nor did they seek redemption away from Jamaica. 'The youth of today must take an active interest in the running of the country' writes the editro, who closed his piece with the words 'one Love', a conventional Rastafarian expression of fraternal greeting. A group of such young people are to be found among the University undergraduates and may be termed *functional* Rastafarians, who have served to secularize the movement away from its strongly religious orientation and to blur the lines yet further between those who want deliverance in Ethiopia and those who desire it in Jamaica. To bridge the gap, the notion of the Africanization of Jamaica is invoked with some of the old Rastafarian ardour though with little hope of total success in a wider society which is confident in its commitment to multi-racialism and cultural fusion.

The influence of the Rastafari movement on the young began to show itself in the mid-sixties in the phenomenon known as the rudies or rude boys.* The University team had found that ganja and the easy translation of the Rastafarian dialectic into orthodox Marxism were ready attractions for middle class youths and Jamaicans of a leftist persuasion. It was further predicted that the trend would 'surely continue so long as Jamaican society fails to provide the young with significant ideals of social justice for which to strive, and opportunities for their achievement'.[110] The rude boys felt that such ideals and opportunities were significant by their non-existence in the society. The scourge of unemployment with all its side-effects was largely responsible for the rude boy phenomenon. In an interview a rude boy defined his set as originating from those 'that are being oppressed'.[111] Another member of the group had this to say: 'There are thousands of them (i.e. rude boys) out there with ambition, seeking jobs, looking work and get none. Some of the places they go, they really turn them away. They feel as if they are not part of the society and nobody wants them around'. The frustration frequently resulted in a turn to anger. 'A hungry man becomes an angry man' explained a rude boy 'and if these boys can't get no way of obtaining shelter nor having food nor clothes and when you look at them their ages just 15 to 20 . . .'[112] Garth White, a young commentator on the rude boys, asserts that this anger assumes proportions as described by Jean-Paul Sartre in his Preface to Fanon's *The Wretched of the Earth*.[113] White says that the majority of youth coming from the lower 60 per cent of the population that shares approximately 19 per cent of the National Income is angry – angry to the point of violence. In

---

* In Jamaicanese, the word 'rude' often refers to anyone who is openly defiant of constituted authority.

fact, violence was a feature of the rude-boy phenomenon in the wake of the mid-sixties. At first directed against members of their own deprived class, the angry young men were soon to acquire a 'higher consciousness', according to one member, and to realize that 'it's not the suffering brother you should really stick up [with German-made ratchet knives and guns, according to White] it is these big merchants that have all these twelve places and living into apartments – all fifteen – with the whole heap of different luxurious facilities'.[114] The speaker continued: 'We no longer going to hold our brothers and sisters up because they haven't got what we want. What we really want is this equal rights and justice. Everyman have a good living condition, good schooling, and then I feel things will be much better as long as we get this right of equality'.

Here is a shift of emphasis from classic Rastafari doctrine. There is no question of deliverance in Ethiopia ruled by a divine Haile Selassie. Deliverance must be in Jamaica. Change must come not by escape from the system but by the shaking up of the system – even if by violence. The Robin Hood morality of robbing the rich to give to the poor is also evident here, where it is absent from Rastafarianism. Nor did the rude boys establish a religious base for their position. Theirs is a secular social and political 'philosophy' that invokes the right to work, stresses the obligation that society has to the individuals born into it, demands equitable distribution of wealth with special considerations for the deprived black majority, and calls for universal justice. Their doctrinal position was, however, inspired and informed by Rastafarian belief. Many a rude boy consciously shared Rastafarian beliefs and practices and meandered quite comfortably between the religious escapism of Repatriation Rastas and the secular and materialistic anarchy of the rudie youth. Although Garth White correctly thinks that the rude-boy is less ambivalent in his attitudes to the wider society (the metropolitan orientated 'other society', as he called it) than, say, the Rastafarian, the ambivalence is there nonetheless. The rejection of 'middle class standards and values' is never complete for either group – the acquisition of middle class education, motor cars, homes with swimming-pools, salaries of four figures and regular secure employment (whether self-employed or otherwise) are still objectives which determine the protest. What Robert Hill said of the world of the rude boy is applicable to that of his mentor, the Rastafari. At its worst it is a 'world of violence, suffering and deprivation, police brutality and the cruelty of the poor to poor'. The rudies have learnt the antidote of 'peace and love' from the Rastafari even though some invoke the weapons of violence against the 'oppressors and the exploiters' (viz., the middle and upper classes). At best the world that was the Rasta's and later the rudie's is said to reveal 'an intensity of feeling and human want, a strong sense of individuality, a capacity for gaiety, hope for a better life, a desire for understanding, readiness to share the little they possess and the courage to carry on in the face of unresolved problems and confusion'.[115]

They survive as depressed people do anywhere through different forms of artistic expression. Garth White reminded the Jamaican upper and middle classes that whatever (they) may have had to say about 'the quality of ska presentations, their usefulness as indicators of thought of the other society – predominantly black – cannot be overemphasized'. The ska as a music and dance form emerging from the urban lower classes in 1965 had its initial responses of sneer and snobbery from the more privileged society, only to be thoroughly appropriated by the wider society and commercially promoted at home and abroad (and into oblivion). What has developed since has been an energetic musical creativity in the pop culture of the young in depressed areas from which the Rastafarians originally came. Preliminary commentaries on this aspect of Jamaican subculture have been done by at least two reliable observers and both have credited the Rastafarian movement with providing the initial and creative drive for these developments in Jamaican popular music and dance.[116] This was repeatedly emphasized by the informant in a recent interview with Count Ossie, the Rastafarian drummer, with this author. It was Count Ossie himself who had provided 'the beat' in spontaneous jam sessions in the Wareika Hills for the early experiments and it was out of this that the pioneer tune 'Carolina' emerged. Even more important, according to Gordon Rohlehr, the Rastafarian environment produced the late Don Drummond, the talented trombonist who is universally acclaimed in Jamaica as one of the country's 'few artists with a genuine vision and message'. It was the message of 'despair, rebellion, and the longing to travel further East, back to the Fatherland', thus showing, according to Rohlehr, that Drummond was steeped in the agonies and hopes of the Rastafarian.*

The compositions of ska and its offsprings, the rock steady and reggae, were to serve as a common mode of artistic expression among a wide cross section of the youth of Jamaica. The ska like its successors had the force of pop music everywhere, what with the promotion by radio stations and the ubiquitous sound system creating common, if unprecedented, bonds between the youths of town and country, between the lower and the middle classes, and at times even narrowing the gap between generations. In the wake of such universal appeal the contribution of the Rastafarians was almost forgotten. The rude boys themselves took on a personality of their own. New recruits into their ranks no longer needed an initial apprenticeship with hard-core Rastafarians, they could go straight into this world of sounds and pressures – pressures of poverty and politics. The anarchy and violence of the mid-sixties were reflected in the rocksteady songs of the rudies. Comment on the injustices of the system, on confrontation with the law courts and tragi-comic representations of personal experience in the depressed gully courses characterized the rudie songs. The sheer hypnotic ritual of the earlier Rastafarian-inspired beat no longer satisfied the needs of protest. However, in the late sixties the reggae songs (musically more akin to the traditional mento than the contemporary revivalist) went back to the Rastafarian themes while maintaining the

---

* Rohlehr illustrates his point by reference to the names Drummond chose for his compositions: 'Beardman Ska', 'Addis Ababa', 'Marcus Garvey Junior'.

rudie social comment on poverty and general distress. The song 'Babylon's Burning' reflects a definite Rastafarian view of the wider society and its likely fate as retribution for its wickedness. The song 'Sufferer' utilizes a common expression of how the Rastafarian sees himself and so does the internationally popular gold-disc winner 'Poor Me Israelites'. In this the lyricist wails his refrain as if in suffering and assures his audience that he would prefer not to be 'like Bonnie and Clyde' (i.e. resort to violence). One could speculate as to whether the young, after a first flush of violence, are going back to the Rastafarian position of 'peace and love'. The language is certainly widely used by the inspired young but it is not always certain whether it is always a positive guide for action. Nor should the young lyricists be invested with a self-consciousness in their compositions designed to give a message. Many of the composers on being interviewed admitted that they were not themselves conscious of the implications of their creations. But there is sufficient recurrence of themes and rhythmic signposts to justify claims that it was the Rastafarian climate of concern that helped to produce what could prove to be a rich heritage of popular music and dance among the youth of the sixties.

Many aspects of the earlier Rastafarianism were to find new expression in the Black Power advocacy of the late sixties, with certain declared cultists publicly supporting the new movement and even writing for the newspaper produced by its hard core militants. Yet many of the older Rastafarians while sympathizing with the young advocates' embrace of black nationalism questioned their sincerity on the key tenets of Repatriation and the divinity of Haile Selassie. Those Rastafarians who had themselves journeyed the road from radicalism to religious quietism were heard to express disapproval of the aggressiveness of the young Black Power advocates. The doctrine of 'peace and love' was by now meant to have literal application in the lives of those who committed themselves to Africa and things African. It was obvious from early that there was an emotional gap between the overriding secularism of the new Jamaican Africanists and the religious doctrine of the African deliverance of the older Rastafarians.

Some Conclusions

After a decade the Rastafari movement may be seen from a somewhat clearer perspective. The notion of polarization of the society into the Rastas and the rest is at best a misleading one, encouraged both by the Rastafarians themselves in their bold rejection of the established mores of Jamaica and by the wider society which ostracized cultists and treated them as deviants from the 'inviolable' norms. Much evidence, however, points to the deep involvement of the Rastafari with the society and to the phenomenon being a natural and logical development from the social, economic and psychological circumstances of the Jamaican society. The Rastafarians have been the barometer of social and economic pressures in the society chiefly among that segment of the population which has long nurtured a feeling of having been wronged and deprived. Supported by a continuous state of economic want and social humiliation, the masses threw up the Rastafari who reinforced their 'moral' position by a strongly religious dynamic giving their movement a momentum and force which was easily conceived as a threat to the society it sought to change. For implicit in the rejection of the dominant values and beliefs of the society was a desire for fundamental change.

In this sense it was revolutionary and as such invited the proscription that such movements frequently receive from Governments and supporters of the status quo.[117] The persecution by the wider society at times assumed proportions of irrationality, paralleling what were too often referred to as the blind and bizarre stirrings of the Rastafari. But the excesses against the movement may be explained in terms of the wider society's uneasiness with the problems of identity which the Rastafarian rumblings indicated. A Jamaican author was right in the view that 'essentially the existence of the Rastafari is a token of our tacit spiritual denial of our African past'.[118]

The ignorance of self and the conditioning process leading to acceptance of this lack of perspective are recurrent themes in all black Caribbean life. 'The truth about Africa and our connection with this continent, the acceptance of ourselves as we are, racially mainly Negro, culturally a mixture of several streams, is the first stepping stone to spiritual independence'.[119] If the wider society regarded this truth as dangerous it was the Rastafari who faced it squarely, as a group of Jamaicans responding to the pressures of a society whose institutions, practices, beliefs appeared to deny the 'sons of Negus' the benefits of a civilization which they have helped to build.

This theme of the contribution of Africans to the building of Jamaican society (and indeed the West) is a recurring one in Rastafarian doctrine and betrays the ambivalence in the doctrine of rejection, specifically in such tenets as physical return to Africa and the non-participation in the social and political processes of 'Babylon' (i.e. Jamaica). Over the decade, many Rastafarian brethren have resolved the ideological conflict and have emerged with a concept of the 'Africanization' of Jamaica. Just as the Kingdom of Heaven is within you (instead of somewhere in the clouds), Africa is in Jamaica, goes the reasoning. Some argue that Jamaica *is* Africa. The fact that the majority of the population is of African descent is used as tangible support. But some claim that they have reached their decision by divine revelation. The Rastafari Repatriation Association encourages its members to build houses and seek employment in Jamaica without compromising its commitment to Africa as 'home'. Claudius Henry has officially abandoned his 'Back-to-Africa' position and is 'building Africa in Jamaica'.*

---

* In a recent interview with the Rev. Claudius Henry, R.B., the author learnt from Henry that he had long decided to abandon Repatriation since he had been told by the Ethiopian Minister of Foreign Affairs on a visit to Ethiopia in 1958 that black Jamaicans should stay and build the country to which they had contributed so much and which, if abandoned by them, would fall into the hands of the white man.

On his release from prison, Henry addressed himself to the 'Government, government agencies and the people of Jamaica in general' giving assurances of bearing no 'animosity, vindictiveness or hatred', though he felt that his aims and objects had been misunderstood and 'wrongly evaluated'.[120] He was determined to carry on his work 'geared to help the less fortunate, regardless of creed, colour or national origin of which there are thousands who, I am sure, will . . . conform to the laws and high principles of our Government'. Henry had clearly decided to work within the framework of the established laws of the land. But his help of the 'less fortunate' would naturally mean the help of the blacks and his later pamphlets,[121] though declaring his International (New Creation) Peacemakers Association as non-political, reveal a concern for the growing problems of violence and the continuing economic deprivation in the society. As a 'prophet' he warns the Government, with appropriate biblical allusions, that only a commitment to peace instead of the use of guns or police, can solve Jamaica's problems. He maintains his millenarian zeal as a 'prophet sent from God' to establish 'God's Kingdom on Earth'. But in secular terms (and these are understood by Rev. Henry) that Kingdom is the African Jamaica. 'Those who are wise and having understanding will understand this, and seek God's kingdom, the *Blackman's* new world of righteousness'.*

---

* Rev. Henry claims some 4000 adherents, though in an interview he admitted 1000 active members of his organization. He engages many of them in his blockmaking and baking establishments at Kemp's Hill, Clarendon. He has since built a school with an enrolment of 150 at Ground Bottom. There is no doubt that he has managed to mobilize the energies of his followers in useful work that could be the basis of economic self-sufficiency at the grass-roots. Supporters of the status quo may fear that his feeling that God is on his side carries with it the usual unpredictability of decisions and action in the future. Add to this memories of a past tainted with a prison term for treason felony, the betrayal in his writings of a point of view that claims that he is doing for the grass-roots what Government should be doing and the fact that he still attracts dedicated followers, and it is not difficult to understand the distrust

The Africanization of Jamaica came to be refined into the Black Power position of mobilization of the country's human and material resources by black people in their own interest. If conditions in Jamaica do not change for the better, the tension is likely to increase between this recent concept of 'Africanization' and the older 'creolization' which, it could be argued, has served to freeze African traits in a position of inferiority and would-be passivity in the cultural complex of Jamaica. (See Essay 'The Melody of Europe, The Rhythm of Africa' below.) It is in this sense that Africanization may continue to be seen in the 1970s as a necessary and vital agent of spiritual liberation. To many there is no spiritual conflict between the original and classic position of physical return to Africa on the one hand, and the later version of employing Africa as a point of reference for the fundamental structural transformation of Jamaican society, on the other. This phenomenon indicates further, the involvement of the Rastafari brethren in the society at large and explains the ease of accommodation between the Rastafari and the wider society in the years that followed the crisis points of 1960 and 1963.

These crisis points had revealed the movement in all its millenarian dimensions. The rebellious rejection of the assumptions of Jamaican colonial society with its belief in white superiority and black inferiority; the protective attitude towards the African culture preserved in the slave experience and said to be threatened by Westernization and by the internalization of so-called 'white values', the call for salvation not passively in the Afterlife but actively in Ethiopia and the freedom from subjection to the foreign ethos regurgitated by the Jamaican middle and upper middle class, have all jolted the society into a careful look at itself, if not at the Rastafari. Much of Rasta belief derives from revelations coming from God (Jah Rastafari) or from prophets like Marcus Garvey and the Old Testament sages. The expectation of the Millennium

---

and suspicions that surround the Rev. Henry's activities. Ironically he operates in the constituency of the present Prime Minister of Jamaica.

was reinforced by the incidents of Claudius Henry and the Red Hills ambush as well as by the Coral Gardens skirmish and the reactions of Government and police. These, the Rastafarians duly endowed with eschatological significance.

The rejection of Jamaica for Ethiopia, the land of milk and honey where the Christ Re-Incarnate reigns and where black people would have respect and abundance has been preached with much ardour while the wider society was simultaneously fed, through the news media, with much information about the state of Ethiopia as an underdeveloped and backward African state struggling out of medievalism into modernity. It therefore took the wider society some time to take the cultist seriously on the matter of Repatriation. But in this the Rastafari were being as consistently Jamaican as could be expected. Repatriation, despite its religious significance, can on one level be reasonably viewed as a typical Jamaican response to social and economic pressures, namely, the urge to migrate – an urge which is not restricted to the peasant and urban proletariat classes though they have been the largest numbers to leave the country in search of work and a better life. In 1969 the Government of Jamaica can seriously talk about migration to Africa as the Government between 1960 and 1962 did. Any such scheme would naturally be broadly based and made open to all Jamaicans willing to migrate to Africa. Much will depend on the incentives involved but it may turn out that Ethiopia in its underdevelopment will require the pioneering spirit and stamina of frontiersmen that only the Rastafarian Jamaicans with their religious motivations will be found to possess. But while the wider society no longer views their cry for Repatriation as idealistic, there is still no sympathy for the view that Repatriation should be at the Jamaican taxpayers' expense and the Prime Minister on his return from his African tour did not equivocate on the matter. Government may, however, have to look seriously at Ethiopia and other parts of Africa, among other places, as alternative outlets for traditional Jamaican emigration. It may even have to offer help to facilitate the transporting and settling of these migrants on the basis of some shared scheme, say, between the Jamaican and Ethiopian Governments. This would fulfil the Rastafarian dream. Yet how many brethren would actually seize the opportunity is still a matter for speculation among the wider society. In 1959 Claudius Henry did manage to attract an estimated 15,000 persons who said they were anxious to return 'home'. With the persistence of unsatisfactory economic conditions, Repatriation (like, though not to be equated with, migration) will continue to be kept alive in the society even though other members of low income groups, finding it difficult to migrate, will increasingly clamour for change in Jamaica itself. Jamaican taxpayers are not likely to agree to financing Repatriation schemes out of public funds. High transportation costs will obviously be a deterrent but the Jamaicans who would be able to afford the fare to Ethiopia may prefer to migrate to the northern industrial countries unless motivated by a strong desire for Africa.

This motivation is not restricted to low-income groups but distinctions need to be made between those Jamaicans of a Rastafarian persuasion who see Ethiopia as the Promised Land and those Jamaicans (many of them middle class) who have a general attachment to Africa, its culture and the place it holds as their point of origin. Such Jamaicans have long been going to West Africa as railway workers, missionaries, teachers, doctors, etc. There is, however, a new though still very small, group of young educated Jamaicans, referred to earlier as functional Rastafarians. Whether they will migrate to Ethiopia, as teachers primarily, in any plan for migration will be interesting to see. Even more than the classic brethren, these new educated Rastas may find it difficult, on graduating from the University, to come to terms with the Jamaican Establishment and are most likely to be discriminated against in their search for jobs (on grounds of dress and wearing of beards and unkempt hair, for example). Many have already responded to or anticipated the Jamaican reactions by adopting what is called the 'culture of poverty' in what sometimes appears to be a parody of the Rastafarian stance, while many of the 1960 vintage Rastafarians have moved nearer middle class aspirations on the acquisition of jobs and some economic security.

There is, however, a Rastafarian life-style that awaits study in depth. Such aspects as the role of women, the family, and grass-roots economic self-sufficiency merit this attention. Estimates of the Rastafarian population have been restricted largely to the male adherents. Their 'queens' and children have been omitted, largely because it is the male who often declares and makes himself a visible member of the cult. These women may on closer examination turn out to be the major effective links between the Rastaman and his Babylon. They may also turn out to be prime breadwinners in their roles as domestic servants, fishvendors, higglers, laundresses and the like. In the 1970s there will be a new generation of adolescent Rastafarians who were born, as it were, into the faith and who will have been brought up under the close care and attention of their fathers; the Rastaman is proud of his offspring, the 'seed of Israel'. A study of these children and the degree of their involvement or otherwise in Jamaican society will be instructive. So will a study of family pattern or patterns in the Rastafarian community. Will these fit into the existing typology of Jamaican or West Indian family structures? Clearly there is no evidence that the Rastafarian views Christian marriage as a goal to strive towards. Nor is illegitimacy a moral concern. Mating habits in an ethos where common sharing is an ideal may even reveal that the Rastafarian is no less fastidious than his Jamaican compatriots in his belief that 'sexual exclusiveness is the ideal mode of behaviour'.[122] The strong emphasis on the male suggests a patrifocal organization and a possible solution to what some people view as a major problem of Jamaican family organization, viz. the household without a man at the head. But any assumption that the Rastafari movement has a strong family organization, effective paternal control and freedom from the wider society's preoccupation about common-law marriage as against Christian marriage is out of place in the absence of carefully observed and available data.

As a potential political organization, there is no doubt that given the intensity of feeling, the justification of the grievances rooted in social and economic ills, and widespread sympathy among the lower classes for sentiments often associated with the Rastafari, the movement could be mobilized into a politically feasible entity. But it is in the nature of millenarian cults, like the Rastafari, to assume a fundamentalist posture and allow every individual to claim divine inspiration. In classic Rasta doctrine then, there is no leader excepting the divine Haile Selassie. When the Back-to-Africa mission was to be selected in 1960 there was great difficulty in finding representatives from among the cultists. There were several Rastafarian organizations with membership of one each. When the self-styled 'Ambassadors of the Rastafari' made their independent tour of certain countsies of Africa they were not accepted as the legitimate leaders by others who had similar ambitions. Not even audience with the Emperor can secure an assertive Rastafarian the position of leadership. It made sense, then, for many of the brethren to dissociate themselves from Claudius Henry's movement since Henry declared himself a Prophet anointed by God. The process of fission (as Worlsey calls it)[123] was to continue throughout the sixties, with groups forming, disintegrating and re-forming in new aggregates, thus ensuring a low and ineffective level of political potential. This is likely to continue in the next decade. In this, Claudius Henry, who is able to mobilize large numbers based on a programme of action, may well be an exception. His admission of attempts to collaborate (unsuccessfully) with the political party in power betrays a political involvement which cannot be ignored. Several organizations exist as stated above but none of them have so far exhibited any real capacity for political action. They now operate as religious groups, socio-economic group-ings engaged in primary co-operative enterprises, or where the activist zeal still exists, they join with newer voices of protest or consciously act as catalyst for new activities. They remain by and large committed to the expectation of deliverance from the ills of Babylon either in Africa or in an improved Jamaica.

The earlier fears that the Rastafari might just be the integrative force heralding the unity of the Jamaican blacks were unfounded. The blacks as working class remain split and poor. Even the attempts at instilling a working class consciousness are thwarted by the bright, if grudging, hopes offered by the society in its thrust upward towards industrialization, and its push outward via migration.

One of the most persistent features of Rastafarianism will continue to be its religious doctrines. The central one turns on the divinity of Haile Selassie, the former Ras Tafari. This Rastafarian spokesmen regard as natural and valid. Selassie as a symbol of black glory and ancient African lineage dating back to Solomon and Queen of Sheba, is important not only to Rastafarians, but it is the Rastafarians who have deified him. The implication for the Jamaican society will continue to turn on whether Rastafarianism can be accepted as a legitimate form of religious worship. It is somewhat tolerated now but as the letter from the Government Radio Station (q.v.) clearly indicates, there are those who view as blasphemous the belief in the divinity of Haile Selassie. Some justify their objection on the grounds that it is a deliberate falsification of the facts since the Emperor is said to have denied any claims to divinity. The relevant fact is that the Rastafarians have declared him so just as others, according to Rasta doctrine, had declared the *man* Jesus to be the son of God. Perhaps the seeming irrationality of the declaration will appear less so with the passage of time and the Rastafarians are not slow to cite the history of other religions to prophesy their eventual success at gaining legitimacy for their creed. Some see themselves as the 'vanguard of celestial selectees', the true prophets, the 're-incarnated Moseses, Joshuas, Isaiahs and Jeremiahs . . . destined to free the scattered Ethiopians who are black men'.[124] The re-interpretation of the Old Testament is typical of such cults and is considered valid, but the results prey on the sensibilities of many Jamaicans. In fact, the religious claims involve wider questions of freedom of worship and conscience. The introduction of the Ethiopian Orthodox Church into

Jamaica would probably provide a compromise for the ortho-dox-minded in the society. But many Rastafarians, even if they became members, would in time bring Selassie to head their own pantheon of saints with possible serious implications for the traditional exegesis of the Ethiopian Church. On the other hand the secular 'canonization' by the Jamaican Govern-ment of historical figures into 'National Heroes' can hardly be said to be a deterrent for the Rastafarians, since this is in effect answering identity needs among another segment of the Jamaican population. Until the society can accept Rastafarianism with ease and in its own religious terms, the dichotomy between itself and the cult will persist into the far future.

On such details as ganja and attitude to work, already the Rastafarians have done the society a gratuitous service by forcing into the open questions which affect the general community and which are now seen as complex social problems of real urgency for public policy. It was the Rastafarians who defied and challenged the society's official view of ganja as a dangerous, violence-inducing drug, deserving of punitive measures usually reserved for the most heinous crimes. In the absence of conclusive evidence to support this widely held view, the problem of ganja (and particularly of the increasing use of it among the wider population) will continue to receive the urgent attention it now has in Jamaica as elsewhere. It is unlikely that Rastafarians will desist from smoking 'the weed' in deference to the law (however stringent) any more than Christian communicants will abandon taking wine. Rasta-farians justify their use of the drug on the grounds of the sacramental place it holds in their form of worship, and will no doubt continue to do so. But as long as ganja is illegal, Rastafarians will be at variance with the civil power.

On the matter of work, the Rastafarians have emphasized that a theory of indolence is socially determined since it results directly from the conditions of chronic unemployment, under-employment and the incidence of low-paying jobs when these can be had. The future existence of Rastafarianism and recruitment into the cult turns in large measure on the future employment situation in the country. While the belief in the divinity of Haile Selassie has no logical connexion with unemployment, Repatriation is directly related to the capacity for true believers to raise sufficient money for their fares, and this depends in turn on the availability of lucrative occupation. Fund-raising by public subscription will achieve limited success in a society whose committed members do not agree with the social rejection stand of the Rastafari. Over a period of ten years only some 20 Rastafarians out of a 1960 estimate of 20,000 have been able to migrate to Ethiopia. It may be that the availability of work could have an opposite effect – i.e. provide Rastas with enough money and opportunities to lay down roots in Jamaica and call it a part of Africa. This does not mean that they would become passive collaborators with a white ethos; they would probably feel themselves stronger and more able to promote certain beliefs about 'African virtues' into the overall value-system.

More generally the role of the Rastafarians has been to bring to the attention of the Jamaican society the urgent need to root identity and national cohesion in a recognition of the origins of its black majority and to redress the imbalance of history's systematic weakening of any claim to achievement which descendants of Africans would otherwise make in the New World. In this they have been a revitalizing force, albeit a discomforting and disturbing one. In addition, their call for improved standards of discipline in the conduct of one's daily life has had wider implications in their disavowal of the double standards that obtain among the more privileged society and in the indiscretions of public life. Many of their numbers have been repeatedly accused of hooliganism and uncivil behaviour but many are committed to a new morality that values selflessness, brotherly love, and communalism above deceitfulness, stealing, exploitation and envy. Such a call for a renewal of spirit can hardly be said not to be in the interest of Jamaica. The experiences of the sixties would suggest that the phenomenon of the Rastafari has itself been the occasion of the society's internal dynamic of change. The rejection by this group of values long deemed sacrosanct has forced the society into self-examination which is still in progress. Without forming themselves into a political party, the Rastafarians have managed to influence the traditional power elites towards a social philosophy that dare not ignore them and their aspirations, and much of this will inform the thinking and even the public policy of the nineteen seventies. On the other hand, the extreme claims by the Rastafari have been tempered with common sense and partly with the passage of time but largely on account of the practical measures that have been taken to meet some of their demands and by the growing tolerance and greater understanding in the society at large. Their concern with self-definition and self-knowledge may in its extremes suggest a racialism which Jamaica is never likely to accept or can condone. But the notion that *what we do* for ourselves depends on *what we know* of ourselves and *what we accept about* ourselves will continue to be of significance for a long time.

One of the things Jamaicans have yet to accept about themselves is what the Rastafarians have long asserted – the recognition of the African connexion in the national ethos. A *Gleaner* editorial in late 1969 summed it up aptly when it admitted the need of 'a psychological rebirth' of the black majority whose racial origins 'are too tenuous for real self-confidence'.[125] How narrow the gulf has become between the Rastafari brethren and their 'Babylonian' captors (the wider society) is evident by the fact that the Jamaican Prime Minister and the Leader of the Opposition should still feel it necessary, ten years after the Rastafarian outbursts and a generation after the call by Marcus Garvey, to weave into the pattern of (their) international travel what has been described as 'obeisance and commitment to the African majority ethnic in the Jamaican multi-racial family'.[126] Could this be a measure, as well, of the inherent logic of the Rastafarian belief-system?

JAMAICAN BLACK POWER OR NOTES FROM THE HORN

A Discussion

Some Jamaican Attitudes. Jamaican
Black Power. The Adherents
and the Role of *Abeng*. National Economic
Independence. Black Awareness and
Self-knowledge. Black Power and Violence.
Black Power and its Jamaican Future.

M.M.   H

THE END OF the decade of the sixties will partly be remembered in Jamaica for the country's involvement with the phenomenon of Black Power just as the beginning of the decade brought Rastafarianism face to face with the society. Much has been said and reported on the Black Power phenomenon with varying degrees of passion and involvement. Whatever may be one's attitude or position in the matter it is clear that to ignore it or to pretend that it does not exist is to defy reality; to insist that it should not exist is to fail to recognize the cogency of persistent historical forces in the development of Jamaica; to embrace it indiscriminately in forms which claim monopoly of understanding of the black predicament and deify racial exclusivity is to be unaware of the complex nature of those very historical forces in the society. Yet any attempt to suppress it with the might of Establishment power is to stockpile collective wrath for future reckoning.

Some Jamaican Attitudes

Many Jamaicans nevertheless see Black Power as little more than the affirmation of blind irrational forces which must be eradicated from their multi-racial midst. Multi-racialism as a result becomes to Black Power advocates the expression of an oppressive 'power structure', 'the establishment', or 'the system', while to the power structure, Black Power becomes a dangerous divisive force. Duly elected representatives of the people have made public announcements about the phenomenon. The most vocal detractors among them are notably junior political party functionaries who have declared that there is no place for Black Power in the society.[1] Though, according to one such detractor, 'if Black Power meant the dignity and social and economic upliftment of the black man then it was good but if it meant destroying the progress Jamaica has made and engendering hatred then it was undesirable.'[2] 'The progress Jamaica has made' refers to the historical situation since 1938, and more specifically since 1944, when the process of transfer of constitutional power from Great Britain actually began with universal adult suffrage, a bicameral legislature comprising a fully elected house and an embryonic 'ministerial system' heralding Jamaican participation in actual decision-taking. These may well be regarded as the institutional pillars of 'the system' or 'the power structure' which has been a main target of attack for Black Power advocates. Fears for the system have been expressed by persons other than political functionaries. A letter in the Press from a citizen read: 'An imported serum has been injected into the veins of our society. It is "Black Power". The Government and people of this country must come to grips with this "new thing". Any reasons given to evade this issue will be most futile . . . Are we going to sit back and let dangerous elements educate our people into thinking that Black Power necessarily means anti-white Power; or are we going to take it upon ourselves to teach them about the intrinsic dignity of the Black Man; his inherent potentialities, his universal importance in relation to his race?'[3] A mere month afterwards, another letter-writer urged that Jamaicans 'aim at Black Dignity and Black Power will follow.'[4] The Leader of the Government of the day has been more positive about his Government's position in the matter. 'As long as this Government remains in power' reads a newspaper report 'we believe in only one power and that is the power of people working for the benefit of the country as a whole and for the stability of the nation'. The speech, as reported, made reference, too, to 'forces in our country today who are spreading divisiveness among us' setting 'race against race, district against district, colour against colour'.[5]

He is quoted elsewhere as saying that 'Black Power advocates are irrelevant. They are pushing causes and voicing slogans that they have adopted from elsewhere. We have a black government; we have votes for everyone, we have got rid of colour discrimination'.[6] On October 16, 1968, the Government barred a young Guyanese history lecturer at the University of the West Indies from re-entering Jamaica. As it happened he was returning from a Black Writers' Conference held in

Montreal and although all efforts were made through the Press and in Parliament to assure the Jamaican public that the Exclusion Order had nothing to do with the man's attendance at the Black Writers' Conference,[7] the general impression that stayed with the public for a long time was that to embrace the doctrine of Black Power was to be subversive. Both Government and Opposition were soon to be involved in a Parliamentary session which gave to the Jamaican public televised information of the young lecturer's activities which the Government insisted could be construed as 'subversive'. The act of explanation was unprecedented in the history of bannings from Jamaica but took place only after a riot which resulted in heavy damage to and looting of property, had occurred in down-town Kingston following a protest demonstration march by some students from the University campus. The events of October 16, 1968, and immediately after were to set the pattern of thinking among many Jamaicans that Black Power was an evil thing. But they also served to crystallize ideas already existing among many Jamaicans about the unfavourable position of black people in the society. The result was a hardening of this position by those (particularly the young) who had by now embraced as their mission in life the task of restoring to the black man his manhood, his dignity, and gaining for him real ownership in the society which was supposed to be his own.

Jamaican Black Power

While October 16 may have hardened this position and given to it positive dimensions, the position was even then not a new one to Jamaica. The Black Power claim, that the phenomenon was in Jamaica from the first day that an African slave resisted his involuntary servitude, may in some sense be putting too much of a strain on history, but it evokes feelings which are deep-delved in the consciousness of many Jamaicans. It also helps to explain the anxiety of the age and the pre-occupations of many of the young people who may or may not even be committed advocates to the doctrine. To refer to the phenomenon as the 'doctrine' may even be too great a claim. For the term, here as elsewhere, spreads over a wide matrix of ideas, activities, plans and even organizations. *The slogan itself is American in origin but the view could be reasonably held that it is as much a 'thing Jamaican' as one could expect.*[8]

Marcus Garvey Jr., the son of the great visionary, insists that it was his father who first expounded the philosophy of Black Power. Quoting from *The Philosophy and Opinions of Marcus Garvey*, the young Garvey cites the following to support his view: 'Power is the only argument that satisfies man. Except the individual, the race or the nation has POWER that is exclusive, it means that that individual race or nation will be bound by the will of the other who possesses this great qualification . . . Hence it is advisable for the Negro to get power of every kind. Power in education, science, industry, politics and higher government. That kind of power that will stand out signally, so that other races and nations can see and if they will not see, feel'.[9] This coupled with the use of other Garvey sayings printed in all Black Power publications particularly since October of 1968, makes Marcus Mosiah Garvey the father of Jamaican Black Power. As a Jamaican National Hero (the highest distinction any Jamaican can achieve for public service) Garvey seemingly gives to Black Power advocacy a legitimacy which further confirms its hold on Jamaican life. The fact that Stokely Carmichael* and black Americans have found the slogan useful for Americans is further evidence, so the argument goes, of the foresight of Garvey.

For Jamaica the danger probably lies in the fact that the capitalization of the first letters of these two now powerful words threatens to take the whole phenomenon of black identity and consciousness out of the ambience of Jamaican life into the mainstream of what some people may regard as yet another vulgar 'ism'. Moreover, the subsequent embrace

---

* The work *Black Power* (*The Politics of Liberation in America*) by Stokely Carmichael and Charles V. Hamilton (Vintage, N.Y., 1967) is on the list of books banned by the Jamaican Government.

by Jamaicans of the American importation may serve to blur the fact of the continuity of this search among the uprooted in Jamaica for self-sufficiency and self-respect. More damning perhaps for some of the Jamaican advocates is that they lay themselves open to the accusation that they, like the reactionaries they berate, continue in colonial fashion to look *outside* of the society for ideas and for original thinking.* For despite the resonance of the clarion call for black people of the world to unite, many black Jamaicans question the desirability of yet another type of 'neo-colonialism', however 'black' and however disguised this may be in such forms as international black writers' conferences or arts festivals of the black world. To them these are mere further projections of the great United States of America on to a weak and vulnerable Third World. They see the American command and control of the communications media as the most important contributory factor to the transplantability of Black Power, as has been the case with American movies and other rituals of the mass culture; and they feel that many personalities in the Black Power movement have largely been the inventions of the American mass media operating in a market which has the advantage of size, global power, technological advancement and a well attuned and receptive audience. The 'imperialistic temper' of many aspects of American Black Power is in this sense seen as little more than a black variation of the current global hegemony by Anglo-Saxon America and as such, invite the distrust of many Third World peoples (including black Africans and West Indians) who may wish to find solutions for themselves in their own way and beyond the dictates of American-style protest and American preoccupations, however praiseworthy and 'universal' these may seem to be. Many Jamaicans do feel that however relevant the American dilemma may be to their situation, their own experience must take precedence over that of others. Nor do they value their own experience any less

---

* Both the Leader of Government and Leader of the Opposition seemingly regard this as an invalidating factor for Black Power advocacy.

simply because it has not had the advantage of instant and widespread exposure through a powerful network of Press, radio and television. In fact, the tradition of black assertion has never left Jamaican life. There were the late eighteenth and early nineteenth century slave rebellions, 1865, and Paul Bogle, 1938, and the black working classes, 1960, and the Rastafarians, 1968, and the young sufferers.

So when a Jamaican in Jamaica calls for black awareness of his history, culture and heritage as an indispensable aid to self-knowledge as well as for pride in his racial origin, without apology for the colour of his skin, the shape of his nose or the texture of his hair, he is reacting to well-known objective factors in his history and in the world at large – factors which would otherwise deny him self-confidence and rob him of a sense of history and therefore of achievement. The call by black Jamaicans to create institutions with black leaders at the helm who will take decisions in the interest of black people is itself understandable. Many of the leaders of 1938 will probably assert that this was a primary motivation for their tasks. Whether these institutions can be *exclusively black* in the Jamaican situation is, however, another matter – a matter which separates advocate from advocate and gives to Jamaican Black Power some of its most difficult moments as well as some of its staunchest opposition. In Garveyite terms such black institutions would ensure black economic power, black commercial power, black industry, science and technology and even black military strength. The notion of Back-to-Africa and the building up of strong homogeneous black nation-states provided Garvey's doctrine with a powerful unity and logic that too often escapes present-day Jamaican Black Power advocates. Today it is the homogeneous black states of Africa (despite tribal separatist factors) that will earn for black peoples elsewhere much respect when these states are able to exhibit viability and internal strength. The methods of achieving this definably *black* power in Jamaica, which has a black majority but also boasts its valid minorities, would clearly be a point of controversy. But that this must be central to any meaningful definition of Black Power in the sixties is incontrovertible. Behind all this there is the notion that black people anywhere in the world have a common destiny and a common aim underpinned by a common racial bond. This view is used to justify the participation of Jamaican blacks in international conferences on Black Power or related subjects. Further it legitimizes in the minds of young West Indian intellectuals their 'right' to criticize and analyze conditions in any territory of the Caribbean wherever they may feel there is perpetuation of black 'suffering and deprivation'. The very 'West Indianness' of some of these people embraces, inevitably, the Black question or the predicament of the ex-slave in the entire Caribbean area. Governments of the Caribbean nurturing their newly-won independence from Great Britain do not readily concede this right and invoke from time to time their Security laws. Only time will decide on the effect of such measures on the Black Power movement.

Meanwhile one of the major contributions of declared advocates to Jamaican life may well be the refocusing of attention on some of the real needs of the society, namely to give dignity, cultural security and economic well-being to the *majority* of people within its jurisdiction (that majority happening to be black and/or of African descent). As a developing country, Jamaica could have its successive governments so easily involved in the vagaries of global powerplay between the industrial giants to the point where they become other-directed at the expense of internal needs and relevant national development. Black Power could well turn out to be a necessary antidote in this particular. More specifically Black Power in Jamaica may be said to be seeking to celebrate the undying concern of the majority of people to give substance to the form of freedom which was won in 1838 when slavery was abolished but which has never attained full reality. It has, after all, been subjected to the vicissitudes of edgy human relationships leading up to the events of 1865 and the imposition, albeit benevolent, of crown colony government. The new association with the British Crown did little to ease social and economic deprivation during the hundred years that separated emancipation from the social revolution of the late nineteen thirties.

One cannot, however, dismiss the social and political revolution of 1938 as a mere bourgeois exercise in the service of the middle classes and underestimate its importance to the notion of black betterment. Marcus Garvey and his movement played a far greater role in this than Jamaican history has up to now been able to admit. The stimulus for greater participation in the civic and political processes of the country did indeed come in a large measure from a black consciousness or a need to ease black deprivation. This was couched, granted, in terms of nationalism or trade unionism. But it was black Jamaicans who largely led in the fight for control of the society in power terms, not white Jamaicans. Many were what would, in the Jamaican social colour-scheme, be called high browns; but they themselves were all too conscious of their Jamaicanness in terms of a past of black-and-white confrontation. The fact that white Jamaicans were in the van of the fight for civil liberties (the right to property not least among them) which were threatened by a strong-arm Governor in 1942, should not make one miss the point. If Alexander Bustamante, the labour leader, was regarded as white, he knew too well that his platform had to be one based on the betterment of black Jamaicans – the *small man* as he termed them, the *masses* as the Peoples National Party called them. Significantly, Bustamante's first lieutenant who helped to give him a toe-hold on the masses (i.e. blacks) as instruments of political action was St. William Grant, a former lieutenant of Marcus Garvey. The experience of mass organization in the Garvey camp was to serve the activities of the mass-leader Bustamante, despite his personal inherent qualities as a crowd-pleaser. Garveyism was in spirit part of the progressive ideas to be found in Jamaica in the nineteen twenties and thirties. Never mind that Garvey had feuds with his Jamaican, as he did with his American, colleagues. They often differed less on ends and more on methods. The progressive movement of the late thirties spearheaded by the Peoples National Party did commit itself to nationalism rather than to sectional black or sectional labour but both blacks and labour were regarded as primary subjects for consideration in the movement. Bustamante specialized unerringly on labour and the Jamaica Labour Party was formed, as he repeatedly put it, in the interest of the 'small man' or worker. The two parties subsequently became national all-embracing entities and today they are criticized by Black Power advocates for achieving less than they could have since they did not commit themselves to the blacks *qua* blacks. But whatever may be the arguments now, there is enough evidence in the sources of the period indicating the progressive movement's concern for the people at the base of the society. The bluntness of Garvey earlier in the decade, in calling a spade a spade, clearly grated on the sensibilities of the newer leaders then. Rather, it was in the nature of the times to achieve ends through formal institutional arrangements. The emphasis on universal adult suffrage by the Peoples National Party was therefore regarded as an advance for the black man who would for the first time achieve, collectively, a voice in the political processes of the country. There were dissenting voices in the Peoples National Party itself and there is no evidence that the popular labour leader Bustamante was himself at all committed to the idea. But universal adult suffrage was achieved giving to the blacks what the whites had had since the late seventeenth century, the Jews since 1826 and the Free Coloureds since 1832.

The 1944 election which followed on the advent of universal suffrage was a three-cornered fight but there was no doubt as to where the black Jamaicans were. They were on the sides of the Jamaica Labour Party, the Peoples National Party and the Independents, many of whom later joined the Jamaica Labour Party.* The Jamaica Democratic Party had a high Jamaican white content in its leadership that clearly had a vested interest in the rights of property. They managed to divert the campaign

---

* Of the 349,127 votes accepted in the 1944 elections, 144,661 were polled for JLP, 82,029 for PNP, 104,814 for Independents, 14,123 for the Jamaica Democratic Party and 3,500 for others.

into the stock correlative of capitalism versus socialism with the Peoples National Party represented as the enemy of capitalism. But the real fight was between the labour leader of the Bustamante Industrial Trade Union/Jamaica Labour Party complex and the nationalist middle-class leadership of the Peoples National Party, with both fighting for the support of the black working class. Some people today see the elections as black against black and for 'brown leaders'. The result has been a split trade union movement, each fragment supporting a political party in a two-party system which, according to the argument, thwarts rather than serves the interests of the black Jamaican. Historically then, the black man in Jamaica is said to have been deprived of what Black Power advocates would regard as his true identity since he was transformed into 'the small man' by Bustamante and into 'a member of the working class or masses' by the Peoples National Party. As such he was organized primarily into trade unions which merely perpetuated the traditional confrontation of slave (now worker) with master in a tidy system of checks and balances called industrial relations. This system, the argument goes, increases wages and even gives the black worker some opportunity to play a game called Collective Bargaining, but the black man still fails to control the workplace because he does not share in the ownership of it. The sixties therefore finds his institution unsatisfactory. The very trade union gains were to produce, in any case, differentials in the wage structure breeding frustration, general dissatisfaction and discontent and the very reassertion of the black essence among the workers.

By the middle and late fifties the black essence was to find expression in what has come to be called the Rastafari movement, which asserted the essential dignity of being black and demanded Repatriation for its adherents to the homeland of black Africa, where Haile Selassie (formerly Ras Tafari), the divine Potentate, ruled in supreme dignity and power. Much of the apprehension that attends current Black Power activities were evident in 1959 and 1960 when the bold assertion of the black essence was conceived as a threat to the very fabric of the society.* The capture of black American subversives in the Red Hills was taken as firm evidence of this. The Rastafarian denunciation of 'brown man governments' (i.e. Jamaican governments) as incapable of perceiving the true meaning and essence of blackness, is the forerunner of the current Black Power position that sees the Jamaican power structure as being under the influence of the white imperialists, utterly incapable of acting independently of the United States of America and therefore without any real power. The social rejection by the Rastafarians was itself an expression of the alienation of these black Jamaicans from a society they had been asked to call home. The alienation argument is central to Black Power advocacy in reference, particularly, to the jobless young from the depressed areas as well as to the more privileged middle class, from among high school or university graduates who find the values of the society in which they find themselves difficult to live by. Today, some people would regard the Rastafarians as an anachronism: they are not. Much of their belief and fight for the recognition and status of the black Jamaican may be said to be continuing in the phenomenon which now calls itself Black Power.

The Adherents and the Role of 'Abeng'

It is not difficult to identify the adherents. The definitions of Black Power vary but where it concerns itself with black dignity and the control of one's own environment, it has a wide range of adherents with varying degrees of commitment, starting from a concentrated militant core that would not hesitate to include revolutionary tactics in its programme and fanning out to the fringes where there may be a not too burdensome commitment to the withering away of the white bias in the society.

Without attempting to place special persons at any given

---

* See Essay 'African Redemption . . .' above.

point in the structure, it is fair to say that concurrence of views on different aspects of Black Power is to be found among the traditional Africanists, i.e. persons who have long displayed an interest in things African and in the fate of descendants of Africans in plantation societies such as Jamaica. These include old Garveyites and people who have been influenced by the Garvey movement as well as the Rastafarians (in all their different modes of commitment). Then there are the young middle and lower middle class persons who are recently evolved from the black peasantry or the black urban 'yard' dwellers. They find common cause with others in their own age-group from the depressed urban areas. There are also those of the more established middle class (perhaps of a generation or more) who throw up some of the spokesmen for the movement. Some of these exhibit a kind of brown guilt at being what they are and seem determined to correct their 'crime' for having enjoyed privilege and benefits in a system which continually denies these to the majority. Closely associated with these are the young intellectuals – many of them black and obvious beneficiaries of the social and political revolution of the late thirties. It is these people more than any other who have given Black Power its present form and intensity. Their speeches, writings in varied newsletters and their positive efforts to make common cause with less fortunate 'brothers' and 'sufferers' among the less educated and deprived classes mark them off as a significant, if not a new, phenomenon in Jamaican social life.* The events of October 6, 1968, gave them a springboard for action and for dialogue and it is through them that certain ills of the society and the aims of the Black Power movement are mostly articulated.

Many of them are deeply affected by a social conscience that

---

* Some adopt the title 'Bongo' to precede their Christian names. In Jamaican dialect the word is an insulting term meaning black, ugly, stupid or 'African' (*Dictionary of Jamaican English*, F. G. Cassidy and R. B. LePage, Cambridge University Press, 1967). There is also a self-conscious effort to develop an argot called 'Bongo Talk' analysis of which is outside the scope of this essay.

was not as evident in University circles or among people of their class less than a decade ago. Many of them are likely to have pursued or are pursuing studies in the social sciences; or they will have read some History which furnishes them with a knowledge of the historical forces in West Indian development and the sociological implications of the historical process on Jamaica, and for that matter, plantation society. They come from varied social backgrounds – many poor but a good number of comfortable middle class. By certain of the canons of the white bias, some would not even qualify as legitimate blacks but this dilemma is usually met by the thesis (long put forward by the Rastafarians) that it is not what one looks like, but how one *feels*. So many fair-skinned Jamaicans are able, so the thesis goes, to feel 'black'. Conversely many black-skinned Jamaicans feel 'white' and are therefore disqualified from membership in the innermost sanctuaries of Black Power advocacy.* Some act like new converts do to an old religion and are fanatical in their novel discoveries. They are many of them highly intelligent Jamaicans and have had the advantage of higher education, which puts them among the elite, an embarrassing fact for them and a further cause for alienation. Some make safaris to the yards of deprived blacks as a kind of ritual of re-unification with the source – a source many of them might never have known. Others have made discoveries of the Rastafarians and the power in the creed of this sect who are now better understood after a decade of derision. Some of them have even declared themselves members of the sect in conscious attempts to identify with what they feel to be the essence of Jamaican life. Some are committed to universal black revolution; others prefer to deal with the specifics of Jamaican (or West Indian) experience and leave the generalities of the international polemics to Stokely Carmichael, Rap

---

* A September 1969 issue of *Abeng* emphasized the point: 'In Jamaica true Black Power does not attack white as *white*, brown as *brown*. All men are equal. The attack is on white, brown or black *as oppressing* the Afro-Jamaican and as an oppressive economic and social *class*'. *Abeng*, Vol. 1, No. 33, September 13, 1969.

Brown and Eldridge Cleaver. All Black Power advocates understandably turn to Marcus Garvey for ideological strength and sustenance.

The educated among them are very aware of what is going on among the young elsewhere and this acts as something of a bolster for their ideological position at home. They know about Marcuse. They will have read Marx or suitable commentaries on his alienation of labour. They follow the developments in American universities with regard to Black Studies; they know the language of the politics of confrontation and echo the distrust in established institutions which they feel are irrelevant to Jamaican needs. They let no facet of Jamaican life escape their scrutiny and criticism: the whole to them is as sick as the parts. The Jamaican Government is particularly culpable, in their eyes. They express amazement at the banning by officialdom of the works of Stokely Carmichael and Malcolm X. They cannot reconcile themselves to the fact that no corresponding Government provision has been made for banning books which may laud white supremacy, Rhodesian UDI or Afrikaaner apartheid. They see the inconsistency as yet another expression of the white bias and moral turpitude of the power structure. They cannot understand why the Government in power could accommodate in its Cabinet a trade union boss side by side with the country's most influential non-black entrepreneur. They cannot understand why the Government should have banned from its shores a young West Indian intellectual, who said nothing that Garvey had not said before and merely preached basic African History which needs to be taught from the level of primary school in any case. Even when they are willing to grant the nation its right to safeguard its security, they cannot understand why the Government finds it difficult to extend to a black West Indian the facilities of due process of law, so as to clear himself and his cause. The same position is held in respect of yet another Guyanese lecturer Clive Thomas, the economist, who was banned some ten months after the Rodney case. They understand this case even less since clear reasons were not given, at the time of exclusion.

They, like Thomas, cannot understand how the Government prefers to 'ban black West Indians and yet welcome with open arms the capitalists of Europe and America who exploit Jamaica's natural resources – the plantation owners who dominate the countryside and the hotel owners who convert their beaches and other natural recreational facilities into play-grounds for the idle rich of North America'.[10] Rodney had reportedly reacted in like manner when he called the Government 'a set of bandits' selling out the country.[11] It is clear that the main targets of attack are the white 'imperial powers of the North Atlantic', particularly the United States of America.

Now, the banning of Dr. Thomas, a black and reputedly able West Indian economist, would seem to suggest grave psychological problems for the future, in Jamaica's choice of much needed skills for her national development; but politicians will no doubt argue that a security risk, black or white, is a security risk and Governments are particularly sensitive to such risks. On the other hand there is yet no answer for Dr. Thomas's reported assertion, that the domination of Jamaica by the imperial powers of the North Atlantic 'has helped to reduce a people of immense vitality and creativity, with a long history of struggle for freedom, to be the servile tools of foreigners.'[12] The language may overstate a case but it is certainly in the tradition of the fight for self-determination. Only now it is spoken out against a black West Indian government instead of the white imperial British administration. The young black lecturer would no doubt say that white or black imperialism is still imperialism. For the Jamaican Government with its legally elected Opposition, like its counterparts in the Caribbean, is regarded by Black Power advocates as an extension of the colonial system. Closely identified with the power structure in the lore of Black Power are those who see themselves as heirs to the European legacy – the middle class, whose boorishness, proverbial lack of social conscience, ruthless acquisitiveness, and perpetuation of white values in the black society are also targets of unceasing attack.

All this betrays, at best, a healthy spirit of criticism of the society; and this spirit of criticism of the society's structure and raison d'être could be the greatest virtue of what is called Black Power. It is well within the tradition of modern Jamaican experience. The newspapers, broadsheets, journals, and speeches of the thirties are replete with this kind of criticism of old colonialism. Even during the process of transfer, criticism of this kind continued. First it was colonial power, then it was the two-party system, the trade union and the vested interests of property. A weekly newspaper in Jamaica intensified the practice, even after Independence, marking out set targets for polemical attack and scrutiny.[13] Scrutiny based on scientific inquiry and depth study was to become a more common thing, following on the establishment of the University of the West Indies Department of History and Faculty of Social Sciences. This new dimension has activated a long-suspected anti-intellectualism among vested power interests in the Jamaican society and it has been suggested that the social sciences be abolished and resources put into such 'useful disciplines' as Medicine and the Natural Sciences. Small wonder that the Dean of the Faculty of Social Sciences, in a public address, felt it necessary to outline the functions of the social scientist as one trained 'to question accepted conclusions, established systems and conventional wisdom. To avoid this kind of scientific questioning and critical analysis' said the Dean, 'is to stagnate and to place a premium on mediocrity at the expense of creativity, dynamism and innovation.'[14] This provoked an editorial attack which is typical of attitudes in certain quarters to criticism of the society: 'Unhappily from what we have seen of the products of social scientists [sic] in our midst, it appears that they themselves are largely incapable of analysis in depth, uncreative in the sense of a true and individual economist such as the late Maynard Keynes and full of Marxist and Fabian dogma and jargon, which had some pertinence in the days of Professor Laski and the London School of Economics in the thirties; but are singularly unhelpful in the mixed economies of the 1960s.'[15] The quotation is indicative of prevailing attitudes to Black Power advocates, some of whom are believed to articulate their position from the safety of the University and from the 'dubious authority' of the social sciences. Some do lay themselves open to just this kind of criticism since the employment of a quasi-Marxian tool of analysis is frequently evident in discussions about Black Power. Society is here divided into two opposing classes – the black race representing the exploited proletarian class while the white race represents the exploiting capitalist class. The absence of original thinking, hinted at in the editorial attack, merely comments on what is a central weakness of the colonial heritage. The paradox is that the accusation is frequently levelled from both sides of combat.

Yet Jamaicans are not unaccustomed to critical analysis of their society. Long before the Black Power phenomenon emerged in its present form, economists, historians and sociologists were commenting on Jamaican society in terms of need for basic structural changes and changes in the value system. The work of M. G. Smith, the sociologist, in his analysis of Jamaican social structure and of Elsa Goveia, the historian, in her examination of historical forces in West Indian plantation life (to name just two) have long informed the criticism by several persons of West Indian communities.[16] It is difficult to believe that members of the power structure were not always aware of the knowledge gained from this kind of research. Edward Seaga's much referred to speech in the Legislative Council in 1961 on the haves and the have-nots, presumably came out of his studies of the depressed areas in urban Jamaica. This he had done in his capacity as a serious sociologist. More recently – and just before Black Power broke – the public controversy on sugar and its future, was merely one in a series of colloquies which flowed from depth study of the West Indian society by scholars, who had banded themselves into the New World Group with a thoughtful quarterly journal.[17] At least one member of that group came to be involved in the publication of *Abeng* which was generally regarded by many as the official organ of the Black Power movement in Jamaica.

Abeng could then be said to be in a sound tradition of criticism of Jamaican society. The inaugural editorial of *Abeng* described its task as being 'to help us discover ourselves – not just the past, but also what we are today and what we can be tomorrow if we can move forward together. . . . in seeking possibilities for change, the newspaper will invite the views of everyone; thereby it will transmit like the original cow-horn used by the Maroons and called Abeng a great variety of ideas!' This made it less original and less revolutionary than its organizers would probably care to admit; and it was to remain a valid part of the Jamaican scheme of things as long as it managed to survive. Survival was itself not a certainty judging from past experience of the birth and rapid demise of newspapers other than the gargantuan *Daily Gleaner*. Perhaps *Abeng* was tolerated by those who wished for it a similar fate. This came in less than a year of its controversial existence.

It did, however, earn some international attention while it lasted. A British newspaper described it as follows: 'The name "Abeng" commemorates the horn which the black slaves sounded in their uprisings against the British long ago. Garvey is the paper's chief hero, for its writers argue there is nothing to choose between the Prime Minister, Hugh Shearer, and the new Opposition Leader, Michael Manley. Its articles have become increasingly anti-white, attacking the foreign owned bauxite companies and naming four volunteer teachers – some Peace Corps and a Canadian couple – as "spies" '.[18] Detractors described *Abeng* as destructive and accused it of failing to offer constructive criticism. Some, no doubt, expected better of the scholars who sat on the newspaper's editorial board. This criticism may, on the face of it, be valid but scholars have also been criticized for transmitting their findings in too blurred, dense and indigestible a manner.* Supporters of *Abeng* would

---

* A criticism sometimes levelled against (*a*) 'Social and Economic Studies' the academic journal of the UWI's Institute of Social and Economic Research; (*b*) 'The New World Quarterly' which examined issues in a scholarly way and sought after a semi-popular projection.

no doubt, defend the paper's position in terms of mass appeal. Moreover, the paper was not a journal or a review publication but a newspaper designed to get the hard facts of Jamaican existence to the mass of black Jamaican people, as well as to any others who might have wished to embrace the cause for human dignity among the majority of the Jamaican people. It also provided a forum for so-called 'black sufferers', whose experience within the constraints of economic deprivation and social injustice need to be communicated to the thousands of Jamaicans who may have no other means of knowing. The paper was also, tactically, a necessary weapon in the politics of confrontation which seems to be the accepted strategy of the young in the early second half of the 20th century. Let *Abeng*, the argument would go, make frontal attacks on the system, question the every move of the power structure, expose the inevitable outflows of black dependence (or Third World dependence) on white technology and imperialism, and some action productive of 'good' is bound to ensue from all this. For some of its readership this approach might well have been something of an endurance test. The constant refrain of 'Government is bad, Government is bad,' can drum up as much boredom as belief.

But *Abeng* was capable of more than this and a series of articles seriously examining the state of the Banana Industry and the social implications, as well as the factual accounts of actual suffering and police indiscretions did earn it respect in some quarters. 'There are another set of people in this country' asserted the newspaper in an editorial headlined SUBVERSION, 'who, from their pronouncements, would like to see a change in the existing colonial situation. They want to "overthrow suffering", to "destroy" the colonial heritage, to "upset" and "overturn" foreign domination of our lives so as to create a dignified existence for the people of this country. In short their ambition is to destroy what has proven bad for us and replace it with *whatever will best serve the interests of all Jamaicans*. ABENG identifies itself with this set of people. And if the purpose outlined here is subversive, we want to be as subversive as can be'.[19] Its weekly quotations from the writings of Marcus Garvey served to remind Jamaica of the depth of this visionary's insight into what is still a major problem of the century – the recognition and dignity of the black man. But this very act endorsed, though unintentionally, the action taken by the power structure to make Garvey into a National Hero – a decision taken long before the advent of *Abeng*. *Abeng* was itself a good test for the Jamaican society's repeated declarations of respect for such basic freedoms as the unhindered flow of thought and exchange of ideas in the system. Government was not foolish enough to censure the newspaper, though there were reports of prohibition in places like the military and in a number of schools. The newspaper itself repeatedly accused the power structure of attempted suppression in the form of harassment of known *Abeng* distributors and contributors. It enjoyed a reported circulation of 15 to 20,000, however, with strong pockets of readers in a number of rural parishes. On the more practical side it offered a group of young Jamaicans the beneficial, if gruelling, experience of organizing the production of a weekly newspaper and this in itself may well be considered a contribution to black people's capacity to organize themselves and sustain their activities in their own interest.

But there were pitfalls. The policy of unabated frontal attack on the Government that 'has no power', on the Opposition which was regarded as hardly better, on the police activities which they always documented as brutal, on the middle class, who were labelled 'white lackeys', on 'the haves' who remained ill-defined but vulnerable, might have deprived the *Abeng* group of much of the support which would have been available for the more substantive issues, such as the need for equitable distribution of wealth, social justice, respect for the black and, by extension, human person, and control by the Jamaican majority of the economic resources of the society. The *Abeng* group was, in the end, preaching more to the converted rather than effectively changing the reactionaries, the apathetic and the very power structure. But such a happening may not have been desired by the more militant among Black Power advocates out of fear of a deeper entrenchment by the status quo and deprivation of a horn to blow.

Many of the sounds from that horn were, and still are, not altogether flawless. Many of the blowers are themselves trained in one intellectual discipline or another and should be aware of the logical fallacies which accrue from analogies which are pressed too far, or from untested categorical statements which seek to universalize unique experience into frozen laws of nature. Tools of analysis are useful as tools, not as substitutes for the phenomena being analysed, and social scientists, because of the nature of their material, are particularly vulnerable. The 'plantation model', for example, is still a useful, relevant (and indispensable) tool for analysing present-day Jamaican society. But it is not present-day Jamaica. The sugar industry in the late eighteenth and early nineteenth century cannot be the same industry in the twentieth century. The 'colonialism' of bauxite-alumina is not the same as the 'colonialism' of sugar. Metaphor does not become fact in one fell swoop of rhetoric. Labelling the elected black representatives of the people and those who exercise authority as 'household slaves' has the potency of polemics, but seldom the usefulness of facts. It may offer the black 'sufferers' an easy explanation of the society from which they cannot seem to reap rewards, but it can equally confuse them when they must decide about working and improving their lot should opportunities to do this arise. Why should they not refuse to work for 'white absentee landlords of the imperialist North America'? The distrust which black people have for other black people, who may have emerged by their own efforts from the 'ghetto', may very well offer an excuse to perpetuate self-hate and lack of self-confidence.

The 'haves and the have-nots' model (if one can so call this over-used jargon) does not take us very far either. In any case it is to be doubted whether Jamaica is so simplistically polarized. 'Have-nots' there certainly are and there have been 'haves' for some time now. Nothing is said, however, about the struggling thousands who on analysis would probably fall into neither

category. Nor does lumping them in the category of the middle
classes offer much assistance. They may have skills and some
earning power which qualify them for the hire-purchase
merry-go-round – an activity which could, in the end, categor-
ize them among the 'have-nots'. For they seldom *own* their
cars, their electric appliances or their houses. Many of them
would insist that they work very hard to provide their children
with a good education and material comfort, and expect to be
respected for this. They are most of them of African descent
and would not expect to be written off as useless and misguided.
They may not openly declare their African heritage or their
love for Mother Africa and many often have ambivalent
attitudes to the black commitment, but they would certainly
care about respect for their own dignity. Many would probably
admit that they are not blessed with much imagination or sense
of poetry, but they would not regard themselves boorish or
expect to be blamed for wanting to acquire the kind of education
and skills, that will facilitate their functioning as ordinary
human beings in a modern world. They would feel it unreasonable to regard their quest for material comfort as a 'white
value', for they are aware that this is an ambition to be found
even in black Africa. In its more chameleon moments, Black
Power advocacy sometimes adapts to these people but hard-
line radicals would prefer to lose this potential support than
treat with these 'traitors of the race'. The otherwise fashionable
Marxian dialectic is not as frequently employed as it might be,
but some advocates do make proletarians of the entire black
race.

Looking at the society as the neo-colonialist does, however,
give valuable clues to the ills. In a lecture entitled 'Black
Power as a political strategy in Jamaica', a young Jamaican
social scientist reminded his listeners that, 'in Jamaica, in
particular, the governmental order, the people who held office
have never been the most significant elements in determining
the way in which the social environment is organized, the
methods and means whereby goods and services are produced
for the satisfaction of popular needs.'[20] His concern is with

making a distinction between black *authority* and Black *Power* as he later asserts. He therefore avoids simplifying his thesis into a discourse on the evils of capitalism and the virtues of socialism. He is, however, more concerned with pointing out the need for black people to control their environment in their own self-interest (i.e. economic self-interest), as well as in their humanization. He, therefore, cannot take seriously the fact of a black Prime Minister, a black Governor-General and black ministers who are actually to be found in Jamaica, since on his own analysis of traditional Jamaican society, it is 'private power which determines more clearly what gets done in society, and therefore, in *economic* terms the collective environment of black sufferers'.

National Economic Independence

In focusing attention on the need for Jamaican blacks to assume economic as well as political control of their country, the phenomenon of Black Power can lay some of its strongest claims to relevance. Jamaicans did seek the political Kingdom first but all things have not followed in the interest of the blacks and so many are now stronger in the view that *economic independence is a necessary pre-condition of any real political independence*.[21] The concern is not exclusive to Black Power advocacy. In fact there is universal outrage at the control of our destiny by foreign exploiters and this is to be found among a wide cross-section of Jamaicans, some of whom are not black. Yet the Chinese and Lebanese (Syrian) Jamaicans are particularly vulnerable in the face of Black Power attacks because they are dominant at levels of economic activity where it is thought blacks should be in control.[22] The dilemma that surrounds any attempt to blacken the distributive trades and other branches of commerce is, however, nowhere examined in the literature of Jamaican Black Power. Instead, a listing is made (from *Who's Who in Jamaica*) of what the advocates call 'intensified white economic power in Jamaica'. Over one

hundred commercial businesses are controlled says the information sheet by 'four white families.* In most cases they are
outright owners. For the rest they are either Managing
Director, Chairman of the Board of Directors or Directors of
these Companies.'[23] The information sheet ends with an
apocalyptic injunction from the Old Testament – 'Riches
profit not in the day of wrath; but righteousness delivereth
from death. Proverbs 11, verse 4.' The question is still worth
asking as to what is to happen to the Chinese† and the Syrians
and the Jamaican Jews who between them command much
wealth and material comfort compared with the blacks. Is their
property to be expropriated so as to accommodate control by
the 90-odd per cent black Jamaicans? The blacks in Jamaica
have not displayed until recently much interest in commercial
life. This was no doubt due partly to cultural conditioning
and partly to lack of facilities to finance businesses. The
understandable preoccupation of blacks with respectability and
status professions probably kept them out of occupations of
profit. But it is said that money in Jamaica produces power;
and without money, say the Black Power advocates, the blacks
are powerless. But it may be that the Jamaican black man will
have to rid himself of the cultural cocoon in respect of his

---

* Two Jewish and two Lebanese (Syrians) families are named. They
are again named by Blackman in his column 'Time Now' who
describes them as 'parasites who rise or fall with American fortunes'.
(See *Abeng*, Vol. 1, No. 33, September 13, 1969.)

† In 1854 the first group of Chinese came to Jamaica via Colon,
Panama, where they had gone to work on the railway. This was a
private scheme which failed. From 1884, however, Chinese
immigration received official blessing and in that year 696 Chinese
arrived from Hong Kong to work as indentured labourers on the
estates. Some 109 women were among them, 508 men, 59 boys,
17 girls and one baby. The Chinese who came after this left the
estates and entered the grocery business which they still dominate
in the island's townships. Resentment against the 'Chinese invasion'
developed as far back as 1911–12. This had disappeared with the
integration of a new generation of Chinese into the society. (See
'Chinese in the Caribbean', *v.p.* Oswald Hoston, Kingston, 1941,
esp. pp. 27, 29, 81, 83, 97.)

dislike of manual work at home and be now concerned with consciously acquiring the skills, other than white-collar ones, that will make him economically independent. He will probably have to be prepared to make sacrifices in the way many of his Chinese and Syrian countrymen did a generation or two ago, without fear of humiliation. It may be that the black man will have to stop littering the countryside with illegitimate children, dull the memory of his proverbial castration by slavery and face the responsibility of fathering a family unit as a base from which to build his social and economic security. It may even be that what is being demanded of the Jamaican black is impossible, since it requires a complete break with a past which has left too big and deep and permanent a scar on his consciousness.

This may be one instinctive reason for Black Power advocates' concentration on the bigger problems of the black collectivity – on the *national* aspects of economic life. The focus tends to be on the big industries such as sugar, tourism and bauxite, which all have the common feature of being foreign owned and foreign directed.* The entire policy of foreign investment and the exploitation of Jamaican resources become then the target of attack. It has been the paradox of national development that the optimism indicated by the statistics of the annual *Economic Survey of Jamaica* bears little relation to the facts of life among the majority of the people. The information that the gross domestic product increased by 9.1 per cent in 1968 as compared with 5.5 per cent in 1967 remains more a discussion point for professional economists than a reason for jubilation among the perpetual poor.[24] Factors such as the increase in general price level and a rise in population are likely to reduce considerably the per capita increase of the GDP in any case. But this in itself is more a matter for attack and counter-attack between Government and Opposition. Problems of unemployment and the maldistribution of income remain realities. The *Gleaner* editorialized a further problem after the 1969

---

* Black Power advocates' strongest case. See 'The New Imperialism' by Blackman in *Abeng*, Vol. 1, No. 33, especially paragraphs 3–6.

Budget Debate. 'Government claims that unemployment is being reduced. The Opposition claims unemployment is rising. Who is right? Government claims the income gap is being bridged; while the Opposition claims that the income gap is widening. Who is right?' The editorial, in conclusion, agreed with the Leader of the Opposition, Michael Manley, that 'signs of discontent which have become manifest over past months indicate that many Jamaicans are not participating sufficiently in the development process.'[25] Although Mr. Manley reportedly disapproved of what the editorial called 'trouble-making instigating', his views on non-participation would be endorsed by Black Power advocates. The Jamaican economy, then, despite its brilliant recorded statistical performance over the past decade and a half, has not lived up to the expectations of an ex-slave society struggling to give full meaning to emancipation and freedom. As the *New World* article on 'Sugar, Our Life or Death' puts it, 'The period which elapsed since Emancipation can . . . best be understood in terms of two interdependent processes; the one leading legal equality to its logical conclusion in full popular political representation (adult suffrage) and self-determination (independence) the other *involving attempts to secure an economic structure which would bring political and economic relations into equilibrium*'[26] [my emphasis]. It is the consistent thwarting of this latter process which angers the Black Power advocates most as it does the entire range of young intellectual thinking in the Caribbean today. It is this which made the economist Havelock Brewster invite readers to take a long hard look at the sugar industry. High production cost, low profits and low wages plague the industry despite the protection it gets by 'unusually high' negotiated price and quota provisions. The call for mechanization has been heeded by the Government but the British investors are loth to invest the kind of money needed to resuscitate the 160,000 acres of very arable land now planted out in what is often described as a dying industry.

'Surprising as it may seem', read a letter to the *Gleaner* from the Manager of the Sugar Manufacturers' Association of

Jamaica Limited, 'for the four years 1965 to 1968, the earnings of the sugar estates as a whole, after offsetting the losses, have been of the order of twenty thousand pounds per annum on a capital employed of over twenty-two million pounds – *an average annual rate of earnings of less than one-tenth of one per cent for the four year period*' [his emphasis].[27] The experience with sugar is indelibly imprinted on the consciousness of black West Indians. Even in its dormant state the slave product remains the ghost that haunts the mind of the aware Jamaican. Such intangible considerations which turn on its slave connexions are too often ignored in assessments by government officials and management alike. Instead workers are blamed for being perverse and workers in turn, not infrequently, expect the worst of the heirs of slavemasters. To make matters worse it is not profitable though it still serves as one of the largest sources of employment in the country.* Sugar's connexion with the past is the surest link with the still unrewarding present in the minds of many critics of the society. As the Cuban journalist-historian Ramiro Guerra y Sanchez said, the final goal of the sugar economy was to 'produce at minimum cost a basic commodity or luxury article for a distant market at a profit, even though that policy will in the long run ruin the producing country economically, socially and politically.'[28]

It is not difficult to see why some analysts see this logic of exploitation working itself through in the more recent bauxite industry which produces another basic commodity for the distant North American market at immense profit. The instruments of exploitation are still cheap labour and foreign capital in search of profit. This results, inter alia, in the loss of land. And if the land is lost, all shall have been lost, including liberty and honour according to the Caribbean historian of sugar. It is in this spirit that Black Power advocates assault the fact of foreign domination and what is seen (and not without

---

* In 1967 the sugar industry employed some 63,244 persons in croptime or 8.8 per cent of the workforce. (*Economic Survey of Jamaica*, 1968.)

some just fears) as the industrial annexation of Jamaica by North America.

So sugar remains a special problem to Jamaicans. After all it did bring slavery and indentureship, the plantation system and colonial dependence. It now brings little returns in terms of living wage for the vast majority of the workers. It remains, despite the rationalization of the labour force (by some 25 per cent) a symbol of servitude for social-conscious advocates of change and many Black Power adherents are among these. The anger is exacerbated by the fact that a suitable substitute seems to elude political decision-takers as it has academic analysts. Meanwhile, sugar remains king in its capacity to employ labour in a country burdened with chronic unemployment. Attempts at mechanization would seem at this point to be a last ditch to resuscitate it if not to its pristine glory, at least to a tolerable position.

Less tolerable is the tourist industry which the Black Power militants see as the curse to end all curses. This, in their eyes, is the direct 'sell-out' of the country by black politicians to the 'white devils' of North America. This attitude is said to have an adverse effect on the industry, particularly in Canada where 'for some time now we've been getting a bad press – inaccurate and exaggerated stories about the imminence of revolution and the influence here of the Black Power boys. In consequence we are losing a lot of tourist business, and even Jamaicans in Canada are writing home in alarm . . .'[29] The statistical surveys show an impressive increase from some £10,000,000 sterling (20 million Jamaican dollars*) in 1959 to just under £40,000,000 sterling or 80 million Jamaican dollars in 1969. Though some of this is attributed to transfer of visitors from a Cuba that went under Castro, tourist promotion has intensified in its hard-sell of sun, beach and old-world ambience.[30] Probably the most apt Black Power comment on the industry is to be seen on the front page of an early issue of

---

* Jamaica converted its currency to dollars and cents in September, 1969.

Abeng which carried a picture culled from a Holiday Magazine dated November, 1968. It shows a black beach boy with shining teeth supporting on his shoulders a middle-aged white female tourist clad in bathsuit covering an unmistakably unbecomingly obese figure but grinning away at the unusual piece of sporting. The *Abeng* caption read 'Tourism on top, we underneath'.[31] This attitude betrays what has been a long-standing dislike of tourism particularly among the Jamaican middle classes. The northern littoral between Port Maria and Montego Bay, a distance of about seventy miles, is still regarded as 'foreign country' by many Jamaicans and the reports of discrimination against local inhabitants have not endeared the industry to many. It remains, however, a big money earner for the country and is even regarded in some quarters as a way of making quick hard currency for more meaningful and long-term development. The fact that the vast majority of tourists are white and North American would naturally go against the grain of Black Power advocates.

The distrust of North America comes out strongest, however, in attitudes to the bauxite-alumina industry. In this Black Power advocates have some of their firmest allies. For many Jamaicans see this as the 'colonial industry' *par excellence*, controlled as it is from multinational bases situated outside of the country.* They know that decision-taking does not rest with Jamaicans and seldom with the white functionaries who reside in the island. The subtle discriminatory practices against native Jamaicans in the matter of appointments and job responsibility are abhorred. While many of the local executives are paid enormous salaries they are said to have no real responsi-

---

* Six companies now operate in Jamaica: Aluminium Company of America (Alcoa) in the parish of Clarendon; Aluminium Canada (Alcan) Jamaica Ltd., in Manchester, St. Ann and St. Catherine; Aluminium Partners (Alpart) consortium of Anaconda, Kaiser and Reynolds in St. Elizabeth; Kaiser in St. Ann; Reynolds Jamaica Mines in St. Ann; and Revere Copper and Brass in St. Elizabeth. (See 'The Aluminium Industry and the Caribbean Connexion', p. 9, Carlyle Dunkley.)

bility and job satisfaction is seldom realized. Pockets of colonial-type housing compounds are all but reserved for white expatriates of the management class and the break-through by a black or brown Jamaican into the haven is often regarded as a major feat. Labour may be well paid, but only after strong trade union pressure, and even then the entire wage structure is thrown out of gear causing serious problems of wage differentials in the economy at large.

'Why', the question is asked, 'the concentration on mining – the stealing of our earth and the raping of the hillsides?' The manufacture of alumina goes further, it is conceded, but not far enough, it is frequently argued. 'Why such small royalties when the situation has changed so radically since 1950 when the first "sell-out" took place?' The unions, it is also argued, are, in any case, in collusion with the United Steelworkers of America who have a vested interest in Jamaica remaining a primary source of supply so that North American workers can enjoy job security. Some militants favour nationalization but this has less support than would be supposed. There is, however, support for an aluminium smelter so that Jamaicans can participate in the full range of the aluminium industry from mining to smelting. Why should Jamaica not negotiate one as Puerto Rico has done?* One point of view insists that a successful lobby could be organized in Washington to obtain from the United States the undertaking to guarantee Jamaica a market of, say, 100,000 tons of ingot annually. Cost factors notwithstanding, this point of view insists that Jamaica could produce competitive ingots. Another point of view holds that Jamaica should emulate Guinea by obtaining controlling shares in the bauxite alumina companies operating in Jamaica.[32] Even if it means financing the shareholding by a loan, the industry is profitable enough to make the debt self-liquidating within a

---

* Prompted by Reports in the Jamaican press that Alcoa planned to build a 2 million-dollar smelter in Puerto Rico that would benefit some 1,000 workers to the tune of 5 million dollars annually. (See *Star*, April 21, 1969. Also letter to Editor, 'Jamaica Bypassed', *Daily Gleaner*, May 19, 1969.)

generation. There has, however, been no Black Power comment on the corresponding sacrifices (e.g. an austere life-style and higher personal taxes) that would have to be made. Yet another point of view sees bauxite-alumina firms being charged a very high surtax which could be ploughed back into development projects that could generate more income and provide more jobs. This would be essentially a government matter but since the Government, in the eyes of Black Power advocates, is a 'stooge of white power', it is unlikely that this point of view would win their support.

At least one of the bauxite owners is optimistic about Black Power and bauxite in Jamaica. Appearing before the Canadian Senate's Standing Committee on Foreign Affairs, Mr. Nathaniel V. Davis, President of Alcan Aluminium Ltd., replied to a question about the rise of Black Power in the Caribbean as follows: '. . . we are alert to some of these developments which are occurring. We believe that areas such as Jamaica and Guyana – the lesser developed areas that are basically short of capital – can use their capital to better advantage in areas other than those in which we may be operating. We believe that, effectively, the governments and the people of Jamaica and Guyana are partners with us in this profitability of our enterprises in the two countries, although the entire risk capital has been invested by us. These forces are at work in many parts of the world, but we believe basic economic sense should prevail and that these countries would use their resources in areas that they can develop better themselves.' The speaker added his belief 'that the equity participation which has come into these countries from Canada has brought not only profits and income and foreign exchange to the countries, but technological and managerial skills as well.' Senator Connolly the questioner from Ottawa West obliged with 'And taxes' and the President of Alcan Aluminium concurred.*

It could be argued by management interests in bauxite that the cost structure of the industry is nowhere realistically

* See *Proceedings of the Standing Committee on Foreign Affairs*, p. 19, Senate of Canada, Second Session, 28th Parl., Tues., Nov. 25, 1969.

discussed by Black Power advocates. But it is doubtful whether in the absence of investment exposure by exploiting firms many of these advocates could be aware of the implications of their demands in terms of national ownership of the industry. Sterling Brubaker in his book *Aluminium Industry* has this to say: 'There is no transport advantage to be had from moving fuel to the bauxite source for smelting ore to metal, for, in addition to the carbon and fluoride used in reduction and the soda and fuel used in the alumina stage, about 4–5 tons of coal would be required to produce enough power to smelt a ton of metal and the metal would still have to be shipped to market. Thus the advantage lies with moving the bauxite or, far better, the alumina.'[33] Persons who inhabit exploited economies would hardly expect otherwise since the advantage lies with the white owners of the smelting plants. But Brubaker seems to be saying that the advantage lies also with the primary producers such as Jamaica, when he further writes 'Apart from questions of prestige then, an aluminium smelting industry is not essential to a country for reasons of defence, industrial progress, or employment. It may help conserve foreign exchange through import substitution, but usually at the cost of more expensive metal; it may earn exchange with only a minimal diversion of domestic resources if it is commercially viable and able to attract foreign capital; or it may permit collateral benefits from river development projects.'[34] Brubaker admits that he understands the desire on the part of developing countries to claim any economic rent arising through exploitation of their resources. But in the same paragraph he expresses summary doubt as to whether 'there is much rent to be claimed in the aluminium industry. *Bauxite supplies are so large and widespread that they have limited scarcity value*' [my emphasis].

Brubaker's work may well be based on the best principles of scholarship and hard-headed statistical analysis, but Black Power advocates would see him as the apostle of exploitation and the defender of white power interests against defenceless Third World countries like Jamaica. The inevitable distrust ensures, then, the perpetuation among Jamaican cynics (black and otherwise) of the grave doubts they harbour about bauxite-alumina and its long-term effect on the economic strength of their country.

Implied in the persistent view that the bauxite-alumina industry ought to be rationalized into a nationally-determined enterprise, is a confidence in the force of the political power which Jamaicans have acquired, but which they have allowed to become frozen in formal institutions. It can indeed be reasonably argued that the elected representatives of the Jamaican people (the majority of whom are black) ought to have enough confidence in their constituents to use their political leverage to the advantage of the people of Jamaica. Even if economics were to dictate otherwise, the power of politics could indeed force a foreign company to accede to the demands of Jamaicans who, at least potentially, own the land from which the rich ore is mined. But then Black Power advocates would counter this with the view that Jamaicans do not really own the land, have no power and never will until they have *complete economic control*.

The advocates share with others the deep fear that the economic aspects of Jamaican life are likely to remain the province of outsiders while Jamaicans are barely allowed to get on with the political and the 'harmless' cultural aspects. This division of labour is grossly unrealistic and unhealthy. For it merely allows decisions about the destiny of the Jamaican people to be taken elsewhere rather than through the democratic process in which many Jamaicans seem to take great pride. The one-man-one-vote principle, the claims for workers' right to strike, the conduct of public affairs through frank, open, free, parliamentary debate would all be meaningless. Some Black Power advocates feel that this is exactly the situation as it now is in Jamaica. In their eyes the gains of political independence are all but negated by the economic satellization of the country by North America (the United States and Canada). This has prompted the declaration that Jamaican politicians have no power and that they are black masks of authority shielding the white faces of power. Yet although neat distinctions between 'authority' and 'power' are necessary intellectual preoccupations[35] they must also be prepared to stand the test of real political experience. Authority begets power and *vice versa*. What is not unreasonable to ask is that the Prime Minister of Jamaica with the authority of office must find the myriad ways of using his office and authority to acquire power. But to deny him and his ministers this capacity is to absolve them from all responsibility and therefore from all blame for the decisions they take. And this Black Power advocates, or any one else, would not be willing to do.

A politician without power may be a politician without respect, to parody a famous Garvey saying. But he also becomes an official without the burden of public moral responsibility. One way out of the intellectual dilemma would be to write off the politicians as public vegetables (and some Black Power advocates do). This, however, does not always relate to realities. Many of these would-be 'public vegetables' are themselves talking the language of Jamaicanization, of self-respect and of the need for Jamaican ownership of economic resources. They do, however, speak in Establishment jargon which blurs the substance with repetitious clichés of rhetoric and it is this which in turn rouses the impatience of the militant and progressive who desire action and quick change. It pleases less those Black Power advocates who do not in any case equate Jamaicanization with black ownership. What may be more usefully examined, however, is the question of whether black Jamaican politicians are not too sensitive to the constraints within which they work and whether they should not muster their creative drive to burst through man-made barriers in dealing with big brother countries and rich international trading partners.* It may be that our black politicians lack the skill to achieve objectives and the vision to

---

* The view of a young black West Indian intellectual is that 'there are no vast, impersonal forces *constraining* Jamaica or any other West Indian country to accept as given the continued dependence of these territories. The solution lies in our hands.' (James Milette in article, 'Exit Norman', *Moko*, No. 3, Port-of-Spain, Trinidad.)

perceive the needs. Perhaps these politicians underestimate the strength of the small nation in the world today and over-value the power that supposedly inheres in military might and technological achievement. It may even be that Jamaican politicians do not appreciate, sufficiently, the twentieth century demands for teamwork and organization. Perhaps old attitudes and prejudices and their very conditioning in the ways of the white man's world, preclude them from grasping, fully, the need for a society like Jamaica to cultivate its intellectual capacities through its university and other educational institutions so that its resources can be maximized – both material, however limited, and human which can be limitless.

Black Awareness and Self-knowledge

Black Power advocacy declares unerring faith in the human resources. The power that seemingly inheres in a certain type of human knowledge is regarded as limitless by many Black Power advocates. Garvey had enjoined the Negroes of his time to know themselves, to become aware of the great potential of their blackness and to enjoy the pride that flows from this awareness.[36] His *Philosophy and Opinions* is full of such injunctions. The Black Power Movement in the United States has aggressively declaimed that black is beautiful in defiance of white arrogance and in support of the new discovery. The Jamaican Black Power advocates also put the striving of a black image through a 're-evaluation of ourselves as blacks'[37] as a necessary precondition of attainment of power. Some share with other Jamaicans the view that this must be the result of a social process. Others settle in the thought that black awareness and black pride are essentially a psychological state of mind. The Jamaican society lends itself to both points of view. It is still a society that needs to be liberated from a strong white bias.*

---

* See my Essays 'National Identity and Attitudes to Race' (p. 17) and 'The Melody of Europe, The Rhythm of Africa . . .' (p. 171).

The value-system is Western which is understandable. But weighting in favour of European habits, mores and idiosyncracies at the expense of the contribution of peoples other than Europeans is well known to be the bane of black existence in the New World. Too many Jamaicans (black and otherwise) have for too long believed the myth of white European superiority and black African backwardness. For most it is now second-nature to think in terms which serve to negate the very fact of their own existence. Yet for a long time, Jamaicans have fought against the persistence of the white bias in the society. Not least among these was Marcus Garvey himself and many who campaigned for self-government in the thirties. The antidote was the positive swing of the pendulum over to the side of Africa so as to redress the balance. The Rastafarians later committed themselves fully and adopted outward signs of the inward grace.

Black Power advocates now follow in the same pattern and so do others with less vociferous attachment to the cause. A major symbol of 'belonging' on this level is the wearing of the dashiki – an American adaptation of the loose Hausa shirt, and this has been imported into Jamaica. Its functional and aesthetic virtues aside, it acts as a piece of ideological protective clothing for many.* It has been referred to by a Jamaican citizen writing to the press as a piece of 'black stupidity'.[38] Others, however, find the newly developed practice in Jamaica quite valid. 'Wearing an African dress', a letter in reply read, 'is a silent and dignified "statement" by a Jamaican of African origin that he belongs to one of the clearly defined, and I should like to think, *great* races of the world. Jamaica has many racial

---

* Black Power advocates find ideological support in Frantz Fanon's analysis of the use of the veil by women in revolutionary Algeria in the sense that it 'protects, reassures, isolates'. (See Fanon's 'Algeria Unveiled' in *A Dying Colonialism*, Grove Press Inc., New York, 1967, pp. 35–67.) It is doubtful whether the dashiki, in fact, achieves all this in the Jamaican situation but the garment has succeeded as a symbol of emancipation from the strictures of formal European dress.

origins, and those who wish to indicate dignity of the African heritage should feel free to do so by way of haircuts, dashikis or what have you.'[39] The so-called Afro hair style now popular among American black women has also found its place among Jamaican Black Power advocates as well as among others who are either in the fashion or have discovered the style's flattering potential. The Rastafarians had gone much further two or three decades before wearing their hair in long and matted braids. They also adopted sandals and knitted woollen caps and sashes of red, green and gold – the colours of the flag of Ethiopia. Like some of them, many Black Power advocates mistake the form for the substance and betray much misunderstanding in what Africa is about. The late Tom Mboya's article written for the *New York Times* magazine was reprinted in the Jamaican leading newspaper. In this he revealed that New World blacks would find it extremely difficult to become Africans. 'Some think,' he wrote, 'that to identify with Africa one should wear a shaggy beard or a piece of cloth on one's head or a cheap garment on one's body . . . An African walks barefoot or wears sandals made of old tyres not because it is his culture but because he lives in poverty . . . White people have often confused the symbols of our poverty with our culture. I would hope that black people would not make the same error.'[40] Many Jamaican black people have made the same error.

It is such people who will have to understand with Tom Mboya that the culture of the black peoples of Africa is 'something much deeper'.[41] It is in this context that one must understand the Black Power call for the teaching of African History, like that of the Garveyites and Rastafarians before this. The tendency in the past has been to look almost exclusively for what one writer calls 'the elements of unquestioned grandeur in the African past"[42] But Mboya in the article cited above seems to give priority to what he called the 'basic qualities' such as the 'extended family ties and the codes governing relations between old and young, our concept of mutual social responsibility and communal activities, our sense of humour, our belief in a supreme being and our ceremonies for birth, marriage and death'.[43]

This was the emphasis placed on the value of African History by historian Walter Rodney who emphasized in his article in the Black Power Journal *Bongo Man* the fact that ordinary African life had meaning and value. In other words, concern about the indisputable grandeur of African antiquity should give place to questions about the actual historical position of the ordinary African before his enforced 'exile'. Did he live in a kind of Hobbesian state of nature, driven by unbridled passions, lacking in any sense of personal security and with a life devoid of compassion and reason? Did he, in fact, live like the proverbial beast without moral awareness and relying utterly on force for his self-preservation, thereby justifying his being encaged in slavery for a period of *taming*? Or, did he inhabit communities which were structured on his proven capacity to abstract from his experience principles which he in turn ordered into maxims of prudence serving as guide for his actions and for his working relationships with others with whom he came into contact? Was he in fact some noble savage? That one-time fashionable image of the pre-Bondage African with his innocence intact may have been useful for disciples of negritude romanticizing the purity of the original and authentic African before his Fall into slavery. But this child-of-nature image also suggests a Man without a capacity to grasp the complexities, obligations, rights and moral implications of social relationship and therefore without the faculty to think (though he apparently feels) or the skill to organize and perceive of himself as a member of society. The reconstruction of African History, if Black Power at all requires it, must as a matter of priority concern itself with establishing for the benefit of human knowledge, basic and undisputed facts about the essential *humanity* of the ordinary pre-Bondage African. 'That is one of the weakest aspects of our perception of the African past' it is said.

It is not surprising since concepts of power and achievement are based on European canons of historiography with emphasis on crusades, conquests, kings and emperors, political in-fighting and imperial annexations. Garvey's very sense of grandeur betrayed the conscious creation of black parallels of certain white trappings of office. Like others after him, he felt the need to emphasize what have come to be generally regarded as some of the real achievements of his forbears. There *were* early Sudanic empires – complex in organization and en-veloping wide expanses of territory. The Benin bronzes are the essence of creativity, craftsmanship and sophistication and it is yet to be proven that these were the work of the Portuguese. Nor were the brilliant Ife heads the creation of Egyptians as some Europeans would have it. The Zimbabwe ruins of Central Africa betray townships, civilization and capacities for sophisticated social organization and Nkrumah's claims of an earlier kingdom of Ghana when Europeans were slaughtering each other are all now documented and accepted as major con-tributions to human history. Before this, as the West African historian K. O. Dike once wrote, 'Many statements on Africa rested not on the evidence of history or the ascertained fact, but on preconceived notions which in other contexts the scholars responsible would dismiss with appropriate academic detachment'.[44]

Jamaicans should be acquainted by now with this approach for the same thing can be said about the early writing of Jamaican and West Indian history. The works of West Indian historians and sociologists over the past twenty years have been to correct much of this wrong. This in itself gives the Jamaican Black Power advocates the responsibility to place West Indian history in the service of their cause. The fact of slavery is too often passed over in an attempt to learn what happened before slavery when both are, in fact, important. The basic humanity of the people, brought as slaves, in terms of their civilization and especially the intrinsic meaning and value of their ordinary life will indeed deepen one's understanding of the sustained rebellion by the African slave against his involuntary servitude in the West Indies. Black Power advocates are right then in asking that this be taught in schools and not just at the Univer-

sity level where a course in African History had been introduced.* But their emphasis on African History even at the
expense of West Indian and Jamaican History betrays a basic
dilemma. It is what Mboya called the *contradiction between
black nationalism and, in this case, Jamaican nationalism*. It is a
contradiction because complete identification with Africa (or
countries of Africa) is difficult in a world of nation states. Yet
it is reasonable for New World blacks to be concerned with
the reconstruction of an African past that can serve their
interests of identity wherever they may find themselves. Their
very identity, wherever they are, is thwarted by an attitude
born of the very assumption by a ruling white ethos that the
blacks have no past beyond that of slavery and degradation.
African achievement therefore has a place not so much for the
sake of the past but for the present and the future; and African
nations, as any African leader would aver, are deeply committed
to the use of their history as a function of modernization. The
call for teaching an African language in Jamaican schools is, in
this sense, an unnecessary relic of the past. Language is an
organic device for meaningful communication for doing things
practical. That is how the hundreds of African tongues are
used, not as museum pieces for nostalgic viewers. Many of the
new African countries find English and French practical and
use them despite their strong cultural commitment to the
'African personality'. Black Power advocates may not agree
but the future of their identity – black, Jamaican, or Jamaican
black seems tied up with the use of English.

This is the measure of the subtle connexions with which
Jamaican Black Power advocates, like all fellow-West Indians,
must learn to cope. Echoing Wilson Harris, the Guyanese
novelist-philosopher, a West Indian economist betrayed
welcome sensibilities. 'What is remarkable about the West
Indian' he wrote, 'is a sense of subtle links, the series of subtle

---

* Paradoxically the banning by the Jamaican Government of Walter
Rodney who was hired to teach this has put a temporary halt to the
programme.

and nebulous links which are latent within him, the latent ground of old and new personalities'.[45]

The perspective is indeed poetic but this is precisely the problem of the Jamaican black. Pedestrian polemics, statistical growth rate and national income columns, as well as broad sociological categories, are techniques that are unlikely to bring ready solutions in the matter of race relations in this part of the world. The dimensions of probing become deeply personal and individual, just as the humiliation of suffering has been, and still is, for many. This is not to underestimate the importance of the collective, but one is not talking simply of tactics and strategy, one is also concerned with final fulfilment. One must indeed take seriously a Black Power sympathizer's warning against confusing 'personal emancipation with collective liberation', but black awareness must turn on self-knowledge. Lloyd Best is probably right in his view that a 'grasp of the cold facts and *knowledge of self* are the true sources of compassion'.[46] Perhaps the Jamaican or West Indian black has advantages he is failing to exploit. He has always had to operate as an *individual* in his struggle for survival. Perhaps greater reflection on this aspect of his past could point some directions without betraying the cause of unity.

Much of what is expressed here would contradict one of Black Power's main tenets – namely the unity of the cause of all black men. But to deny persons who are black some form of individual uniqueness is in itself a kind of injustice. It is true that, although the blacks have been scattered, slavery, the plantation system and colonialism have thrown up a common framework of suffering and humiliation. Yet factors of time, place and circumstances have produced differences of life-style, of orientations and even of aspirations among people though they may look alike. The blocking of black creative wellsprings by the tyranny of dependence may now be perpetuated by the tyranny of a 'black culturalism' which sets goals without due concern for the feelings of the people involved and the objective factors that might go contrary to those goals. The richest cultures of black Africa, as of other peoples, are the fruits of cross-fertilization. Black Power militants may well exploit the creative potential of their black brothers in the West for they are the very expression of this continuing process of cross-fertilization. One God, one aim, one destiny in some things perhaps but not in all and to further deprive the black man of the agony of individual choice may be to deprive him of his humanity. One need hardly worry that European commentators interpret contemporary tribal conflict in some countries of Africa as manifestations of pure atavism. The Africans, as human beings, presumably have it in their nature to make choices and among the choices open to them, as to people everywhere, is good or evil, peace or violence.

Black Power and Violence

Black Power in Jamaica has been accused of making a *choice for violence*. Panic, among the established order in particular, has produced blame on the movement for crime and misdemeanours which attended the nation in the nine-month period following October 16, 1968, and for which it could hardly be held responsible. It is true that among the heroes of the movement are Malcolm X, who is too often remembered for his language of violence than for his words of wisdom, Che Guevara, who was a practising revolutionary and has written a manual of revolution, Stokely Carmichael, whose activities added violent dimensions to what used to be called the Civil Rights Movement in the United States, and of course Frantz Fanon, whose experience may even be more relevant to Jamaican blacks than to the Americans. Yet Fanon's advocacy of violent action by the oppressed referred to specifics of time and place that would hardly equate the Algerian or Angolan situation to that in Jamaica. There is nothing in the literature of Jamaican Black Power which advocates the essential need for violence in the achievement of goals. But the objective of total change anywhere has far-reaching implications. The call for basic structural transformation could presumably be achieved by a change of heart among incumbents of the present power structure but, according to Black Power views, this is itself a cultural-psychological impossibility. The answer then clearly lies in the attainment of power by those who are true believers. Provision for peaceful assumption of power exists through established institutions but Black Power advocacy denies these institutions any legitimacy or moral justification: as part of 'the system' they would have to go. The change implied would therefore be fundamental, all-embracing and even final. This clearly is in contradiction with the current views of the people in the power structure who have declared their commitment to change[47] but could hardly be expected to bring it about with Leninesque style or haste. Neither Government nor the Loyal Opposition can in fact be committed to change by violence.

An appeal to Jamaican history may well give the fearful some hope. The Jamaican past reveals a marked poverty of a will to violence and no impressive record of major achievement by violence. The Maroon rebellions gave to the runaway slaves a treaty, confederacy with the ruling British against blacks, like Paul Bogle and increasing obsolescence.* The slave rebellions, praiseworthy in themselves, were not supposed to to be a major contributory reason for Emancipation as *Capitalism and Slavery* affirms.[48] The Morant Bay riot was made into a 'rebellion' only by reason of Eyre's disproportionate reprisals against the rioters, and the event merely resulted in the imposition of crown colony government. The events of 1938 were not followed by Independence but gave, instead, a far too protracted period of phased transfer of power so that by 1962, when the real thing came, it had all but lost its force. Much of the argument above betrays cynicism but also raises serious doubt as to whether very much in Jamaica has ever been achieved for Jamaicans by violent means. A one-time Minister of Finance seems to think otherwise. Disagreeing with his former Party Leader's interpretation of Black Power, he

---

* This does not in any way detract from the significance of the Maroons' refusal to accept their enslavement.

affirmed that any 'attempt to identify Black Power with negritude was in line with the general policy that history should be forgotten; that in some remarkable way constitutional documents and modern institutions (including a Jamaican army) had wiped out white dominance of the society. *But it is well to remember that the slave revolts were Black Power.* The Maroons represented the success of Black Power. Paul Bogle canalized Black Power when he made his trek from Stony Gut to King's House. Black Power was shot down outside the Morant Bay Court House. Marcus Garvey made his indelible mark on Jamaica with Black Power. Bustamante in 1938 was a leader of Black Power . . .'[49] [my emphasis]. Black Power's *authenticity* is here made to find its roots in a history of *black revolt*. Another commentator sees Jamaican history serving the cause in a different way, however. Achievement is seen to be more on the side of oppression or 'legal violence' as it has been called. The lawful but inhumane punishment meted out to slaves, the hanging of Bogle (George William Gordon, the brown man who was also hanged is not mentioned) and the incarceration of Marcus Garvey after the due processes of law are cited in support of the view. Legal violence is then a part of the historical oppression of the blacks in Jamaica according to this view and since no 'oppressed class' has ever liberated itself without a struggle, the words of Marcus Garvey one of the national heroes of Jamaica (so the thesis suggests) takes on a certain relevance: 'Any sane man, race or nation that desires freedom must first of all think in terms of blood'.[50]

The language, despite its ambiguity, carries in it something of the violence of revolutionary rhetoric but nothing that Garvey did, revealed the use of revolutionary methods, reminiscent of guerilla warfare or the Fanonesque transference of a repressed aggressivity to rituals of violence against the oppressors.[51] Garvey's Black Star Line was just one of these many conscious efforts at building institutional frameworks through which his ideals and aspirations could materialize. On his return to Jamaica he ran for municipal and national elections providing the country and posterity with a manifesto that mirrors much of what was subsequently achieved in the political movement that succeeded him.[52] There is no evidence of his being influenced by the revolutionary tactics of the Russian Revolution and infiltration of his movement by the Communists would not have been his idea of progress.* But much has happened since Garvey's time. Brotherhoods of men have justified their fellowship by successful onslaughts against imperial masters and old institutions have eroded or are forced to change themselves radically under the raids and faith of guerilla armies of true believers. No place has been too sacred for the pitched battles. The universities in the most powerful nation on earth have been the most recent to lose their halo under a barrage of bullets and sheer youthful energy. The experience is not lost on the Jamaican power structure which, even if it wanted to be tolerant, would not wish to risk the almost legendary 'stability of Jamaica' which has been painstakingly built up on a series of institutions born of an early commitment to parliamentary democracy and supported by the conservative tendencies of rural dwellers – peasantry and planter class alike. The threat to such institutions was once offered by the Rastafarians,† or so things were interpreted in the late fifties. The Black Power movement is now deemed to present a similar threat and so inherits the wrath of a populace which still comprises thousands who remember the struggles and sacrifices of nation-building less than a generation ago. Violent language from vociferous militants is therefore interpreted as action and people are likely to be tried on their intentions rather than on their deeds. It was in this light that Walter Rodney defended himself against what he said was the

---

* Garvey had this to say of the Communists: 'The danger of Communism to the Negro . . . is seen in the selfish and vicious attempts of that party or group to use the Negro's vote and physical numbers in helping to smash and overthrow by revolution a system that is injurious to them as underdogs, the success of which would put their majority group in power, not only as communists, but as white men.' See *Garvey and Garveyism* by Amy Jacques Garvey, United Printers, Kingston, Jamaica, pp. 87-88.

† See my Essay, 'African Redemption . . .', p. 39 above.

Jamaican Government's charge that he had consorted with persons who had 'plots and plans to prepare a violent revolution in Jamaica'.[53]

The Prime Minister in putting his case before Parliament, however, did not divulge the specifics of such plots and plans: he was not able to reveal them 'without gravely endangering the nation', he said. But the Prime Minister, with or without such facts, knew that Jamaicans sometimes take seriously the use of language.* They had so done many years before when the Rastafarians used the fire-and-brimstone language of the Old Testament. Now they would do likewise. The Prime Minister therefore quoted from one of the speeches allegedly made by the Black Power revolutionary – 'Revolution must come. We must be prepared to see it through. We must stop talking and indulging in academic exercises and act. Who will be the first to come with me downtown and take up a machine-gun?'[54] A Jamaican solicitor offered the view that he did not think that 'one can properly say that in these circumstances the Rule of Law was breached.'[55] But by then an Exclusion Order had been issued, a riot with damage to property had taken place in Kingston, and the Government of the day had won the confidence of 'the nation of Jamaica, through its accredited representatives in the House of Representatives for the action taken on Tuesday to declare Dr. Rodney an undesir-

---

* So concerned is the status quo with resort to violence by dissidents that the *Daily Gleaner* saw fit to headline a report on the UWI's new 26-clause Statement of Principles in the following way: 'Officials, Departments in accord: UWI CANNOT SUPPORT ADVOCATES OF VIOLENCE'. (Friday, September 5, 1969.) The statement, as the paper's Education Reporter accurately stated, 'deals with the functions and purposes of the UWI, staff-student relations, relationship of colleagues in the academic community, relationship of members of the academic staff to the general extra-university community, the university teacher and political activity, political and public office, and responsibility of members of staff in relation to the university.' The singling out of the statement on violence is a reflection of attitudes to student militancy and Black Power advocacy both of which are closely identified with the UWI especially since October 16, 1968.

able inhabitant of, or visitor to Jamaica.'[56]* A newspaper report from Toronto, quoting the banned lecturer as saying 'there is bound to be an explosion [in Jamaica] whether I have anything to do with it or not', could not have helped his cause.[57] Before the Black Power movement got on its feet in Jamaica then, it was tainted in the public's mind with the tinge of violence.[58] Later it was to be associated with all types of violence. 'Since the inception of Black Power doctrine in Jamaica' wrote a citizen in the newspapers, 'the incidence of certain types of crimes has escalated. Vicious attacks are made on people of all ranks, *particularly the white and fair-skinned*'[59] [my emphasis]. But just as many of the Rastafari sect had taken pains to clear themselves of the taint of violence and declared themselves against violence in 1960, so in 1969 many Black Power sympathisers preached peace and love over destruction. As late as September, 1969, what was described as 'the first Black Power Conference to be held in Montego Bay' declared against revolution: 'Black Power does not mean revolution . . . it means black dignity and black pride'.[60]

Yet there are people who are still unsure whether the energetic and committed will take to the hills, not so much in passive isolation to worship their God and smoke ganja, but to find a base of operation from which to strike against what they know Black Power advocates regard as an oppressive society. Some would no doubt welcome such positive action by the advocates if only to be able to identify the target and narrow the area of conflict to purely military considerations. Black Power militants would probably respond that the dimensions of the conflict cannot be so simplistically viewed nor should foolhardiness be confused with courage: the time may just not be opportune.

---

* The Opposition after initially disapproving of the Government's action, reportedly concurred with Government's decision though deploring the way in which action was taken. The Leader of the Opposition disapproved of the excluded lecturer's 'activities which involved violence to overthrow those things we cherish highly in this country, in which a man is not as good as his skin, but as good as his merit'. *Hansard*, Oct. 17, 1968, and *Daily Gleaner*, Oct. 18.

Black Power and its Jamaican Future

The question of time (and timing) may well be the Black Power movement's most elusive threat. For time, void of positive action, may render *Black Power advocacy the victim of pre-emption.* The very society it seeks to overhaul may appropriate beforehand much of the ideal of change before the movement itself succeeds in putting it over. Already a colloquy of Roman Catholic Bishops of the Antilles has expressed a willingness and intention to 'Seek out and vigorously promote the good to be found in the Black Power movement.'[61] The Statement released by the conference of clerics did not fail to remind its readers that many Christian ministers had dedicated their lives in the cause of racial justice and equality. 'In fact', the Statement continued, 'it might be said that it was the work of such dedicated men which created the climate in which the nobler aspirations of this movement might be realised.'* Pre-emption is one of the oldest weapons against political enemies and Black Power is particularly vulnerable in the light of Jamaican circumstances. For although the Jamaican power structure is uneasy about talk of violence and echoes of other aspects of the American black revolution, it can afford to take in its stride talk of black beauty, black pride, black dignity and concern with the African heritage. In fact, much in Government policy and Opposition beliefs have reflected the encouragement of things African even when they are placed within the nationalist perspective of 'things *Jamaican.*'

---

* The Recording Cleric reportedly resigned on the issue of the Statement some days earlier. The Statement saw ignoble aspirations in the Black Power movement, especially the call to 'inverse racism, *separatism* between the races and philosophy of "licence to hatred and violence" '. This was a misuse of the term which in the eyes of 'thoughtful advocates' meant 'the eradication of racism and all its social, cultural and economic adjuncts . . . a political and economic programme . . . intended to put an end to a history of degradation and minimal progress for black.' The Statement concludes that 'such a philosophy is basically Christian'. *Abeng* gave qualified approval of the show of episcopal interest. (Vol. 1, No. 33.)

Respective Governments have long taken the Rastafarian cry for Africa seriously and a wide cross-section of the Jamaican populace is now attuned to the idea of Africa regaining its rightful place in the value-perspective of Jamaicans. Many would indeed support a political programme which could really put an end to a history of degradation and what has been minimal progress for the blacks. To many, the very notion of who is Jamaican is inconceivable without the recognition of some actual African ethnic connexion. But the other notion of 'multi-racialism' is equally very strong not only among those in authority but among the general citizenry. Black Power militants are yet to offer conclusive arguments against the objective fact of the existence of Jews, Europeans, brown men who do not wish to be called black, as well as Syrians, Chinese and others in the Jamaican racial complex. Whether these people have made a contribution worthy of consideration in determining the Jamaican ethos, may not be simply a matter of statistics; no more than the 11 per cent of blacks in the United States can be conceived as a minority position worthy of consideration commensurate with numbers. The minority psychology of the Jamaican black majority presents a unique problem, but one is here the victim of definitions. The hybridization (some prefer creolization) of the black is itself an objective fact: the change is irreversible, as Tom Mboya has reminded all Afro-Americans. To start from that point is the very essence of common sense and may well be the prevailing consensus of Jamaica. But the Black Power advocates are correct in saying that imbalances are yet to be put right in favour of the majority (i.e. the blacks). And these are indeed in the realm of economic opportunities.

Pre-emption is certainly not impossible in this area of concern. Jamaican political parties have long been declaring against poverty; the trade union leaders would assert that their wage negotiations are conducted on the recognition of the need to spread income to the poorer classes. The language is not dissimilar to that of the Black Power advocates. Nor is the concern with the hegemony of multi-national enterprises restricted to Black Power advocates. Many native Jamaicans feel strongly about the need for increasing negotiated royalties and advocate the stringent use of the Work Permit Law to ensure job security for qualified Jamaicans. The new increased revenue from the latest bauxite-alumina plants may be regarded as inadequate, the price paid in trade union rivalry with result-ant violence may be regarded as too great, the very terms of agreement between the North American giants and the Jamaican government may be considered not as good as they might be, but what has been done is an attempt to better some of the in-adequacies of the past. Political leaders, past and present, can perhaps be accused of treating ineptly with the industrial giants but they would regard it as unfair if accused of inaction.[62]

Knowledge of and disgust at the weaknesses of the Jamaican economy are not the monopoly of Black Power. Even the *Daily Gleaner* which would be regarded as 'establishment' has declared its concern by warning that 'those who lead the nation's affairs must recognize the chasm and vacuum in the economy'.[63] Black Power advocacy, by hammering away at the ills, has no doubt had its effect: the debates on the 1969 Budget would seem to suggest this. The Government's obvious attempts to shift the burden of taxation from the small (i.e. black) man to the large Companies and the entrepreneural class in general and the measures designed to have private firms go public are clear enough evidence of the politicians' awareness of the need for some action. The Opposition's indications of thinking in terms of a robust and new economic nationalism also reveal the universal concern with many of the issues that are central to the Black Power anxiety. But on both sides of the House the nation's 'accredited representatives' denounced any scheme or attitude that would advocate change other than by peaceful means. The Opposition Leader did not equivocate. 'We are opposed to violent revolution, or indeed any form of political violence, as irrelevant to Jamaica's situation.'[64] After emphasizing the need to make an assault on the class-oriented economic system which feeds 'the delusion that race is the enemy' he deplored 'the sad product of a colonial history which makes Jamaica forever seemingly prone to the slogans and solutions of *other* people in *other* lands, in *other* situations.' An imported Black Power doctrine that would advocate racial exclusivity, for example, clearly does not have the support of the Jamaican Leader of the Opposition. Black Power advocates may underestimate the reservations that Jamaican people have on racism even when they betray strong pride in being black. This, perhaps, is a function of the contradictions born of a heritage of subtle and myriad links.

Black Power through its newspaper *Abeng* has made gains in the trenchant criticism of the maladministration of justice, but this is not an exclusive province of concern. The dramatic renunciation of his appointment as Queen's Counsel (a high professional award) by a young distinguished barrister probably did more to focus attention on the canker than many a Black Power outpouring.[65] The Bar Association itself seems unhappy about developments. Some highly placed Jamaicans see the erosion in the administration of justice as a sign of the erosion of political ideals long treasured by the new nation. It was after all a brilliant Jamaican lawyer who gave form and articulation to these ideals in many of the institutions which now serve public life.[66] A threat to the Rule of Law is therefore considered a threat to the very fabric of the society. Many Black Power advocates who call for the entire overthrow of the system – two parties, parliament and all – seem to fail to appreciate the organic connection here implied. Black Power advocates' appeal to the Rule of Law, when their supporters are banned, is itself an appeal to one of the fundamental notions (or institutions) which prop up the political and social arrangements in Jamaican society. The concern with its falling into desuetude or being abused can only be supported.

The Jamaican Black Power belief that the political leaders operate in the shadow of the might and power of the United States of America is a widespread one among public-minded Jamaicans and the dislike or resentment of this is not restricted to the militants. Not all Jamaicans are in agreement with the 'American position' on Cuba for example, and few would support the view that Jamaica should break diplomatic relations with one of its nearest neighbours. The withdrawal of the passport of a University lecturer, because of a visit to Cuba, resulted in much public support for the lecturer, and though the Government could be more liberal in granting permission to visit Castro's country, there is supposed to be no outright prohibition. There is a deep dislike for Communism among the members of the established order but Black Power itself has no necessary organic link with that brand of social organization. The American intervention in Santo Domingo reminds many Jamaicans of American might in the Western Hemisphere and concerns many, who are not Black Power advocates, out of fear that Jamaica might suffer a similar fate, with or without the connivance of those compatriots 'in power'. Accusations against the activities of the CIA are not to be found only in Black Power literature. Many Jamaicans having no connection with the doctrine themselves would prefer not to be the targets of American Intelligence. The hegemony of the North Atlantic powers as an expression of neo-colonialism earns the abhorrence of Black Power advocates and non-advocates alike. The cultural and artistic domination by Europe (Eurocentrism) is a target of attack by a wide range of people as well. Black Power advocates see all this as an extension of the white technological domination of the entire Third World; non-advocates see it as a usurper of the right of Jamaican nationals to determine their own destiny. The influx of tourists, missionaries (peace corps and CUSO), executives and capital merely intensifies the apprehensions.

Black Power then by its very nature and by the issues it rakes within its ambit, possesses a relevance which accounts for its persistence, and explains in part the fear it arouses. In the hands of the young it is of special significance. Its young adherents, educated and alienated, share ideals with their counterparts elsewhere in the world in their demand, as a Jamaican writer puts it, 'not only a re-distribution of wealth and political rights (which are what most revolutions up to now have been about) but a transformation of the morals, values and behaviour patterns of their societies'.[67]

166

Even in this there are signs that the Establishment, old and new, are willing to concede the point. The founder of the nation's oldest party on his retirement all but 'handed to the young generation' the nation which he was instrumental in shaping. He seemed to have been on the wavelength of the anxieties of the young and even of Black Power advocacy more than *Abeng*, in an uncompromising obituary, seemed willing to admit.[68] Norman Manley in his last days repeatedly pointed out that *his* generation's mission had been to create a national spirit for the purpose of achieving independence. With that mission accomplished he admitted that the new generation had the right to expect its leaders to proceed to the social and economic reform (and some would say transformation) of this country so as to put an end to what he himself described as 'the continued denial of economic power in our own land'.[69] His successor* was soon after to reveal his own awareness of problems which confront Jamaica – the alienation of the young, the gaps in income levels and the corresponding frustrations, the chronic unemployment and underemployment and the general psychological state of the country.[70] But all this spells change, the Black Power advocates insist. The commendable work of the past thirty years under the earlier leaders 'like the work of any historical stage, must yield to the new times it helped to create, or be destroyed', warned *Abeng*.[71] This is not a novel idea. The entire mood of the country since the late fifties has been one that would countenance change. Members of the old Establishment seemed aware: 'I can almost see history being made in Jamaica, daily' the older Mr. Manley had said addressing the 29th anniversary banquet of his Party in September, 1967, 'and I sense profound changes ahead of us. I am convinced that Jamaica is going to change'.[72] By 1969

---

* Opposition Leader Michael Manley was reported as saying, 'The basic directions of the Jamaican economy show that we are still running a colonial-type economy, relying increasingly on foreign goods, foreign markets, foreign capital, foreign ideas and foreign outlets for labour'. See *Public Opinion*, Vol. 33, No. 16, June 6, 1969.

the mood for change had grown more intense and Edward Seaga, the Minister of Finance and Planning in the Government of the day and one who had gained a sound political reputation by his earlier call for change, reminded the nation in presenting the Budget of the important changes since 1938. He, however, conceded the right of the young to expect change and the need for change being 'part of the character and make-up of youth . . . when a society stops changing it will decay and die.' Black Power as an instrument of change and a political strategy would therefore seem to possess an undoubted relevance in society. But it is as a political strategy that it clashes head-on with what it calls the system. 'It is now a question of change, how?' said Edward Seaga, concluding with a statement which apparently won him much applause and concurrence: 'In all these things a pendulum effect can be obtained; it is a movement that swings from one extreme to the other and must eventually swing back and settle in the middle and it will always be found that the position in the middle is no farther forward than if one had moved in moderate terms. Jamaica has had and continues to enjoy a reputation of stability. *We want to effect change without despair* [my emphasis]. These are our objectives for the future. We think of it as part of the dreams of the things that are to come, but in those things, we don't want to destroy, obliterate or wipe out the institutions that we have and start something new that sets us back almost forty years. The rebuilding of a society is not something that is to be done overnight. The good sense, responsibility and wisdom is there to shape and redirect the forces that can build within a society.'[73] The Black Power organ *Abeng* was not impressed. Instead, it headlined an attack on the so-called Reform Budget with 'CHANGE WITHOUT HOPE', and blew out the perennial query in conclusion 'To whom, then, does the Government of Jamaica belong?'*

---

* The *Daily Gleaner* later asked a similar question (see Editorial of May 20, 1969) when angered by a suggestion by the Governor of the Bank of Jamaica that was interpreted to mean that U.S. currency should be made legal tender in Jamaica.

It is clear that part of the strategy of Black Power is to brook no accommodation with the Jamaican power structure. This seems to be an intuitive response to the threat of pre-emption. The fact is that both Black Power advocates and the political leaders are appealing to the same constituents. Both appellants have identified and uncovered the ills. The question now may well be which one of them is going to do something about the ills, *how* and *when*. The power structure has undoubted advantages. But the power structure, whether as Government or Loyal Opposition, is vulnerable on its acts of omission as much as for the decisions actually taken. Black Power advocates, untried and untested, do not have the institutional framework within which to take effective action. They are likely to find support for justifying rebellion on grounds of colour discrimination but it is to be seriously questioned whether the matter of race is the real issue at stake. But even with the disadvantage of a distrusted, though at the same time fashionable, slogan, Black Power advocates would have ample reserves of strength in the grave unemployment situation existing in the country at large, the continuing correlation of poverty with blackness and the increasing dominance of foreign (white) capital and the accompanying executives in vital areas of Jamaican life. Instead Black Power advocacy is tempted to restrict itself to polemical chronicling of the ills rather than committing itself to action that would correct such ills. Infiltration of existing institutions is ruled out on doctrinal grounds and the same applies to the chance of forming a Black Power party, as the movement has been repeatedly invited to do by the leading members of the two Jamaican political parties.[74] Doctrine aside, strategy considerations could hardly support such a move on the part of Black Power advocates. Both the ruling Jamaica Labour Party (JLP) and the Opposition People's National Party (PNP) with their strong trade union bases have the advantages of organization, experience and financial backing. Strategy would also dictate against engaging in guerilla warfare, it would seem at this time, and if there were plans for this it would be suicidal to let it be generally known.

In the absence of action of one sort or another then some enemies of the movement find it easy to dismiss the phenomenon as irrelevant. This may be more wishful thinking than accurate assessment for, when stripped of the glamour of its slogan, the movement reveals an underlayer of deep concern with live issues which are fundamental to Jamaican life. *Abeng* might be accused of overstating its case but this is not the same thing as not speaking the truth. The country is said to need a new political strategy and emergence from colonialism naturally dictates this. Many would agree that power of 'property' as enshrined in the Constitution cannot be that strategy. And while many will even share doubts about the capacity of the existing two party, two trade union system to continue substituting for the much needed political alternative, they will also query the claim of Black Power to the prize. The question then remains: can it offer the new political vision which Jamaica seems now to need?

To dismiss Black Power as irrelevant in a country which is inhabited and governed by black people is to beg the question and indeed possibly to play the proverbial ostrich. Better to examine whether the phenomenon can at all provide the definitive *revolutionary ethic* or that desired *strategy for change* not only in Jamaica but throughout the entire Commonwealth Caribbean islands which have shared many aspects of a particular experience. No simple answer is likely to emerge out of the textured complexities that characterize the Caribbean. But in examining the situation it will be useful to dissolve the current image of sandy sunlit playpens for the affluent from the North Atlantic, and bring into sharp focus the predicament of resourceful but frustrated groups of people who are determined to break the protracted malady of poverty and an imposed self-doubt. For this is the measure of the difficult task facing the native Caribbean inheritors of the British authority and power: they must now bring within the pale of their people's immediate experience material self-sufficiency and spiritual rebirth.

THE MELODY OF EUROPE
THE RHYTHM OF AFRICA

But every John Crow tink him pickney white

THE BLURRED focus of the Jamaican's perception of himself frequently invites metaphors for description. 'Every John Crow tink him pickney white'* is still among the most expressive and has been for generations the most brutally accurate. 'The melody of Europe, the rhythm of Africa' is a more felicitous, if a less spontaneous, phrase seeking to catch in language all too inadequate, the dynamic of the quavering existence that some people loosely label 'Jamaican'. To some, the phrase suggests a counterpoint harmony, the dynamic interplay of elements in varying degrees of attraction and repulsion creating a third dimension of beauty that can be textured, rich and life-giving. To the music purist, melody cannot exist without its own rhythm and therefore melody and rhythm cannot be regarded as mutually exclusive phenomena.† Europe and Africa in this context would then form an organic whole inextricably bound up and expressive of a new and rich phenomenon which is neither Africa nor Europe, yet embodying the two in unprecedented and creative modes of relationship. Yet, to other types of purists, the enduring elements of Europe and Africa are seen quite separate – each in its distinct sphere, making contact when necessary, but existing in a complex of decided duality which gives just this character to the society that the elements are used to describe. Again, to the music purists, rhythm can exist without melody, i.e. conceived as the articulation of movement. As such it may be said to appeal to something fundamental and atavistic – no doubt the provider of that soul

---

* An old Jamaican proverb meaning everyone thinks what belongs to him is of the best (literally, every John Crow thinks his child is white). The John Crow is a popular vulture, a scavenger, whose rich black plumage and bald (peel) head are said to have been named after a Baptist parson, the Rev. John Crow. To call one a John Crow is to equate him with a scavenger, a low-bred, worthless fellow and the term turns up in Jamaican folklore and speech with a certain frequency.

† I am grateful to Miss Pamela O'Gorman, Director of Music, University of the West Indies, for helping to clarify my thoughts on this.

energy that is demanded of music by many today. Rhythm so
conceived is more likely to affect the listener physically and
viscerally than intellectually. To other types of purists the
physical-visceral stimuli of rhythm develop logically from the
analogy as the very role played by the rhythm of Africa in the
Jamaican cultural complex. Melody, on the other hand, is said
to be associated with mind, emotion, insinuation, rhetoric,
lyricism, and for some this becomes the melody of Europe.
And so it has been in the minds of generations of Jamaicans
(as well as Europeans) that the European melody and the
African rhythms have produced a harmony of a kind that
maintains for Europe a superior and for Africa an inferior
place in the composition of the complex. The sociologists
have put it more expertly: the mixture has produced a Creole
culture in which European and African elements persist and
predominate in fairly standard combinations and relationships
with things European gaining ascriptive status while things
African were correspondingly devalued, including *African racial
traits*.[1] One important outcome was to be the culture mirroring
race, Europe taking precedence over Africa, melody over rhythm.
Today, despite declarations to the contrary, the 'harmony' has
been weighed in the balance and found wanting.

For generations there have been attempts to liberate the
society from a predisposition, deliberate and otherwise, to
maintain the mutual exclusivity between melody and rhythm.
But many times the attempts to find the formula that would
adequately describe and catch the elusive harmonies echoing
from the counterpoint meeting of Europe and Africa, have
been thwarted. The development of an indigenous life-style
(called 'creolization') during the late eighteenth and early
nineteenth centuries was a recognizable shaping of such a
'harmony'. It took place against a background of slavery, the
plantation system, and the imperial connexions with Britain.
The major fault with the harmony was that the melody of
Europe rasped loud and dominant over Africa's rhythm. Even
though this rhythm was steady, haunting, quite audible and
in many instances subtly interwoven, it was largely Europe's

melody that was deemed important, valuable and fit to be heard. Nearly everything conspired after Emancipation to militate against the creation of a viable organic third dimension that would reflect a balanced and harmonious relationship between the enduring elements. If the early post-Emancipation years merely attested to the submergence of the rhythm and its threatened extinction from any accepted annotation in the scheme of Jamaican social composition, 1865, and the imposition of the Crown Colony system amplified into a blaring crescendo the melody of Europe through the entrenchment of British colonial government, education, law, and language as well as ideas about property ownership, family and kinship. African elements on the other hand remained merely observable in such things as language, diet, folklore, family and kinship, property, marketing, medicine, magic and religion and some grass-root economic organizations.[2] The 'rhythm' was here threatened with further loss of definition: it gave flavour but what mattered was the melody of Europe, with its own rhythm and producing a harmony with less and less African component.

But the tenacity of the African rhythm/flavour was evident in the entire cultural complex which according to Tyler includes 'knowledge, belief, art, law, morals, custom, and any other capabilities and habits acquired as a member of society.'[3] The Jamaican society had assumed a culture, however ill-defined, and in that culture were embedded the albeit submerged forces of Africa from whence the majority of its members had in fact come. These submerged forces have at different times of the last century's history attempted to break through. Today some would have one believe, despite the self-evident brute facts, that Jamaican life is all Africa's rhythm and little else. The fundamental atavistic, physical-visceral yearnings have burgeoned into Garveyism, Rastafarianism and Black Power advocacy.

> And then the revolution. Black
> and loud the horns of anger blew
> against the long oppression; sufferers
> cast off the precious values of the few.'[4]

Europe's melody is drowned out, as it were, and the haunting ritualistic repetition of Africa's rhythms in the protest of these black soothsayers merely serve to conjure up in the minds of the so-called true Jamaicans dark and unpredictable irrational forces that are said to augur revolution, bloodshed and cultural regression. The traditional carriers of Europe's melody (largely the brown biological and the black cultural hybrids) are many of them among the voices raised against what is termed 'too much emphasis on Africa' in Government's and the society's sometimes self-conscious search for an identity and the national heritage.*

Fears are, however, easily allayed. For officially, the country is committed to *multi-racialism*† which is the latter-day attempt to describe the Jamaican ethos conceived as the occasion and outcome of the meeting of peoples with different racial-

---

* Especially the introduction by Government in 1969 of National Heritage Week and the establishment of National Heroes Day which begins it. A minor controversy developed over a Jamaican barrister's reported questioning of the wisdom of the self-conscious building of a national image. She repeated in a letter to the *Gleaner*'s Editor her concern over the notion 'that a cult of selected heroes is felt to be necessary as the emotional peg offered the young on which to hang their attachment to their country . . . My plea to my audience – and to everybody – is that we should all think carefully about this self-conscious creation of an emotional centre for our national life which might have the effect of creating a problem of minorities'. This was in fact a fair summary of how a wide cross-section of the articulate Jamaican populace felt. See letter from Gloria Cumper to Editor, *Daily Gleaner*, November 1, 1969.

† Like our predecessors, the young political leaders do not equivocate: 'Our country has already embraced much of the elements of African and Western art and culture . . . We are already established as a multi-racial community but to be a complete whole it is necessary that it should be multi-cultural as well.' (Speech by H. L. Shearer, Prime Minister, opening the Chinese Benevolent Association Arts and Culture Centre, Kingston, Jamaica, August, 1967.) In his Budget Speech, May, 1968, the Leader of the Opposition, M. M. Manley, had this to say, 'We are opposed to any form of racialism and opposed to the claim of any race of superiority, or advantage by natural right, over any other race.'

cultural memories who live in the society.[5] By definition, then, not only Africa, Europe and their miscegenated offsprings must be taken into account, but also India, Lebanon, China and the biological additions which they have made through various admixtures.[6] Yet such a definition merely stipulates an aspiration rather than reality, for the dominant theme of Jamaican life continues to be Europe playing on Africa, producing a Euro-African cultural pattern. This now grows into sharper focus following on the increasing black awareness among the majority of Jamaicans who are of African descent, in objective conflict with the strongly embedded institutions of British origin which govern Jamaican life in the twentieth century. But if Europe here governs it is Africa which rules in the sense of spiritual motivation. The Creole culture of Jamaica is Euro-African and all comers since the middle-nineteenth century have had to (and still do) adapt to this culture. As such they become 'creolized', or simply 'Jamaican-ized'.* The Chinese, the East Indians and the Lebanese communities may have produced new biological additions to the racial strains of the country, but they cannot be said to have affected the cultural pattern to the point of fundamentally altering the value system. In so far as culture mirrors race or *vice versa*, the new biological additions further complicate the racial identities in the way the mulattos of an earlier era did. But in time wealth and education help to determine their place in the society which is now usually at the top, making functional whites and browns out of the admixtures. So the society vacillates between exaggerated claims of a cultural consensus and exaggerated claims of a harmonious racial heterogeneity, the racial harmony being the result of the cultural consensus.

---

* This is no different with the Indians as of now in West Indian territories such as Trinidad and Guyana where to be Trinidadian or Guyanese means a creolization around to the Euro-African ethos, though with the rising Indian populations of both territories a truly multi-cultural ethos mirroring the multi-racial composition will emerge in a few generations hence. This could produce societies as distinct from the Jamaican society as they and Jamaica now are from the mestizo societies of, say, Mexico and Peru.

Yet the experience of the last decade and before gives little support to this claim of consensus. The frequent call for cultural fusion is not a semantic shift from racial harmony. It is a call that recognizes that in the absence of the former, the latter cannot be realized. 'Out of many, one people' becomes, then, little more than a pithy epigram for speeches of exhortation and official brochures, when it was really intended to describe and inform the spirit of multi-racialism and cultural integration among the Jamaican people. The black majority may find little cause to feel that multi-racialism has anything to do with them when 'multi' conjures up a complex in which they hold an inferior position on grounds of class which in turn dovetails with race origin. The problem is compounded by the fact that any indication of a specific common identity with the more privileged classes is quickly offset by the problems born of 'the continuous changing relations between the middle class and lower class identities' which make up the Euro-African complex.[7] In the contradictions and chaos that result, the members of the African segment reflect on the fact that it was essentially the blacks who were required to be the carriers of the white culture and not the other way around though the whites were undoubtedly tainted with an African flavour, making them palpably different from their metropolitan counterparts. The society that followed from the mutual conflicts and mutual memories of Europe and Africa have revealed European transplants and survivals in all their strengths while Africa seems, in juxtaposition, a mere fragment of its former self in tolerated spurts of syncretized or re-interpreted folklore – some music, some dance, some story-telling, some syntax and some religion.

This had merely served, goes the argument, to perpetuate in the New World myths about racial inequality based on measurements of cultural achievement as well as on biological theories. Commenting on this Eric Williams, the West Indian politician, asserted in his *British Historians and the West Indies*, that between Emancipation and the outbreak of the Second World War 'the West Indies could not be considered without slavery

on which they had been built up until 1833, which Carlyle
had wished to restore, whose abolition Trollope had deplored
and which had left behind a legacy of social relations and
emotional prejudices that Eyre had sought to preserve by his
policy of terror'.[8] Yet Eyre's 'policy of terror' had in fact
served to remind Jamaicans in the nineteenth century that,
other than the negrophobic Carlyles and Trollopes, there was
the liberal tradition that opposed slavery as morally wrong,
rejected racialism in the form of white superiority/black
inferiority, and believed in representative government for all
rational human beings.[9] Men like John Stuart Mill condemned Governor Eyre for his part in the 1865 Morant Bay
riot. Lord Olivier, a later Governor of Jamaica, is said to have
followed in the tradition by exploding the myth that the negro
was lazy, profligate, barbaric and not fit for self-government.
This liberal tradition continued despite the pugnacious imperialism of Churchill and Rhodes, which Williams chronicles
with carefully chosen documentation.[10] Its existence also
made possible what Professor Elsa Goveia, in a scholastically
more satisfying study of West Indian historiography, called
'the momentous alliance' between the 'liberal white official and
the politically conscious West Indian negro'.[11] For Jamaica,
this blending of sentiments was occasioned by the influence
which Lord Citrine the British trade unionist had on the 1938
Moyne Commission (of which he was a member), by the
rapport between the Socialist, Sir Stafford Cripps and the
PNP hierarchy in 1938, or between Norman Manley the Chief
Minister and Sir Hugh Foot the liberal English Governor in
the last stages to full internal self-government, as well as by
the frequent contacts between the Jamaican and West Indian
politically-oriented trade unions and leaders in the British
TUC particularly during the early years of agitation for self-
government. Professor Goveia's 'momentous alliance' has been
a valuable instrument in fighting, not unsuccessfully, the
vestigial traces of the pro-slavery ethic as well as exploding
the myth that non-white peoples were unable to govern themselves. This last position was the base from which the Crown

Colony System was introduced into Jamaica, declarations made about the backwardness of Indians (in India) and Trinidadian cries in the 1880s for self-government thrown overboard.

It was partly on this last issue that 'froudacity' reared its ugly head in 1888 with Froude, the historian, as the standard-bearer.[12] Dr. Williams quotes with gravity and pardonable ire, long passages from the eminent historian's collected views on black inferiority, white supremacy and the inappropriateness of British Parliamentary institutions in the hands of inept West Indian blacks. Professor Goveia with scholarly detachment, dismisses it as bad history though admitting the merits of the writer's literary style. She finally places it in welcome perspective as nothing 'more than the brief recrudescence of a moribund tradition in West Indian historiography' – her point being that the realities of social change since Emancipation 'were at last making it possible for a combination to emerge in which the recognition of the claims of racial equality was united with a firm attachment to the cause of self-government'.[13] It is this unity which now supports the claims for multi-racialism in the Jamaican cultural complex and justifies the hope for it to be a viable ethical variable in the goals which the society sets for itself.

Yet one suspects that current voices of protest would quicker side with Eric Williams against the fulminations of Froude, the negrophobic vulgarities of Carlyle and the peregrinating prejudices of Trollope. For these would be seen as logical antecedents of the present-day persistence of views which promote notions of white racial supremacy in the United States, United Kingdom and South Africa. If 1865 has been avenged in the attainment of self-government, goes the argument, it is yet to be avenged through the achievement of racial equality.

At the same time it is difficult not to view 1865 with mixed feelings. A Mr. Osborn, a coloured member of the Jamaican House of Assembly, spoke gallantly in favour of preserving democracy in Jamaica through a fully elected House of Assembly, in which the people of Jamaica – like the '(brown) class' to which he belonged could participate.[14] Five days later in

a final condemnation of the threat to abolish the Assembly
Mr. Osborn predicted that laws of the kind about to be passed
would be to no avail since the white population was disappearing
and that 'in years to come . . . the government of the colonies
will fall into the hands of the blacks'. He said it appeared to
him that that was the decree of God, whereupon a member of
the Assembly shouted 'sedition' and one Mr. Wellesley Bourke,
to cries of 'hear, hear', indignantly added the retort that 'as
long as Britain exists this island will never fall into the hands
of the negroes to the exclusion of the other classes'. Mr. Osborn
persisted in his prediction, however, that in 'a hundred years
hence the country will be governed by what we now term the
lower orders'.[15] Now one view, following on Osborn's prediction, could today hold that the lower orders, through universal
adult suffrage, are in fact governing Jamaica. Another view
will, however, give credit to Mr. Bourke's prediction, for
today the governing has not by any means fallen into negro
hands 'to the exclusion of the other classes' – other classes
being browns and whites to which have since been added
Lebanese, Chinese, etc. The doctrine of multi-racialism with
all that it implies may then be said to be the measure of the
fulfilment of Mr. Bourke's little prophecy.

Of course the fulfilment may be seen as having been made
possible by the way in which the imposition of Crown Colony
Government served to resuscitate and promote more intensely
the process of shaping the ethos increasingly around to European
(i.e. English) thought, habits, prejudices and institutions. More
and more the term 'negro' came to connote a Europeanized
African, rather than a true cultural hybrid sufficiently of his
own kind to differ radically from his European and African
counterparts. Instead he was the product of a system which
could boast not only Creole white Englishmen but black, brown
(and later Chinese and Indian) 'Englishmen'. True, the
English-oriented ethos provided something of a consensus that
managed to cut across colour and race lines but that ethos was
closely identified with at least one class in the society – the
non-black privileged class. It makes historical sense, then,

that the protest that first erupted to question the claims of white superiority, came from the non-privileged and came in terms of a race consciousness coupled with the whole question of identity which the half-black, half-white middle class embraced. By the nineteen thirties the question was being asked, on what grounds would there be a justification for regarding things Jamaican as identical with things English.[16]

The answers were not and still are not easy to find. The civilizing mission assumed by the middle classes throughout the early ferment of ideas on nationhood, itself betrayed an equation which identified brown vision with the national good. But while 'brown' has meant a disdain for white claims to superiority, it has also been identified with contempt for the black connexion. This in particular has never been forgiven or forgotten by the blacks whose 'every john crow tink him pickney white' seemed a damning enough description of the total Europeanization of the aspirations of almost everybody in the Jamaican society. Not all Jamaican blacks, it is now known, wanted to be white. While some Jamaicans were declaring for a Jamaican nationalism, others were finding alternatives either in Ethiopianization or later in attempts to 'Africanize' the ethos.* But it is clear that this approach is as much an error as the older and still persistent Eurocentrism of Jamaican creole culture. The danger of a polarization of European and African descendants into irreconcilable camps need not be feared but one could envisage a situation where the only real Jamaicans able to give some reality to the ultimate Jamaicanism, are those who are racially outside the Euro-African complex.†

---

* Marcus Garvey flourished from the early twenties. Rastafarianism dates back to 1930. The mass politics harnessed by Alexander Bustamante had its cradle in the Garvey movement in a sence. See Essays above.

† The situations in Trinidad and Guyana are instructive where a Chinese and a Guyanese white respectively proved ideal as Governor-General. In each case the incumbent was not of the dominant racial-cultural complex – Euro-African-Indian in Trinidad and Indo-African in Guyana. The numerically dominant blacks in the

Some of these, however, seek still to escape the resulting confusion if not to preserve their own cultural-racial memories. So total assimilation of the Lebanese into the existing complex is yet to be achieved: whenever he can, he resists it by furloughs to Lebanon and marriage to Lebanese either from the home country or from neighbouring Latin-American communities. With the Chinese this has been far less the case ever since travel back to mainland China under Communist rule proved difficult. There was a period of local factious sorting out of ideological positions among Jamaican Chinese but this now seems to be a thing of the past and the new generation are integrated at the top, marrying into the post-Independence expatriate white group or to other evolved Jamaican members of their own race. The old biological union of Chinese shopkeeper and black concubine no longer seems to be a practical necessity in the process of integration of the Chinese into the Jamaican society. The choice left open to the Chinese-Jamaican has been between white rich and black poor: he can hardly be blamed for not choosing the latter. But as a result of his choice he has been the target of much lower class black envy, since he will have left his black colleagues behind on the road to economic independence. He then becomes a member of 'the exploiting class', in the language of Black Power advocacy.[17] So does the Lebanese who, like the Jew, is considered white. Of the later Jamaicans, the East Indian (the estate Indian) has fared best as far as black protest goes, and worse as far as economic progress is concerned. The two are interrelated for by remaining with the blacks at the base the estate Indian has gained virtual approval from the majority. This is not true of the more recent immigrant East Indians who are largely of the merchant class and who, by maintaining a primary and almost exclusive interest in commerce, earn in return an outsider status from the black-brown-white complex

Jamaican Euro-African complex facilitated, on the other hand, the appointment of a black Governor-General though a 'brown' Establishment type of incumbent might have been preferred by some Jamaicans.

which still meets the structural conveniences of the society. Where Lebanese Jamaicans (Syrians) who are involved with national life can graduate into the upper white echelons, rich East Indians seemingly remain a detached group without any cultural importance. They are neither 'negrified' as their racial counterparts on the estates nor whitened as their mercantile counterparts among the Syrians.

The term 'negrified' is used deliberately to express a special feature of the Euro-African complex. It implies a metropolitan European perspective of the African essence in the New World and more generally of the creole culture. The term 'negro' itself is losing its former status of acceptance among many New World blacks. Though Garvey preferred it to 'coloured', the Rastafarians have rejected it and Black Power advocates in Jamaica, as in the United States, have all but expunged it from the dictionary. The term may be said to conjure up an involuted identity – since the black man is made to see himself as the European conceives him (the black man) as perceiving himself. In this sense Africa may be for Africans at home but seldom is for those abroad. The exiled African ('negro') not infrequently discovers that he prefers life back in his creole society. Such problems are not restricted to the black or coloured West Indian; the creole (i.e. native-born and native-reared) whites are no less confused in perceiving themselves as identical with their metropolitan counterparts only to discover that they in turn have been 'negrified' or transformed in the special way into a Euro-African. They in turn see themselves as the negro sees them. East Indians attempting to identify with the land of Ghandi and Nehru will no doubt suffer the same disillusionment as must the sephardic Jamaican Jews if they were to attempt to make Israel home; and so would the third generation Jamaican Chinese in any effort to embrace the mores of the Cantonese Valley or Taiwan. For they too have been 'negrified'. The force of this process probably stems from the fact that the 'negro' (black and Afro-European) has been the prime carrier of the Creole culture complete with its strong white bias.

In the absence of a strongly preserved cultural memory and in the wake of the deliberate uprooting of ancestral institutions by the slave system among the African immigrants, the African slave was to become the nearest thing to a *tabula rasa* on which the new vocabulary of creole existence could be written. As a result, some of his descendants today boast the claim that of all comers to the Plantation societies of the New World, the African has been the prime agent of creativity through which all the experiments in the new living have been carried out. He therefore becomes the richest expression of all the contradictions, the failures, successes, the fears and hopes of the new society. He is black man, white man, brown man and all the 'in-betweens' rolled into one.* He is Europe's melody and Africa's rhythm, at once the dissonance and the harmony of both. He thinks 'him pickney white' fully knowing that everyone else knows he is black and that he would probably prefer to have him 'brown'. It is through the negro, then, that the new society is said to express itself most. Negro does not mean exclusively African and could never mean exclusively white – it is the other dimension emerging from these dominant elements. This perception of the society through the many-sided negro is strong enough to build a faith in multi-racialism as a social creed even if 'multi' means two (culturally speaking); and it is this perception which perhaps serves to convince people that Black Power, in its wilder claims for identity, on the basis exclusively of race, runs a poor second to the former doctrine of white supremacy and its offshoot of brown power. Yet despite all these cultural claims made on behalf of the negro he still finds himself fighting for recognition and status more than a century after legal emancipation. His own racial identity still coincides, naturally, with his society's fight for independence not only from European Governors, Colonial

---

* Compare the claims made by the Mexican philosopher Jose Vasconcelos in reference to the Mexican Creole as a new race 'made of the treasury of all previous races, the final race, the cosmic race' quoted in *Race Mixture in the History of Latin America* by Magnus Morner, Boston, 1967.

Secretaries and Chief Justices but from the whole matrix of metropolitan customs, prejudices, preferences which are proving irrelevant or may be stifling of creativity in his new society.

The global backdrop, as a point of reference, is mirrored in attitudes in Jamaica; though the society, like the rest of the West Indies, has displayed its own internal dynamic for change through the movement for self-government. Gains have certainly been made, what with the political liberation and cultural recognition of black Africa, the new advances by the negro in the United States of America as well as the decline of the old-style European imperialism and with it some of the untenable notions about the 'white man's burden'. But against all this are the growing Third World poverty of blacks (and coloureds) vis-a-vis the technology-based wealth of the white world, the deepening of neo-colonialism with its extra-territorial areas of decision-taking based in the white centres of financial, managerial and political-military power; the persistence of South African apartheid despite the multiplication of African states and the humanitarian pronouncements of the United Nations, and, of course, the easy recrudescence of the white supremacy ethic in times of crisis especially in places like England with its Enoch Powells and the United States with its Governor Wallaces. Many Jamaicans are apt to see their society as a microcosm of the wider world and so they grow cynical about the goodness of multi-racialism when such evils as poverty, lack of opportunities and the attendant low status for the black members of the society serve to perpetuate belief that blacks are inferior to whites, Africa to Europe, Jamaica to England. There are hopefuls, however, who see the national motto with its multi-racial ethic as productive of good and capable of bringing changes in attitudes not only with regard to the blacks but also to the entire society with respect to its own inner dynamic and potential. *No more the melody of Europe in grand superior isolation separate and apart from the so-called savage atavistic rhythms of Africa, but the two together interacting into a powerful other dimension and reinforced*

*by newer elements operating in the service of our present and
generating at least some of the goods for our future.**

It is in this sense that the artist-citizens of Jamaica and other
West Indian countries make their oft-repeated claims of their
own relevance and of that special gift of foresight. This is not
altogether unjustifiable. In the literary sphere writers like
Roger Mais, Sylvia Wynter, John Hearne, Andrew Salkey, Vic
Reid and Louise Bennett have in their widely different ways
plumbed and expressed, unconsciously or otherwise, the
society's predicament in attempting to find this third force – its
essence.† In this they can only be assisted by a tradition of
criticism that is able to tune in on the same wavelength and
help sharpen the tone and pitch of their intent. Such a tradition
is yet in its infancy and no doubt promises growth and flowering.
Yet L. Edward Brathwaite, the poet-historian, had reason to
express grave misgivings (which I share) about the prejudices
and the guiding canons of a school of English literary criticism
which seem to dominate some of the better minds among the
West Indian talents now addressing themselves to the criticism

---

* Since writing up these essays I have become more convinced of the
validity of the view put forward by Wilson Harris, the Guyanese
writer in his Writer-in-Residence Lectures at the UWI (1970) that
there is an unhealthy 'cleavage between the historical convention
and the arts of the imagination in the Caribbean'. The exploiter/
exploited framework of Caribbean history invests the West Indian
experience with more ills than are worth recounting but that very
experience has also produced forces with tremendous potential for
creativity and originality. As I have suggested throughout this
essay the adventurous exploration of this potential is the dynamic
of West Indian contemporary life and possibly the only way out of
what Harris calls the 'stasis' of the conventional ways of looking at
Caribbean society. My notion of a new dimension with its own
inner logic and consistency emerging out of the contact and conflict
between the dominant groups in the West Indies and the interaction
with other groups that came later (or existed earlier), is the measure
of the creative potential.

† In the wider West Indies, Wilson Harris, George Lamming, Vidia
Naipaul, Edgar Mittleholzer, Samuel Selvon *et al.* are significant
contributors.

of works by West Indian writers.[18] Dr. Brathwaite's point of departure is the little compendium of critical essays called *Islands in Between*, with a well-meaning Introduction by Louis James, the English editor, and with a range of essays by West Indian scholars covering a wide range of West Indian writers among whom the Jamaicans, Mais, Hearne, Reid and Salkey are included. Brathwaite bemoans the fact that Selvon the Trinidadian folk-novelist is not included at all; and I am tempted to believe that despite James's brief introductory discussion of Louise Bennett,* Jamaica's poet of utterance, still seemingly does not rate consideration in the scholarly exercise. Brathwaite's suggestion is that the essays betray a conventional view of the 'West Indian' complex – a one in which the critical variables of Europe and Africa interplay with pre-determined victory for Europe. The West Indies, of which Jamaica is an integral cultural part, is here made to remain the extension of Europe as it has long believed itself to be. The culture as a result remains non-definitive and non-exclusive.[19] The writers are deprived of individual wills (as it were) and are seen as exact mirrors of this parlous state of existence.

Brathwaite tries to give the idea of culture more dynamic dimensions by rendering it as a 'complex of voices and patterns held together by geography, political force and social inter-action'.[20] This is in fact a mere redefinition of the problem though such emotive words as 'voices', 'patterns', 'force' and 'interactions' imply limitless possibilities for artistic explorations of self both individual and collective. It presumably gives to the critics in *Islands in Between* a wider range of choice than they assumed in commenting on the totality of West Indian life as presented by the authors. This is of course assuming that the writers themselves offer intrinsic matter with such wide-ranging possibilities. Mais, Salkey and Vic Reid are often said to offer such possibilities. But Brathwaite is more positive,

---

* See *Jamaica Labrish* – Poems by Louise Bennett (Sangster, Kingston, 1967). Introduction by Rex Nettleford.

rightly or wrongly, in his claims that 'West Indian writers are concerned with . . . constructing an *alternative* to their imposed inherited condition'. Out of the content must come, then, alternative forms in artistic terms – 'dialect, rather than standard speech, "folk" rather than middle class characters'.[21] Such a prescription will, no doubt, churn up welcome dialogue among the Jamaican literati about the meaning of 'dialect', 'standard speech' and 'folk' and much valid argument will be found for all sides. What cannot be denied is the dynamic nature of the very dialect and its current interplay with standard English as well as the changing shifting relationships between so-called folk and so-called middle class.* Such perceptions of identity within the society are less static than is usually supposed. Language is somewhat central to the problem here expressed. A Jamaican linguist sees the serious study of the Jamaican creole in the service of providing 'satisfactory English Language texts for the island's schools',[22] and journalists and hard-headed businessmen see Standard English as the language of progress in the twentieth century.[23] True enough, the ordinary Jamaican grows up regarding Standard English as the standard in all things that apparently matter – in his Five Year Plans, his Constitution, his text-books, his *Daily Gleaner*, the Bible, his collective bargaining agreement, his letter applying for a job, his letters expressing his deepest feelings of affection and intimacy. But it is equally true that he *speaks* and *listens* a lot. So up to now, much of himself comes out in a language less 'standard' but which some poets, novelists and playwrights would exploit more quickly to uncover the truths about ourselves.[24]

For this is the language which occasions the underlying rhythms which are a combination of an Africa suppressed and

---

* As other West Indian writers before him, Brathwaite can certainly be credited with attempting new expressions in his well-received poetic trilogy (*Rights of Passage, Masks, Islands,* published by Oxford University Press) but the English he employs is likely to be regarded as more 'standard' than 'folk', despite the tonal and rhythmic 'resonances' of the African heritage.

the native-born (creolized) Jamaican or West Indian milieu, thus making sense of Gilberto Freyre's dictum – 'while Europe governs, Africa rules'.[25] The hidden history of Jamaica is here seen as the history of the struggle of the African component to emerge from the subterranean caverns into which it has been forced. Where it seeps through it reveals itself largely in the folk. For some people it is the peasant folk, for others it is the 'yard' people among the urban proletariat with or without peasant antecedents. For Brathwaite it is the challenge and full measure of the writer's craft. The West Indian writer (and one could supposedly extend it to all West Indian artists) in his exploration of his real and creole self is said to attempt to 'liberate the consciousness of the submerged folk'.[26]

That consciousness does not always escape the Eurocentrism of Jamaican creolization. One major tragedy of plantation life was the degree to which the system could work because a large enough number of slaves were successfully coerced around to believing that they were inferior.[27] This fact is instructive of the dimensions of the problem. For not only European-trained literary scholars writing literary criticisms are culpable. An entire society in fact is. A wide cross-section of the population would probably instinctively support the Trinidadian writer Vidia Naipaul in his now legendary contempt for the so-called barrenness of West Indian life. Having achieved nothing, we have created nothing, goes the argument based though it is on a questionable premise. The future may not after all be with Naipaul the brilliant but alienated East Indian who seemingly finds it difficult to see the creative contribution of Africa in the West Indian complex. The future may well be with Samuel Selvon who writes with the soul of a Trinidadian or Kenneth Ramchand, the creolized East Indian, who can write passionately and with scholarly integrity of the work of the black Jamaican poet Claude McKay.[28] The intrinsic merit of McKay's work is the critic's central point of reference, naturally, but it is an arch cynic who would fail to credit the society, which nurtured McKay, with its proven potential for creative achievement. One aspect of the story of

McKay, the now universally declared poet of the black renaissance, is itself of relevance to the understanding of social interaction in the society. It was Tom Redcam (Thomas Henry McDermot), a white Jamaican and the country's first poet laureate and former editor of the *Jamaica Times*, who encouraged and guided Claude McKay the black Jamaican policeman-poet. A white creole, McDermot regarded Jamaica as home and could write in 1899 addressing his white and mulatto compatriots: 'Today we lead; tomorrow we advise; and the day following we are co-workers together with our black countrymen . . .'[29]

Multi-racialism as a guiding ethic for Jamaicans identifies the present times with McDermot's 'the day following'. It is part of the current dilemma, however, that to many Jamaicans the present remains what was Tom Redcam's 'today' and 'tomorrow'. For many blacks deem themselves still to be *led* and *advised* and aspire to be true partners in the complex. They grow confused and resentful of the reactions of Eurocentric Jamaicans to any assertion of black consciousness. The introduction of African art into national heritage exhibitions, the emphasis on folk expressions of life in radio and television programmes, the projection of the rich and developing pop art among the black urban folk – all invite responses of uneasiness or outright objection from the culture-establishment. On the other hand, no such response is reserved for the Eurocentric emphases or other exclusive cultural manifestations by racial minority groups in the society. The predicament of the black Jamaican is still the problem of finding himself in Jamaican society without the disabilities of his racial-historical connexions. If multi-racialism is to be taken seriously in the society, Jamaica must rid itself of this predicament.

II

There are problems, however. The tendency generally is to fall back on the strong visible peaks that focus the vision of our existence, ignoring the ravines and mountain passes that lie hidden in the distance. The call to walk the land in a spirit of adventure and discovery is much too difficult for most. Some start out boldly on the road but the first discovery of an African survival behind some concealed hillock is used as reason to end the quest – to set up camp complete with red, green and black flags of conquest staking out an area of alienation to celebrate the long ignored African past. The vision becomes just as limited and limiting as those who had always headed straight for the peaks that spell Europe, 'civilization' and advancement. Hopefully there are those who will still explore, blazing trails and leaving negotiable tracks for those who may come after, defining the topography with landmarks and milestones as guides for the people of tomorrow.

Such is the role carved out by many for the artist in the West Indies whether he be poet, novelist, musician, painter, sculptor, or dancer. The same role is assumed by, or given to, the creative academic, historian and social scientist in particular, but also to all others who may wish to discover anew rather than regurgitate the swallowings of Europe or Africa. The politician, if possessed of imagination, sometimes sees his role in a similar light and he who does not spend time consciously conditioning the Europeanized élite around to the syncretic home-spun folk habits* may stay dedicated to his academic discipline, like the potent one History is, lecturing on the past and reconstructing through lectures and books that past, in order to throw light on the present.† Not all Jamaican artists, academicians or politicians see their roles or accept the challenge in quite this light. Not all Jamaicans expect them to, either. So those literary critics who have disappointed Brathwaite and others could well answer that they prefer to choose the tried and tested in English literary criticism rather than deteriorate

---

* As is the case with Edward Seaga, Jamaican Minister of Finance and Planning, with special interest in culture and folk arts.
† See Eric Williams's more popular histories. He is Prime Minister of Trinidad and Tobago and author of the well-known *Capitalism and Slavery* (Deutsch, London).

into a fanciful myth-making that is more aptly the province of pedestrian politicians in their promotion of heritage weeks and national heroes. Such critics probably believe that the rigorous canons of evaluation must apply to Jamaican and West Indian writers as they did to Wordsworth and Conrad. Brathwaite has himself been assessed as something of a *public* poet with the word 'public' taking on an uneasy signification in the minds of many a reader. Louise Bennett has long been regarded as little more than a spinner of jingles and (gratuitously) a first-rate entertainer. The view that the artist speaks for himself first and foremost is everywhere invoked and the creative artist is seen primarily as 'an artist' rather than as a socialized agent of his society's deeper feelings and emotions.* The perspective is praiseworthy but it is one-sided. Such a deliberate critical choice of artistic narcissism to the exclusion of the collective realities that give to the artist's work ideal, form and some purpose, serves merely to tie artistic evaluations (in all areas of art) to metropolitan prejudices and values which are nowhere as inviolate as ingenuous imitators make them out to be. This attitude finds expression in other art-forms. Romantic classical ballet (with all its colonial class and colour connotations) is likely to remain for some a permanent yard-stick for all movement patterns – and this among a people who cannot keep a rigid back and who may wish to have their

---

* Mervyn Morris, himself an acclaimed poet from Jamaica, is particularly sensitive about this as can be seen from his recent review
of Gerald Moore's book, *The Chosen Tongue, English Writing in the
Tropical World*. According to Morris, Moore hardly values John
Hearne, one of the West Indies' most sophisticated and accomplished novelists because Hearne presumably writes from 'an angle
which somewhat detaches him from the mainstream of popular
life'. Morris's biting retort speaks for itself – '. . . we have quite
enough West Indian cant valuing writers according to the degree
of their *obvious* commitment to West Indians and the West Indies
without having it added to by an Englishman as well'. (See *Sunday
Gleaner*, December 13, 1969.) This does not mean that Morris
believes that commitment to one's society is incompatible with
genuine artistic achievement and excellence which, after all, is all
that West Indians need expect of their artists.

movements explode with centrifugal force from the regions of the pelvis rather than through extended arms and legs. Music is judged by the capacity to play indifferently (or soullessly) such status instruments as the violin, the piano and the cello while the drum is regarded as base, bastard, unsubtle and incapable of 'music'. The rhythm of Africa must give place to the melody, as it were.

Where the two have merged in fusion to produce something recognizably unique, tradition has imposed on the results a stigma of inferiority or has granted these a barely tolerable existence. Who would think of Jamaican patois as the national speech of Jamaica? There are undoubtedly sound practical reasons for not even contemplating the possibility but reason too often gives place to motives associated with the class-colour correlation. Who could think of Pocomania being the national religion of Jamaica? If ever there was a homegrown form of religious expression, here is one! The vain attempts by at least one politican to legitimize it has met with a modicum of success particularly in the performing arts and as theatrical backdrop in election campaigns but it is yet to be accepted on the level of Jamaican religious orthodoxy. A British television documentary on the ritual invited strong letters of protest from Jamaican immigrants* in England who felt that it was bad for the Jamaican identity abroad and for their own position especially in English society which was growing hostile and whose members regarded Jamaican black immigrants as primitive and merely once removed from the orang-outang. Pocomania worshippers themselves will most likely list themselves as adherents to the accepted religious groups in any census record. The European (Christian) choices in the complex are that strongly pre-determined. The Anglican Church has long been dis-established but it is Christian orthodoxy, whatever its variations, which is the dominant religious force in the prescribed value-system of the Jamaican society.

---

* In contrast Jamaica migrants were proud of the 'good image' projected of them by the winning of the 1963 Miss World title by a Jamaican beauty queen who was near Caucasian in appearance.

Like Church, like State: the concepts of political organization and social obligation are British to the core. The old Vestry form of local government administration coupled with representative government has given place to the later English forms – local government authorities, the two-party system, a Jamaican House of Commons (The House of Representatives) and a Jamaican House of Lords (the Senate), a Jamaican Queen (currently the same as the British Queen), a Jamaican parliamentary executive (also called the Cabinet with Ministerial officials operating on the twin principles of collective and ministerial responsibility). In short, the Westminster model as it is known all over the Commonwealth has been transplanted to Jamaica. Ideas of law and justice are rooted in British precedent and practice. Queen's Counsels are still the cream of the legal profession though the voluntary surrender of the honour by a Jamaican Barrister need not make him lose caste. In Independence the entire political system may indeed develop into a truly creole (native) institution. Where there is a beginning, however, voices label the results as a bastardization of the legitimate British model.[30] The Senate or upper house has no hereditary or titled members but it has the distinction (dubious to some) of being the repository for unsuccessful candidates at the polls or a training ground for politicians on the make. The working classes who helped to win self-government for Jamaica maintain their involvement in the area of effective power and in the loyal Opposition by perpetuating the trade unions' organic link with the political parties, throwing up Prime Minister, Opposition Leader and other ministerial material. Employers naturally object but so do others who regard the structure as non-British and wrong. Public quarrels between a prominent journalist and the Speaker of the House of Representatives over the criticisms of the Speaker's rulings in the House betray that there are innovations, even if disputable ones.[31] Other innovations, this time by the Attorney General and Minister of Legal Affairs, have been the subject of acrimonious dialogue both in and outside Parliament as well as of censure on the part of the legal profession.[32] All this shows that the transplanted Westminster model will undergo and is undergoing environmental changes. Whether these are for the best is another matter and one that must remain the province of public concern and debate among the governed. Politicians who feel they have the essence of the national image in their hands will find criticism of themselves and their innovations tiresome. But they could well view this to be an inevitable feature of any society in growth. Already the style of political decision-taking is shaping itself out of the specificities of the issues and affairs of state as faced by Jamaican politicians and eventually a political culture peculiar to the society's needs must of necessity reveal itself.

But for this to happen there must be necessary validating conditions. The premises of the colonial plantation society must give place to ones conducive to a modern complex. The emphasis on entrepreneurial exploitation of labour in the interest, exclusively, of uncommitted foreign pockets as well as the authoritarian paternalism of a foreign ruler must give place to a society in which opportunities exist for mutual respect among its citizens, for individual achievement, self-realization and recognition, and for rational economic exploitation of the society's natural and manpower resources. This must in turn bring equable compensation for energies and talents expended. This will only be done with the energizing of wills around to achieving this just society. But the majority of those wills belong to black Jamaicans whose sense of history is flawed enough to make them believe that the society is designed least of all for them, since white people are still the privileged group, brown people the only slightly less so, while they remain the refuse at the bottom. A historian's warning in the sixties turned on just this view which many had of themselves. '. . . Sooner or later we shall have to face the fact' observed Professor Goveia, 'that we are courting defeat when we attempt to build a new heritage of freedom upon a structure of society which binds us all too closely to the old heritage of slavery'.[33] At the turn of the century a Jamaican Editor of the *Daily Gleaner* (and a novelist) saw his emerging Jamaica as a land in which 'Caucasian and Negro may live and work side by side, with no deliberate injustice on the part of the former and no *insolent self-assertion* on the latter's part . . .' [my emphasis].[34] Were he alive today, fifty years later, he would no doubt regard the self-assertion of Jamaican blacks as 'insolent' giving many white Jamaicans a 'feeling of inferiority' according to a letter to the newspapers.* Race prejudice is here turned on its head, inverting the dilemma rather than solving it.

In terms of solution, Sylvia Wynter in a discussion on heritage once said a desirable thing: 'The paradox is that, if we are to inform our society with that motive force which can transform the unjust system we have inherited, which divided and still divides us, if we are to become conscious to ourselves as a people, as an entity, then we must confront ourselves with our origins, must lay claim to and *take hold of our history*'[35] [my emphasis]. What history and whose history is the question frequently, even if tacitly, asked. The question comes up on the matter of 'beginnings'. There has been a choice of: 1494, Columbus and the Arawaks; of 1655, slavery, representative government and the English; 1838 and Emancipation; 1865, William Gordon and Paul Bogle; 1938, self-government and Manley, the working classes and Bustamante. The Jamaicans have been exposed to protagonists of different eras. 1865 with its villains and its saints has certain epic advantages which were quickly grasped by those in charge of public policy. The period gave to the society two nineteenth century scions of the creole ideal as symbols of the national identity – the coloured gentleman George William Gordon and the black

---

* See letter to the Editor of the *Gleaner* from a Mrs. Elspie Salmon who reports on the embarrassment of a white Jamaican youngster who was accosted with 'You white people don't have no heroes. All the heroes are black men.' The letter-writer rues the fact that the five national heroes seemed chosen on their work in politics, their 'rebellious frame of mind' and their negro parentage. She appeals to the multi-racial ethic in the question'. . . are we going to look around and find at least one fairskinned hero and perhaps one Chinese hero?' She was sure 'such people could be found'. *Daily Gleaner*, November 19, 1969.

Christian deacon Paul Bogle. Former 'heroes' like Dr. Bower-
bank the white Kingston politician have since come in for
denunciation. Yet some militants among the black majority
are dissatisfied with the exclusion of such old Maroon warriors
as Cudjoe and Nanny who were early symbols of freedom in
their outright defiance of the English authorities and, by
implication, of Europe's effort to enslave Africa.*

On another level of history-making it has been suggested
that 'the meaning and character of the new nation of Jamaica
should transcend even the African and slave origins, as important as they were, and should be sought in the more universal conception of the extension of equal rights to all men.
The facts of history seem amenable to such an interpretation'.[36]
But if the facts of history ignore the beliefs of those whose
origins are African and slave, amenability to such intellectual
abstractions are likely to prove difficult. Eric Williams's essays
on British historians and their ideas about the West Indies
seem to be the sort of history that provides a relevant need,
speaking as it consciously does to an embattled and embittered
audience. Yet the voice of Elsa Goveia is no less effective in
her *Historiography of the West Indies*. But where Williams
speaks with the shrill of a practising politician consciously
creating an image, Goveia is the superb academician analysing
in depth and with the imagination of an artist, the malaise as
well as the great potential of the human condition, expressed
in the work of outstanding historians of the West Indies. Her
work is on balance a necessary corrective to that of Williams's
if good sense is to prevail and if the races of the plantation
societies are ultimately to find themselves a harmonious ethos
which they all can share in peace.

---

* *e.g.* Letter to Editor *Daily Gleaner* (November 14, 1969) from
C. G. L. Harris of Moore Town pleading the case of Cudjoe and
Nanny; and letter November 23, 1969, to the *Sunday Gleaner*
from Bruce Barker supporting it and debunking three of Jamaica's
five National Heroes. Here Bogle is made out to be a 'simple-
minded Baptist deacon', Gordon a near bankrupt, and Garvey's
financial activities are put under suspicion. The letter-writer
clearly disapproves of these heroes.

In the meantime politicians and others will tend to pander to what may be, or to what they feel should be, the needs of their constituents. Not all people in search of themselves will want their historical achievements, real or imagined, spelt out in clinical intellectual abstractions. Many will wish them to be portrayed in the exploits of national heroes. To this desire the Jamaican Government responded with despatch virtually establishing a National Hero order in 1965.* It does not matter to the politicians (though it must to professional historians) that the officially accepted photograph of Paul Bogle, one such hero, has not been confirmed as an actual facsimile of the man. After all it shows a sensitive and, by Jamaican Euro-African standards, a 'good-looking' visage; and the subject is dressed in the habit of a nineteenth century gentleman of quality. The photograph of Bogle therefore passes as historical *fact* despite the lack of evidence to support it. The people 'believe' it to be the picture of Bogle and it becomes *fact*. On the other hand the statue in *ciment fondu* and modelled partly on a seemingly more accurate description of the times and partly on the artist's impression from her reading, did not meet the approval of the people of St. Thomas. It was too ugly and too black, said some passers-by when the statue was finally erected.

Distortions are of different kinds. The period from 1938 onwards, for example, is in danger of the grossest myth-making. A split-edifice is being created out of this period by supporters of the two men who dominated the times† and the effect is to make it difficult for many, particularly the young, to negotiate the period intellectually. There is hope, however,

---

* This was conferred on Marcus Garvey before Gordon. The practice was later regularized into law – December, 1968.

† *i.e.* William Alexander Bustamante – trade unionist, leader of the Jamaica Labour Party and many times head of Government both under Colonialism and in Independence and Norman Washington Manley, Oxford-trained lawyer, founder and leader for a generation of the People's National Party, chief spokesman for self-government and one-time Head of Government just before Independence.

with the research that is being done, placing emphasis not merely on who did what but also on what was done. Even now there are threats that the brown middle class who were identified in the nineteen thirties with the self-government movement will be forced into a line of defence of its historical position, for this position has been falsely opposed to the claims by the black working class for better conditions of work, higher wages, employment opportunities and social mobility. The two aims were in fact never mutually exclusive but represented instead, a totality of vision which contributed to the whole process of growth out of colonialism. Yet the history of 'thirty-eight' is already being used, on grounds of this mutual exclusivity, in the service of protest against the very fundamentals of the society. This is a result partly of historical amnesia (a malady of succeeding generations), historical ignorance, and some distortion when the events of the period are recounted.

Where history is not distorted it is severed, and the blacks are frequently among the most guilty. For while some blacks in 1969 root everything in slavery others prefer to forget that slavery ever existed. The amnesia has of course been helped by an educational system which taught colonials more about the people of the Mother country than about the colonials themselves. Today many black students over-react against this by harking back to a history of themselves before the fall, i.e. before the beginning of slavery. It is generally assumed that it was only then that anything that is worth knowing really happened to the black man. The brown Jamaican's genesis, rooted as it is in concubinage and household slavery, also gets severed and nothing is here regarded of value until Edward Jordon the coloured businessman, editor and patriot, entered public life.* The whites, as part of the British extended family overseas, tended to see their history as relating to

---

* Edward Jordon was one of the earliest free coloured Jamaicans to enter the Jamaican Legislature and was Speaker of the Assembly after slavery 1861–64. See 'Members of the Assembly in Jamaica 1830–1866' by G. Robertson (Institute of Jamaica, cyclostyled 1966).

Britain's achievements rather than in the growth of the creole society. Where it was recorded, by Edward Long and Bryan Edwards in the late eighteenth century, for example, it was with a definite and understandable bias in favour of the white planter class which formed the status quo – the one in his expression of the 'pro-slavery racial myth which replaced the humanist tradition', the other in his attempt to find a 'more benevolent rationale for slavery', according to Professor Goveia.[37] Much of their work is valuable, notwithstanding. Yet circumstances now would probably make many a white Jamaican abandon his early history, out of guilt.

III

In the face of severance and threat of distortion and in the absence of a past that could be deemed totally respectable, totally heroic and totally worth remembering, Jamaica sometimes seeks refuge in a history conceptualized in wider frames of reference.* A currently popular frame of reference is delimited as *Plantation America*, as distinct from such other 'culture spheres' as Euro-America (where the racial strain is largely European and the ethos correspondingly so) and Indo or Mestizo America (where the transculturation process between indigenous Amerindian and European civilizations has produced a distinctive hybrid with strong and *recognized*

---

* Three early West Indian historians (none of them Jamaicans) reflected this quest for a wider framework. C. L. R. James's Marxist commitment provided him with a global perspective for colonialism and exploitation of the non-privileged. His 'Black Jacobins' (the title reflects his historical perspective) is said to have rescued Haitian black revolution from obscurity. George Padmore operated on a level of pan-Africanism – the liberation of Africa (and by extension black people) from colonialism, the white supremacy ethic, and a defeating balkanization. The third is Eric Williams, who wrote about the wider Caribbean instead of any one territory, though his theory of economic determinism in his assessment of slave emancipation has been regarded as limiting in perspective.

contributions from both.[38] Jamaica, a plantation society, is studied then largely from the point of view of the history of slavery, its subsequent creolization and the different roles played out by slave and master in shaping the hybrid culture. This frame of reference has been consciously nurtured more by sociologists than by historians though the work of the latter is essential to an understanding of that of the former and both disciplines do in fact inform each other, making a complementary contribution not only to the field of scholarship but to the greater understanding of the societies studied. Elsa Goveia's fine study of the British Leeward Islands under slavery provides a case study for a much wider theory of slave society in the Caribbean. It will not fail to inform the work of sociologists and historians alike. More recently such works as *The Sociology of Slavery* by Orlando Patterson[39] and the historical survey by L. Edward Brathwaite of the Jamaican Creole society between the latter part of the eighteenth and the early part of the nineteenth century seem to draw heavily from both disciplines either for their tools of analysis or simply to inform their perspectives.

One important feature of the Plantation America frame of reference is the 'multi-racial' nature of the societies, with a large number of people of African descent and an outnumbered group of European landowners. 'Everywhere there is a multitude of "social race" categories – categories based not upon scientific fact but upon social values for given characteristics'.[40] And this, suggests Charles Wagley, the author, would be as true of Jamaica as of Brazil and the other West Indian communities. The East Indian populations in Trinidad and Guyana and the Japanese immigrants in Brazil are said to underline the multi-racial factor rather than dissipate it. These societies all in fact share such other features of Plantation America like a monocrop economy, a rigid class system, multi-racialism, weak community structure (which is supposed to explain the paucity of 'community studies' of the West Indian territories), small peasant proprietorship (on a cash-crop subsistence level) and a matrifocal type family form.[41] They are said to be so much alike that more exchange of findings from academic studies are recommended for frequent exchange between Brazilian and West Indian scholars. This is, of course, echoed by several who see Jamaica and the West Indies in yet another perspective, namely as part of the Third World. Certainly for our literature and for literary criticism, some see much more to be gained by exposure to some of the Latin American, French West Indian and African as well as or even rather than European writers. At best, Plantation America and Third World perspectives can offer the riches of comparative studies but at worst they can deteriorate into the congenital habit of looking outside the society for the answers.

Methods of approach are therefore central to all this and the refinement of methodology becomes as important as the phenomena of raw historical or sociological experience that are to be worked upon. The danger of the society being explained out of existence is a very real one when propagandists take a hold of our history and when, as I have said elsewhere,[42] the 'plantation model', indulged without a sense of history, abuses rather than uses history. By so doing guilt is instilled into the Jamaican white, a sense of inferiority bred into the descendants of free coloured 'houseslaves' and 'housekeepers' while banks of hate and a persecution complex are built into the minds of the sons of slaves. It also threatens to dispossess those descended from indentured labourers, of any legitimacy in the cultural heritage. For while by sheer weight of numbers this cannot be so in places like Trinidad and Guyana where the Indian population is large enough to be a potentially dominant political and economic force, by the very weight of numbers this is quite possible in Jamaica where the blacks together with the Afro-Europeans outnumber all others nine to one.[43] Yet all three territories as of now could be said to have an ethos which is Euro-African creole. Already this Euro-African dominance is undergoing changes in Guyana and Trinidad. Time may indeed render them significant with a resurgence of a strong East Indianism which may be now dormant but not dead. Yet the forces of West Indian creolization (i.e. Euro-African) are likely to succeed in the end with the growing maturity of West Indian political and social institutions. Perhaps they will be no more able to 'Indianize' those communities than Jamaican blacks will be able to 'Africanize' Jamaica.

The strong similarities between West Indian territories have therefore been the basis of the strong regional-federal frame of reference which has informed political, economic and social life for over a century and more. The first flowering came in 1958 when the West Indies Federation was formed and regional institutions which preceded the formal union came into their own. Not least among these was the University of the West Indies educating for West Indian nationhood with commitment and a definite consciousness. The region as a culture-unit was accepted as such and Jamaica assumed this perspective itself but only for three short years since by referendum the country seceded resulting in the final break-up of the political union.[44] There is no doubt that the dissolution of the political federation deprived many countries of the English-speaking Caribbean of a desired wider focus. Many Jamaicans do not share this view. Their strong nationalist aspirations are instead felt to have been dissipated in a fruitless flirtation with the rest of the West Indies and since then efforts have been made to restore the spirit of 1938 (with its nationalist fervour) to the society. Independence in 1962 was designed to help in this but by then the society seemed to have been outrun by events following on a difficult economic situation.[45] Indeed, the failure to invest the Jamaican society with a new sense of cohesion is sometimes blamed on attitudes which are felt still to reflect a preference for a wider West Indian frame of reference rather than a Jamaican one. The uneasy relationship of the Jamaican Government with the University of the West Indies is part of this bigger problem and the demand by Jamaicans for the Mona campus to identify with its immediate environment – Jamaica – is an expression of many Jamaicans' unwillingness to sink their country's identity totally in a West Indian context.

Yet if Jamaicans are serious about taking a hold of their history it would be worthwhile also to take a hold of the history of the wider West Indies, including the Dutch, Spanish and French Antilles who share with the people of Jamaica an historical experience and the contemporary consequences commonly arising out of the plantation system, slavery and colonialism. The failure of the West Indies Federation did not abolish West Indian History, as some detractors of Federation would have had it. It is part of the paradox that colonial masters historically treated parts of the West Indies together as a unit, thus assuming the federal principle before West Indians were probably ready for it. There is little doubt that as long as the federal experiment was regarded as an extension of the colonial principle whereby the British authorities encouraged an administrative federation as a cradle for full independence, the West Indian experiment was doomed to failure; and this, despite the insular jealousies, prevarications and somewhat petty bargaining among the territories. It may be that the co-operation, union, or whatever form of association which might be chosen in the future by the West Indian communities *for themselves* will prove a better solution than something pushed from outside, however good. Some Jamaicans would no doubt pride themselves on their instinctive political wisdom in thwarting the first attempt and Eric Williams's early and consistent plea for an association of all the Caribbean including the Spanish, Dutch and French-speaking territories may probably be at last realized.

The possibility remains and is given expression in new forms of co-operation with Jamaica participating, ostensibly in no fear of losing her identity in a farflung disparate West Indies. The Caribbean Free Trade Area (Carifta)[46] is one such example and it is just possible that, what the historians, politicians and West Indian artists were not able to do, will be achieved by the men of commerce in search of profits. This is historically (and ironically) apt since the raison d'etre of most West Indian territories was for a long time commercial profit. The West Indies as a frame of reference for Jamaica's history is therefore as invaluable as it is inevitable. It will not necessarily swamp Jamaican history or Jamaica's concern with itself. The reason why Jamaica with its majority of blacks differs from Trinidadian, Guyanese or Barbadian societies will itself be part of that history. So will the differences between British, French, Dutch and Spanish colonization and the societies they have produced. The prehistory of the West Indian communities will now need to include Africa before the slave as it has long accounted for Europe before settlement and conquest. But African History cannot be pursued at the expense of the history of Europe before colonization, or India and China before Indentureship. All have their place in any attempt to understand the society in useful ways. The early mistakes made by the projection of an exclusive European history cannot now be made with African History. The law of Moses can have no place in the society's struggle to find itself. Most important, naturally, will be the history of Jamaica itself and nothing can be wrong with the rational and sensible use of all available data and tools to help shape an identity out of that history. That identity may very well be conceived as the principle of change underlying the purpose and adaptive processes of which Goveia speaks. 'To discover that principle', she said, 'it is necessary to do as so many of the West Indian historians (that is up to the 19th century) did – to seek beyond the narrative of events, a wider understanding of the thoughts, habits and institutions of a whole society'.[47]

And here comes to mind Wendell Bell's recommendation that this identity transcend 'even the African and slave origins' and should be sought in the more 'universal conception of the *extension of equal rights to all men*'.[48] Implicit in this is a Whiggish interpretation of history with the assumptions of progress affecting, in time, more and more people in the society. There are of course those Jamaicans who will say that this is not their experience or reading of history and that progress has been consistently in favour of one group or class of people over another. This is the Rastafarians' argument and although the utopian millenarianism of their position makes them into outsiders, close analysis reveals some validity in this position. The notion of so-called basic rights has had different meanings to the different societies and even to people living in the same societies at different times. The abolition of slavery was in 1838, as it would be today, regarded as the acquisition of a major right. But freedom from chattel slavery has not resulted in the acquisition of the full capacities to enjoy that right. Some of these capacities, like equal opportunities, freedom from want and from fear, are regarded as freedoms in their own right today. The rude boy will say in his expressive language that a hungry man is not only an angry but also an unfree man, and that a man who lives in fear of police brutality is little more than a slave. The language of freedom and rights is maintained but meanings have changed. Bell further states that the history of Jamaica can be written in terms of denial and subsequent acquisition of rights by whites (including the Jews), blacks, Asians and Arabs who have come to live in Jamaica since Columbus discovered the island. But in terms of the facts, the experience of denial of rights by succeeding groups cannot be equated. A bondsman (white) was free after a contract period of *service*, not of *chattel slavery*. The slave (African) had no such contractual understanding between himself and his master. Laws of manumission and amelioration helped the situation of the slave but as long as he remained a slave, he was a piece of property. The brute facts of his intrinsic humanity played a tempering role in the ultimate relationship between slave and master but he (slave) still suffered, conceived as he legally was as chattel. By the time of indentureship enough lessons were learned for safeguards to be instituted which helped to shield the East Indians and Chinese from some of the hidden, and for that reason, disastrous consequences of slave labour.* Although cruelty was

---

* After Emancipation a policy of immigration of indentured labourers was embarked upon. The largest numbers of such immigrants came from India. But there were also Chinese in 1854. After 1911 a sizeable movement of free Chinese entered Jamaica, Europeans came between 1834 and 1844 from Germany, Scotland and Ireland;

meted out to bondsmen as to slaves, the distinction between contract labour and chattel slavery is an important one to make. It helps to keep in perspective the predicament of the blacks whose history of bondage is said consciously or subconsciously to feed his present attitudes. Their brown offsprings (who were sometimes slaves, sometimes Free coloureds) are themselves not free of the consequences of this brand of slavery and they too, whether they wish or not, share the predicament. Even the Europeans, despite their vested rights, shared in the mutual demoralization of master and slave, thus lending substance to the view that he who guards the prisoner is himself a kind of captive.

It would not be surprising then, if the Jamaicans most likely to find amenable a history interpreted on the model of progressive acquisition of rights, are those descended from post-slavery Jamaicans and particularly those who are of the privileged classes. The non-privileged blacks in the nineteen seventies are no more likely than they did in the sixties to see their history in terms of the particular abstraction. They have their own abstraction: it is the plantation system rooted in the eighteenth century and perpetuated in twentieth century colonialism. The danger here is a history reconstructed or a sociology devised largely in terms of the black experience. But the substance of Jamaican history was never simply the black experience. Its diversity reflects the heterogeneity of the social phenomena and for that reason defies any facile structural rationality. People still cross and criss-cross in ever-changing levels of aspirations and relationships. There is an assumed

some 4,100 entered and is of little more than historical interest for the subject under review. Africans also came, especially after 1841. Black Jamaicans in the parish of St. Thomas, especially those of the Kumina cult, claim they were never slaves. The numbers were small compared with the creole blacks who by 1838 had formed the bulk of the population. Total indenture immigration figures between 1834 and 1914 are East Indians 36,410, Africans 10,003, Europeans 4,087, others 2,050 (total 52,550). See George W. Roberts: *The Population of Jamaica*, Cambridge University Press, 1957, pp. 103–132, 335.

underlying unity in the diversity and this seems to express the national perspectives of West Indian territories. H. G. DeLisser, the Jamaican, had expected little more than 'a homogeneity of sentiment' which he hoped would produce the unity and self-conscious pride in 'the achievements of any of its people, whether Jew, Christian, black, white or brown'.[49] This is the pulse of the multi-racial ideal which some Jamaicans will pitch battle to defend even against the claims to certain human rights. Already the acquisition of one set of rights by the black masses in 1944 has given rise to militant and politically oriented trade unionism, which has effectively circumscribed some of the rights of the white and brown traditionalist economic power interests and former ruling classes. The traditionalist elite fight back through strong employer interest-groups as well as through a rash (since Independence) of 'Service Clubs' whose programmes of community service and weekly luncheons do not allay the fears concerning the great 'backroom' influence their members seem to have on the power structure. Certain discriminatory practices in the exercise of legal rights have at the same time produced champions of the poor, and more precisely the *black* poor. The-one-law-for-the-poor-and-another-for-the-rich argument is a common one among the voices of protest. Moreover, it is generally asserted by those voices that for equality to be realized, the class-colour correlation of the traditionalist structure will have to undergo basic change so as to meet the new demands of social justice. It is indeed a 'tragedy of our history', as a Jamaican leader has stated, 'that the masses are predominantly black and the privileged classes predominantly fair-skinned . . . and the disadvantages of class freeze the members of the disinherited, the sufferers in a self-perpetuating poverty'.[50]

To many who are optimistic there is the glorious future that must come. To others, lack of faith in any such possibility finds expression in social rejection or spiritual iconoclasm. Still to some that glory of multi-racial harmony had existed but has been rendered obsolete by recent developments of protest and a corresponding change of mood:

'Colour meant nothing. Any one
who wanted help, had humour or was kind
was brother to you; categories of skin
were foreign; you were colour-blind
And then the revolution . . .'[51]

Europe's melody here seems to have found new challenges from
Africa's rhythm, creating vibrations – unprecedented and, to
some, awesome. Sometimes the drum tones are deep, steady
and haunting. At times they take on a rapid, breathless, frantic
sequence of seemingly unstructured polyrhythms. At other
times it is that dry, sustained and high-pitched sound called
'ciye' by the Haitian voodoo drummers, *as if* coming from
choruses of castrati deprived of their manhood in the wake of
bondage. The operative words here are 'as if'. For the realities
of the situation point to possibilities of a cultural fusion rich
and cohesive in its diversity. Yet this will be so only if the
people involved will and wish it to be so. It is true that there is
enough evidence to suggest that Jamaican life has been determined by a process of assimilation with one culture absorbing
another rather than by one of mutual acculturation which
could produce that new and vital other force after which so
many hanker.

One way of meeting the problem is for the society to reject
all abrasive and indefensible notions of natural superiority of
one element over another in the complex and build con-
structively and realistically on notions of equality, self-confidence and a basic respect for the individual person. On
another level, a timely voice with another message is gaining
attention among the young who should lead the future generation. It is the voice of Wilson Harris, the Guyanese writer,
who is credited with a fresh life-giving belief in the ancestral
validity of the aboriginal peoples of the West Indies and their
relevance to the contemporary quest for an identity.[52] It is said
to be rooted in the writer's equally firm belief in the essential
unity of man and the felt continuities of human existence
whatever the racial origins or special historical circumstances.

This puts him on the side against claims of racial exclusivity of whatever vintage since such claims merely oversimplify existence beyond full appreciation and serve to rob the human experience of its natural and opulent complexity. This position would therefore invalidate the seemingly exaggerated claims by certain Jamaicans for the primacy of the African heritage in the Jamaican identity just as it has disavowed the long-standing Eurocentrism of West Indian colonial value systems. Following on Harris, a Jamaican writer employs known historical data to restore the Amerindian ancestral position to West Indian life challenging, in effect, the current notion of an Afrocentric Jamaican ethos! The challenge comes in the declaration that the Maroons are 'factually, the mythic descendants of Arawaks and Africans' since their deeds separately or co-operatively do serve to bolster 'the myth that pays tribute to the invincibility of the human aspiration to be free'.[53] This contribution merely serves to bring the society full circle around to its responsibilities as a society which habitually fancies itself as a sane, self-contained and rational unit.

One thing is certain: there must be the liberation of the Jamaican black, whether he be peasant, proletarian or struggling middle class, from the chains of self-contempt, self-doubt and cynicism. Correspondingly, there will have to be the liberation of Jamaican whites, real and functional, from the bondage of a lop-sided creole culture which tends to maintain for them an untenable position of privilege. Then the harmony which so many well-intentioned Jamaicans claim to exist will begin to transform itself from fiction into fact. Melody and rhythm will no longer be regarded as mutually exclusive phenomena and best of all, no john crow living will feel a need to 'tink him pickney white'.

MIRROR MIRROR
A POSTSCRIPT

Mirror Mirror
on the wall
Who is the fairest
of them all?

JAMAICANS squabbled publicly over the answer to the riddle for well over a fortnight in 1967. This was not the first time that the nation's pre-occupation with its own image assumed disputatious proportions.[1] The leading newspaper reported on its front page as follows: 'Changes in the judging of the Miss Jamaica beauty contests were recommended by a Press conference called . . . yesterday morning to discuss the omission of a popular contestant for the Miss Jamaica 1967 title . . . from the final six from among whom the Festival Queen was chosen.'[2] The last of the three recommendations stated that 'a special campaign to persuade more dark-skinned girls to enter the contest should be waged' [sic]. According to the 'sponsor' of the ill-fated contestant, his candidate had suffered a decided disadvantage on account of her colour – and natural hair style. A journalist saw the rejection of the contestant as 'a monster attack on a large group of the people'.[3] Others contributed to the debate, readily, attacking the Chairman of the Beauty Contest Committee for overlooking in his reactions to the Press Conference, the 'charges of (i) racial bias and (ii) snobbery in the administration of the contest . . .'[4] Another contributor was equally frank in his view that 'many are convinced that in Jamaica whatever is black is not beautiful . . . Beauty in Jamaica is judged on European standards and seen through European eyes.'[5] There were those who were understandably facetious in their comments but the controversy drew serious views from many Jamaican non-blacks, one of whom was forced to ask in a long letter to the editor of the *Daily Gleaner* 'I want to know, can I be white and still be Jamaican?'[6] One contributor insisted that to expect beauty queens to be representative of the so-called 78 per cent of the population (i.e. black) was to miss the point not only of beauty contests but of the multi-racial ethic expressed in the national motto.[7] At least one newspaper columnist[8] deplored the disproportionate publicity given to what he regarded as a trivial issue though another[9] saw the matter as a reflection of persistent attitudes in the society and charged the judges with racial bias and class snobbery in the rejection of the black beauty contestant.

The reader might well wonder why a newly-developing nation like Jamaica with pressing problems of unemployment, illiteracy, overpopulation, urbanization, agricultural underproduction etc., should run the risk of transforming trivia into dimensions of moment in the national affairs. Yet such are the trivia which reflect the underlying problems of deep concern not only for economic and cultural poverty but also for the persistence of the *blackness* of this poverty. The strong commitment to the multi-racial ethic among the established order has often misled observers into believing that Jamaicans have no real interest in the moral and spiritual implications that colonialism, slavery and the plantation system have for the collective experience of the negro, let alone in the universal relevance of this experience. It would, however, be unjustifiable to assume that Jamaicans are unmoved by the important gains made for black dignity in the United States and independent Africa. Nor are they any less affected by the increasing racist attitudes which Britons are reported to be adopting towards Jamaican migrants in the United Kingdom or Canadians to West Indians in Canada. These are likely to deepen racial awareness in Jamaica rather than to dissipate it. Such awareness invited throughout the sixties public outcries in numerous letters to the Press about the inclusion of, say, South Africa in the 1968 world Olympics. Jamaican officials responded positively to the widespread view that Jamaica should not participate if South Africa were allowed to enter the Games with racially segregated teams. This decision cannot be attributed merely to the existence of the liberal tradition in Jamaica. Such a tradition does indeed exist but so does race consciousness and a concern for the black man's destiny

in the world at large. In commenting on Jamaicans' reaction
to the 'politics of the Olympics' and the 'Rhodesian scandal',
an editorial in the much respected *Daily Gleaner* pointed out
that 'the people themselves are moved by events that affect
peoples rather than policies and *more so peoples sharing the same
racial strains*.'[10] The editorial dilated on the difficult position
of the Jamaican Government in exercising its function as a
member of the United Nations. Its declared alignment with
the West and the emotional ties with the emergent coloured
Third World in addition to its geographical placement in the
Latin American bloc presumably leads generally to a foreign
policy of equivocation. But, asserted the editorial, '*issues of race*
cut through the vacillation. The identification becomes clear'
[my emphasis]. The sentence that followed, however, summed
up the position of Jamaican governments and the society at
large. It read, 'and since this nation has often repeated a
boast of exemplary human relationships it can ill afford to
shrink from the challenge of *extremist doctrines that deny simple
human justice particularly for racial reasons*' [my emphasis].

Two comments follow from this statement. Firstly, it is
essential that the established order admits that considerations
of race-awareness, race-pride and the cry for black recognition
and status are important and even fundamental to the aspirations and life of a sizable proportion of the Jamaican populace.
To ignore this fact is not only to rob itself of the capacities to
understand the very society it purports to nurture but to lose
as well the opportunity of guide-lines to positive action. To
assume that it is only a lunatic fringe of the vast black populace
that believes (and resents the continuing evidence) that there
is a conspired correlation between blackness and poverty, is to
indulge fantasies. As for the elected governments, their
attitude in the United Nations to race policies reveals a political
evocation which could well be extended to conditions and
policies at home so as to mobilize the deep, if latent, feelings
held by the majority of Jamaicans about their racial dignity
and pride. A country which professes belief in multi-racialism
cannot, for example, appear to condone a system which effec-

tively perpetuates notions about the inferiority of any one racial group in the complex. Yet to admit the significance of the race factor in Jamaican attitudes is not to indulge or condone extremist doctrines; and this leads to the second comment.

Extremist racial doctrines that 'deny simple human justice' have not been able to find a comfortable place in a multi-racial Jamaica. Rastafarian black nationalism and narrow Black Power advocacy are naturally disqualified in this context. Perhaps it is for this reason that the reactions by the established order to these two phenomena of the sixties at times approached panic. In both cases it would appear that the society made little effort to evaluate them in depth before taking action against them. For one thing, it was always necessary to ask the question whether the assertion of black nationalism or of Black Power were forms of strategy or the substance of the protest. In each case, the society on superficial evidence decided that it was the latter rather than the former and even ruled out the possibility of a complex combination of both.

In the meantime, the voices of protest throughout the sixties were all too conscious of the strong tactical foundations that the argument of race has for protest in Jamaica. Developments since the early sixties tend to support this view: in less than a decade 'the fulminations' of the Rastafarians against the white anti-Christ Babylonian enslavers have transformed themselves into injunctions of 'peace and love' not only for the black man but for all humanity. The 'Brethren' are even willing to work for 'Babylon' whenever work is available though the notion of the Africanization of Jamaica introduces into the Rasta dialectic a level of sophistication and complexity that merits further study. The 'rude boys' seized on similar tactics and invoked the Rastafarian doctrine of the Babylonian captivity whenever it suited them but for them redemption was to be in Jamaica. They wanted the (black) poorer classes to enjoy the fruits of the economy and this has been the substance of their cause. Black Power advocates extended this line into a resourceful ritual of polemics against the foreign exploitation of the country's resources, maintaining the language of the black–

white racist confrontation but substantively campaigning for native (i.e. black) ownership and control of the country's economic and intellectual resources. None of this is in effect foreign to what were the ideals of the movement of political and social liberation which had its roots in the late thirties and to which some of the now panicking citizens must have themselves given support in the past. But frustration and impatience have widened the rift between the spirit of 1938 and the aspirations of today. If the ends have remained unchanged, the means adopted or now conceived vary radically from what were acceptable at an earlier period. It is in this light that the notion of Black Power as 'political strategy' should be seen, for it is as strategy rather than as utopian ideal that Black Power makes sense in a society as complicatedly 'black' as Jamaica. A major problem is that any plan for a forced and instant black control of the society would not prove compatible with the methods to which the established order of Jamaica has been committed since the early forties, viz. evolutionary development through parliamentary institutions and a part-planned free enterprise economy.

It is this incompatibility rather than any known plan for action which gave to the polemics and ferment of the late sixties more of a spirit of revolution than did the earlier Rastafarian protest which, despite the Henry episode of 1960, was seen largely as an escape into millenarian fantasy. Both in fact betray extremist temperaments which have lost force in the face of the society's strong predisposition to a spirit of moderation in handling its political affairs. Closely associated with this is that strong pragmatism in the leadership of both political parties. Some leaders, if asked, would no doubt regard this penchant for political practicality as a priceless virtue to be treasured as one of the more worthwhile legacies of the British heritage. A distrust of ideas and ideology (and of those who carry and harbour them) has been a dominant feature of at least one major wing of Jamaican politics. Here there is a corresponding preference for institutions which work over and above those prescribed, and there is an almost exaggerated respect for the intuitive approach in national decision-taking. For many leaders, theory must follow fact and not *vice versa*. Those leaders who display some faith in ideas usually betray through their utterances a strong dose of nineteenth century English liberalism which still informs Jamaican public life as can be seen in many of the political and legal institutions carefully nurtured since 1944. The 'socialism' of the PNP that finally prevailed was itself a Jamaican version of British Fabianism rather than of the more radical left-wing brand. Some would indeed label official attitudes as liberal conservative more akin to Edmund Burke and the strong peasant population of the country is sometimes believed to be a major agent of this conservative tradition.

But such predispositions are not inviolable and many of the established and much cherished principles have been challenged by the new pressures from alienated youth, many of whom are from the urban lower and middle classes and whose only sense of land-holding may be based on their life on squatters' plots or on mortgaged housing-scheme lots. Then there has been the well-known phenomenon of rising expectations and a new home-grown independent intellectualism identified with the University of the West Indies but by no means restricted to it. They all added up to a fairly widespread urge for substantial change. How the established order meets these new challenges in the seventies and after will determine the society's future character.

There are lessons from the sixties, however. The so-called daydreams of the Rastafarians at the beginning of the decade were to become glaring realities by the mid-sixties, providing a logic for the protest at the end of that decade. The apocalyptic fervour of the bearded brethren was not so far from reality that it could not be transformed into justifiable cries for a paradise realizable not merely in Jamaica but in one's own lifetime. The intuitive truths enunciated by the cultists about the society were later to find a seemingly more logical, if less poetic, articulation among a social-conscious intelligentsia, themselves in search of redemption of a society which they sensed to possess great potential but which they felt displayed too little concern for those who comprise it. Yet the protest, in so far as it has entailed questions of identity and race, may be said to have instituted trends which are irreversible. For one thing, the established order, despite its misgivings about race consciousness, dares no longer to see itself psychologically as an adjunct of Great Britain. For another, it must tread warily in its involvement with the United States which is generally regarded to be a variation on the white Anglo-Saxon ethic. Moreover, Jamaicans of future generations will not grow up to regard Africa as the continent of cannibals and cultural backwardness. There is this, too, that whether leaders see the masses as deprived blacks or simply as voters and trade union members, the fact of black poverty vis-a-vis a predominantly non-black prosperity will force them to take decisions designed to effect black mass betterment in the seventies. Anything short of this will only serve to perpetuate the disastrous myth that to be black is to be ill-starred in Jamaica. Euphemism will no doubt be used to temper what is for some people a jarring semantic admission about the poor people of Jamaica. But the brute fact of poor people's blackness will simply continue to take on disproportionate prominence if elected governments fail to meet with positive action the depth consciousness of this state of existence among the so-called 'sufferers'. Nothing that will in effect perpetuate the self-hate and the lack of confidence among the Jamaican blacks (the masses and the new middle class alike) must be allowed to take a hold of public policy – whether it be in education, in the training of young skills or the retraining of old skills, in the creation of job opportunities at all levels of industry and the allocation of these jobs (particularly those in top management), or in the overall maximization of economic resources. Increasing demands are going to be made for Jamaican nationalism to be more assertive in the interest of those who carry the bloodstains and colour of the vast majority vis-a-vis the traditional *Jamaican* holders of social privilege and economic power. And this will be so even though the battle will be waged primarily against the white expatriate entrepreneurs who are the servants of the much distrusted multi-national business enterprises.

There are other developments as well. Values born exclusively of European experience and long embraced with undiscriminating fervour can no longer maintain their accustomed position of eminence. And though not all that is black can be reasonably regarded as beautiful, it is to be doubted that an entire moral system can ever again be based on notions of goodness that is white and evil that is black. Granted, symbolic transfigurations of portraits of a white Christ into black representations of 'Our Lord' or white Santa Clauses into black St. Nicholases will hardly solve the problem;[12] and in this not even 'soul' with its so-called transcendental mysteries will be adequate. For much must be based on solid achievement, not in the sense of building empires at other people's expense but in the production of work through creative activity and sustained application. The souls of Jamaican black folks will continue in confusion and debilitating turmoil unless they find roots in a discovery and understanding of self as well as in the nurturing of a capacity to exploit that *self* to levels of human excellence. It is in this sense that demands made of the society to transform itself into an environment conducive to such human achievement can be said not only to be reasonable but inevitable. The argument here seems to be in favour of more enlightened views about the quality of human life. The sacrifice of human life in the name of great inventions (imperial and technological) now seems a thing of the past and the Jamaican society like so many Third World communities will have to find the answers by painlessly (and realistically) relating those high human aspirations found among its populace to the practical realities of limited resources, material and human.

Succumbing too much to the one or the other carries with it obvious pitfalls. Over-indulgence of unattainable ideals will offer little in the way of positive decision-taking. But the error on the other side can also lead to disasters. On the one hand, there is indeed a brand of political pragmatism that would quickly divorce imagination from power, forgetting that ex-colonial politicians must themselves be artists, moulding from the ill-defined mass, shapes and patterns of a new existence. On the other, the society's pragmatism may indeed save it from the sway of violent upheaval though, if over-indulged, could deprive it of the usefulness of reason functioning in the service of a more enlightened exercise of power. Warnings of the inherent dangers in this need constantly to be made. For a society which is too committed to a pedestrian empiricism may indeed throw up governments who will find subversion in every genuine idea. This will in turn force many genuine citizens to deny themselves of their inner convictions and further lead to an unhealthy temporizing among people whose talents are vital to the transformation of a society from a subject colonial mentality into a productive independent spirit. There could be, too, an imposed silence and this could hardly enrich the texture of the market-place in which ideas for creative action flourish. Power exercised without imagination and debate can only lead to sterility in public life. The paradox is that political imagination has so far expressed itself in those very disturbing 'utopian fantasies' Jamaica has known in such forms as Garveyism, Rastafarianism, and even the *early* cry for self-government.

Jamaican governments in the seventies will after all be heavily burdened with how power, political and economic, is administered. They will also be concerned with how it is shared and distributed. Now that political power has been transferred from Britain, the natives must work out ways and means of apportioning it. In a two-party system, with the two major parties of almost equal strength, it is important that the acquisition of power by the one or the other be the result of means fair rather than foul. Otherwise any doubts as to the validity of a victory can only lead to mental distrust, frustration and endemic strife. The 'revolution' is then likely to come not from the alienated outsiders but from that deprived section of the power structure which may feel that it can never attain political power under existing institutional arrangements. It is political imagination as much as integrity and fair play that will save the society from the cruel circumstances of a system in which law and order become demoralized and in which a resulting tyranny is justified as the life-giving response to a threatened revolt. This matter of the capacity of the society to create institutions which will make possible the peaceful sharing of political power between contending aspirants through free, open and honest modes of operation is germane to any discussion on protest in Jamaica. Already part of that protest turns on questions about the capacity of such existing institutions to serve the society, not least among them the party system and the device of democratic parliamentary debate. Members of the established order and of the power structure would indeed offer more grist to the mill of protest should nothing be done in the seventies and beyond to clear up doubts on such questions.

Those with unerring faith in the 'good sense' of the Jamaican people may feel that the national character though elusive is strong enough to offset any upheaval. But catastrophes are the respecter of no society. Like societies before them, twentieth century colonial societies are fully aware of the long-standing revolutionary principle that there is a 'binding force of mutual complicity in one act of violence.'[13] Jamaica is no stranger to this emotionally charged and binding force. There also were in evidence those universal eccentricities of the revolutionary temperament which characterized the moods of protest in Jamaica throughout the sixties – the frustration of the poor, the scourge of envy among the 'have-nots', the megalomania of the Rastafarian brethren in their assertive claims as the true Israelites – the Chosen People, the resentment of a continuing colonialism by the educated young, and the growing alienation not only among the under-schooled and poverty-stricken but also among the privileged youths who reject the accepted value-priorities of the established order.

Many see the solutions in an economic determinism and, in response, the country's elected government has indicated plans for reversing the chaotic state of sugar, reforming the banana industry (with special emphasis on markets), revitalizing the declining agricultural sector, constraining the urge for conspicuous consumption, emphasizing the need for local saving, mobilizing Jamaican investment resources both at home and among migrants abroad, developing financial institutions for the attraction and generation of capital in the society and easing tax burdens among the low-income groups while increasing them among big companies. The Opposition Party has itself projected a policy of economic nationalism in which the thrust of industrialization and bold economic development will be tempered by considerations of social justice, human freedom and self-realization. The root of the new policy could reportedly be 'humanism, self-reliance and economic nationalism to create a society of personal freedom founded in the security of the family.'[15] Those who regard themselves as outside of the power-structure give little credit to the Government of the day for its efforts and display little hope for the new Opposition policy. Instead a spate of critical observations from Jamaicans and visiting journalists[16] has endowed the popular literature on Jamaican contemporary life with cliches about the haves and the have-nots, the acquisitive nature of the prosperous elite hankering after durable consumer goods, and the jobless state of the squatting poor.

Many leaders of thought see the answer to these problems in the economic integration of the Caribbean area and support Jamaica's participation in Carifta and the Regional Development Bank. Others expect even greater results from the country's membership in the Organization of American States which is seen as something of a protection against the so-called imperialistic hemisphere policy of the United States. On this, Jamaicans will have to educate themselves to acquiring perspectives which will free them from the psychological uneasiness they experience in their relationship with the giant to the north. For although the Alliance for Progress could be said to have operated more in the interest of the benefactor (and particularly American business) than of the Latin Americans, the intended beneficiaries, and although American attempts to export and promote liberal democracy have sometimes confused and insulted rather than sharpened the political sensibilities of hemisphere communities, the power of the mighty giant cannot always be used as the scapegoat for doing nothing with one's own political destiny. Jamaicans must decide to determine their own future despite the constraints of foreign capital, foreign technology and foreign markets. An American historian observed correctly that 'Washington has a limited power, too often exercised, to prevent change [but] it has much less power to compel change.'[17] The call for change in Jamaica will require from Jamaicans themselves a new political consciousness and a new purpose, with which the vast majority of their people can identify. Anything short of this will merely frustrate the efforts of the policy-planners, however good their intentions and their schemes. The black masses believe that they exist in an ambience of irretrievable futility. To correct this view the society must change in ways that will decrease the hegemony of the entrenched business oligarchy (both local and foreign who are overwhelmingly non-black), provide everyone in the society opportunities for equal access to education and to political power, and exploit overseas investment (capital and skills) consciously *in the interest of Jamaicans*. A revolutionary approach to reform may indeed be the new political style needed and Jamaican leaders will have to acquire this, even if it means exorcizing from their minds endearing shibboleths that might have served the country well in an earlier era. Political leaders have no monopoly on the job of transformation but must be prepared to provide the creative leadership necessary in new countries and to forge new methods of achieving set goals. This goes, too, for those who protest from the safety of their position as 'ordinary citizens'. Indeed the criticism by politicians of the irrelevance to Jamaica's needs of some of the imported creeds of protest is not always unjustified. Programmes of change whether from the status quo or from the alienated will matter little if they bear little relation to the problems and needs of the society.

These essays have been concerned mainly with problems of the Jamaican black majority and the uncertainties and contradictions of their role in what is supposed to be their country. The sixties, goes the argument, was marked by the threatening trinity of identity, race and protest. The years following will demand of all who care continued attention to the threat – whether through the piecemeal social engineering of a government in power, economic nationalism of a party in opposition, cultural rediscovery and definition by sensitive intellectuals and artists, or through the cleansing purge of instant revolutionary action as some of the arduous young would have it.

As for the mass of Jamaican black people whose champions assert the right for them as a group to look to their own interest, it may be worth their while to ponder seriously the matter of exploiting the wellsprings of real power – the brain. What offers great potential may well be the use of education as an investment in the human being which often gets the service of the lip but too little of the courage of the will. Developing peoples (and millions of them are black people) have a vested interest in this investment. Only by this can such people hope to exercise the ability to exploit their own resources and inventiveness. *For the power to create and innovate remains the greatest guarantee of respect and recognition.* One would hope that this challenge would not be avoided by black 'souls' on the grounds that it is 'a white value' born of white experience. Nor should the choice to excel in this particular be bypassed on the spurious excuse that the choice means 'excellence on the master's criteria.' The black masses had better develop and maintain a vested interest in the education of themselves.

One may, with some justification, argue that there is no necessary correlation between economic prosperity and mass education, say. The argument could root itself in the experience of Western Europe whose labouring millions, including the slaves, indentured labourers and their descendants in the dependencies were illiterate at the height of those countries' industrial revolutions. Japan's phenomenal adaptation to the West and its successes as a significant industrial power have also been achieved despite its illiterate labour force. Even the great United States did not have to depend on an educated mass to open up its frontiers, the argument could run. But while the argument might have held good for the period of the industrial revolution leading to industrialization, it is clear that it is invalid in what is regarded as the post-industrial period dominated by the electronic computer, resulting in societies that will be able to experience very high per capita incomes, a shorter work week at less hours per day, a possible work year of 39 weeks with some 13 weeks' vacation. Not all countries, we are told, will achieve this in the next generation but it will become the objective of societies whether they be pre-industrial, transitional, industrial or advanced industrial.* Third World countries will wish to take advantage of a late start and apply methods that will quicker realize such objectives as high revenue from exploitation of resources, industrialization over primary production, responsibility for an application of technological innovations and the decreasing of the appalling differentials between high and low wages. Service industries, research institutes, non-profit organizations and the increasing involvement of the public sector and social services all turn on the need for a large supply of rational, educated human resources. These would be expected to have the capacity to exercise choice between competing objectives, to use their leisure for their own creative ends, to innovate newer resources that can be ploughed back into the system. More electronic computers may very well demand more educated persons to work them. *Economic development for the future is therefore something different from industrial development of the past. And Third World countries may very well decide to invest in the future rather than commit themselves hopelessly to the past.*

For even the economic expansion of the past depended on a *quality* of education – the kind that produces creators and innovators. It was the bane of dependent colonies that by

---

* The typology suggested by Daniel Bell in his book *The Reforming of General Education* quoted in *The American Dilemma* by J. J. Servan-Schreiber (*q.v.*).

definition they were deprived of this important activity. Individuals who rose above it did so largely as a result of their performance in the metropolis. Recognition of such achievement under colonialism was tied to metropolitan mores and prejudices in every field of endeavour. Since nothing creative could by definition come out of the colonies, innovations and inventions received their sanction in metropolitan centres.

Independence implies therefore a transfer back to the colonies of this recognition of the capacity to create. The Americans, fresh out of colonialism, knew that a climate for innovation had to be created. Land grant colleges, universities, varying educational institutions were created to grapple directly with the resources of that society. The investment apparently brought satisfactory rewards by opening up the opportunities to a wider area of human participation. The narrow elitism of higher education long associated with Europe has come to characterize West Indian development in this field.[18] It is indeed an elite who will innovate but to stake out arbitrarily the sources from which that elite must be drawn is to deprive the country of the unpredictable resourcefulness of the human being, whatever his station in life or his social origins. This is the virtue of mass education which Third World countries like Jamaica dare not ignore.[19]

Another virtue is the preparation of a citizenry ready for participation in the political, social and economic processes of its country. In an age of democratic participation and the cry of individual initiative this is vital. It is also vital in an age of rapid change when people must be ready to adapt at a moment's notice to the new discoveries man makes of himself and of his environment. Third World countries will in any case have to work out methods of controlling their economic destinies in peaceful, rational ways that avoid the fact of destructive revolution at any price. The proverbial breaking of the egg can be achieved with such clumsiness that yolk and white could run off leaving only the shell and depriving us of the omelet.

Education then becomes a primary factor in economic

development and closely associated with this is what has been called the growth of knowledge or the expansion of education to include adults, making the new discoveries of technology readily available to them. The old Chinese proverb frequently quoted in United Nations exhortations does make sense after all. If you give a man a fish, he is likely to have a single meal. But if you teach him how to fish, he will indeed eat all his life.

The need for access to higher education (technical and academic) becomes essential. Equally important is the reform of education to make this available to children in the lower income group. But this will be of limited value if the child with a free place to a school has no facilities for leisurely and proper study, is lacking in enough vitamins to stimulate biological growth, and is deprived of facilities for cultural and individual integrated development so that he can emerge an unalienated, less confused and more assured member of his society. Children from low-income homes, however highly motivated, will lack the capacities for coping compared with those from higher income groups who may possess the security of an environment which facilitates individual integration. The schools have to substitute where the home cannot help. This is expensive but the price must be paid for future societal mental health.

Jamaican Black Power advocates have not been as strong as they might on the matter of education as an investment in man. Black people's greatest need may well be to acquire skills to make them functional (i.e. free) agents in the society. But the concept of a liberated or free being must be tied to the social context of operation. It is pointless rearing black imbecilic 'kings' or black metaphysicians who are experts on the glories of an African past or chroniclers of white ills. Black men must acquire the kind of education, and insist on the kind of society, that will invest in them as resourceful human beings so that excellence of achievement can be realized and the capacity to create ensured. It is not enough for education curricula to be 'relevant' in terms of black history, of the past crimes of plantation society or the white devilry of the pernicious system of slavery and its offspring. *Education must be relevant first and foremost in its capacity to make the individual realize his powers to innovate.* Throwing off the inhibiting concepts of inferiority born out of an unwritten history with a white bias as well as out of a present frozen in unsubstantiated myths about relative racial worth, becomes a necessary part of that education. But it can never stop there. Education must also make black people really capable of controlling their societies – as administrators, managers, skilled labourers, inventors, as creative artists, scientists, teachers etc. The black Africans understand this. Wherever black people live such societies must be made to provide opportunities in which black people can achieve these things. For freedom cannot make sense without its pristine connexion with achievement. Otherwise we are left with a metaphysical state of existence that belongs more to the philosopher's treatises on the natural state rather than to the realities of human existence.

The priceless gift of *brain power*, or capacity to use one's mind, is not restricted to any one race. Experience illustrates this beyond contradiction. But something constructive must be done with it and whatever the education, it must seek to enable the educated to make something of the gift. Therein lies the relevance of education as should be reflected by the policy-determiners in Ministries of Education and in educational institutions (primary, secondary and university). It should be dynamic in approach and substance and susceptible to continuing examination and change. Change is at any rate the child of that instant communication that advanced technology has imposed upon the far-flung enclaves of the world. Human experience is easily crystallized in less time and in unprecedented ways. Faith in this or that theory is likely to be shaken by instantly communicated new discoveries. Despite the persistent gap between declared policy and practice more people in the world, though still not enough, now know that blacks are not inferior to whites. The sophisticated working out of the new relationships made necessary by this new and important knowledge may very well be the occasion of a rearguard action already instigated among reactionary whites as well as of an escalated militancy evident among a more confident young generation of blacks. We all now know more about ourselves and about each other. The disciplines of the much maligned social sciences and psychology as well as biology and the medical sciences have informed this new position adequately.

There is nothing inferior about the black man's intellectual creativity. It is constantly under threat, however, by his belief in the superiority of all things excepting those peculiar to him. This lack of self-regard, this conditioned inadequacy is a real threat to the capacities of the black communities in the West to transform ideas into practice. This is what much of colonialism was about. Indeed, the persistence of a colonial situation through foreign investment (and foreign fads) is a justifiable concern of Black Power advocacy in any West Indian country. Black Power advocates outside the mainstream of the power structure would purport to be looking further than Governments and their loyal Oppositions. Yet more thought and action is needed for Jamaicans (black or otherwise) to promote and safeguard their intellectual creativity. Many of the ideas about black control need just this dimension. While it is essential to protest governmental banning of scholars (black or white) in the interest of academic and other basic freedoms it is even more necessary that institutions like the University and technical institutes put their own houses in order in respect of the service they give. The relevance of the University of the West Indies to the needs of the territories it was designed to serve deserves the priority in any strategy of change conceived by Black Power or any other kind of advocacy. Meanwhile, short of a complete take-over of the present power structure by revolutionary seizure of power, the framework of existing arrangements will have to find the means of promoting black intellectual creativity and the power structure must itself show its capacities to transform ideas into practice.

Black Power advocates may well argue (and in fact do) that opportunities for the blacks in Jamaica are still limited; for example, the degree of effective participation by non-blacks over blacks in the processes of Jamaican development is still far in excess of the former's numbers. It is further asserted with some justification that rewards are in turn meted out in like ratio, leaving the majority of the blacks still at the bottom of the economic, and, by extension, the social and political heap. It is the correction of this which could mean not so much black domination but harmonization of the society which is constantly projected as an integrated multi-racial unit. The reported prediction by a Minister of Government that this will be so in thirty years[20] may be realistic but it emphasizes the cause for impatience among the young Jamaican blacks in the late sixties. It emphasizes even more the argument against bad management by those who lead. It also calls for the society's mental health to be measured less by its frustrations, endemic dissatisfactions and alienation of its young, and more in terms of a sense of commitment born of the confidence in an environment which can offer its citizens a decent standard of living, a real sense of personal security and an opportunity to create. The importance of this opportunity was early understood by the Rastafarians whose so-called misdirected rebellion against Jamaican constituted authority revealed itself soon enough as an expression of a will to create. It is not surprising that their creed, the vehicle of an inventive value-system, finds support among the young in search of a frame of reference that will liberate them from what they feel to be the irrelevancies of the established order. They share the Rasta defiance of the attempts of established authority to corral them into an atrophied orthodoxy, though they sometimes fail to share the Rastafarian respect for knowledge and self-discipline in the achievement of their goals. It is not by any means a coincidence that the Rastafarian tends to involve himself if he has a choice in what are regarded (at least in a democracy) as the highest expressions of the creative spirit[21] – religion, branches of the arts (painting, sculpting, performing), literature (particularly poetry) and philosophy (though many members of the established order would still not take them seriously on this). In the more practical matter of earning a livelihood, the Rastafarian will prefer to achieve the indices of prosperity *by his own efforts* in a self-employed situation, and in creative ways.

The power to take effective decisions is said to inhere in the power to create wealth and this in turn inheres in the ability to make reality out of ideas – an activity which is the triumph of the human spirit, anywhere. The investment in education, in brain power, here takes a central place in a country's national development. The distrust and fear of ideas betrayed by members of the Jamaican established order is probably one of the most potentially tragic things about Jamaican life. It threatens the society with a pedestrianism, cynicism and moral blindness which can only rob the conduct of public affairs of the imagination and principle foundations from which it could benefit. In the sixties the weapons of combat employed by the established order against the different forms of protest extended at times to expressions of anti-intellectualism, government bannings (of people and of books, some of which dealt with the black predicament with commendable candour) and charges of subversion as well as stringent penalties under the Dangerous Drugs Law and the law against treason felony. Between government and the rest of the society reactions ranged from total resentment to grudging tolerance and even outright indulgence of some of the millenarian 'fantasies' as well as from the strict application of the law to a skilful preemption of the ideals and aspirations expressed in the youthful revolutionary spirit. Yet, in its own self-interest the society can ill-afford to indulge an active anti-intellectualism. Nor can it muzzle independent thought or betray undue intolerance of those who question the very status quo, if it means to be the stable democracy it claims to be. Such an action by either government or public opinion will only further emasculate the process of learning – an effect which colonialism had all but achieved in the era before independence. Educated Jamaicans (especially university-trained persons) on the other hand, might well rid themselves of an indefensible arrogance and abandon the tempting postures of omniscience.

Still, the Jamaican society like all ex-colonial communities, will have to decide whether it wants among its institutions of growth, institutions of learning which are serious in intent – institutions, which, even at the risk of some disruption of the status quo, can help to produce the innovators and creators and forge a quality of mind so widespread among its citizenry that there can come a quick end to that threatening mediocrity which is the bane of much that is Jamaican existence. Such an end, it seems, is the hope of that beginning when a new opening can be found for intellectual daring and creative action.

REFERENCES

Preface

1. Gross Domestic Product at factor cost by industrial origin 1963–68
Current prices (J$ million)

SECTOR	1963	1964	1965	1966	1967	1968
Agriculture	53	52	50.8	55.4	57	55.2
Mining, Quarrying and Refining	45.6	52.2	57.8	62	65.4	72.8
Manufacturing	78.8	84.4	89.2	99.2	101.6	112.4
Construction and Installation	52.2	58.2	63.6	69.2	73.8	92.4

Increase of the gross domestic product of mining, quarrying and refining by J$27.2 million over the six year period, of manufacturing by J$33.6 million and construction and installation by J$40.2 million, is generally interpreted as economic progress. The G.D.P. for Agriculture increased by a mere J$2.2 million over the six year period. See *Economic Survey, Jamaica*, prepared by the Central Planning Unit, Government of Jamaica (1963–1968)

2. e.g. Wendell Bell's 'study of the sociology of (Jamaican) nationalism' entitled *Jamaican Leaders, Political Attitudes in a New Nation*. See chapters III–VII in particular. In the long run the value of this exercise by Professor Bell may be exactly what he had in part intended, i.e. to have the 'conclusion drawn from the survey . . . (give) direction and impetus to research being carried out in Jamaica and the West Indies'

3. See *Poverty American Style* edited by Herman Miller, 1969, Belmont, California, Wadsworth Publishing Company. View expressed in Introduction by Miller himself

4. See my Essay on 'The Rastafari and the Wider Society' on page 39

5. 'This Menace to our Future', statement to the *Daily Gleaner* by Alexander Bustamante, Leader of the Opposition, in *Daily Gleaner*, October 26, 1960

6. Statement from the Council on Afro–West Indian Affairs – a reply to Bustamente's statement in *Daily Gleaner*, October 26, 1960

7. 'The Question of Colour and Race', statement by Hon. Norman W. Manley, Premier of Jamaica in *Daily Gleaner*, October 31, 1960

237

National Identity

1. M. G. Smith: 'Our National Identity and Behaviour Patterns' (Lecture), University of the West Indies, Radio Education Unit (mimeograph)
2. Bryan Edwards: *History of the West Indies* (4th ed.), London, 1807, Book I, Chapter III
3. Anton V. Long: *Jamaica and the New Order 1827–1847*, University of the West Indies, ISER, 1956, pp. 15–16 (Monograph)
4. E. B. Underhill: *The Tragedy of Morant Bay*, London, 1895; S. H. Oliver, *The Myth of Governor Eyre*, London, The Hogarth Press, 1933
5. Jamaica Constitution (1944), Order in Council
6. Speech made to the National Press Club, U.S.A., by N. W. Manley, Premier of Jamaica, in April 1961. Report in *New York Times*
7. Jamaica Report to the United Nations on Racial Discrimination. Report in *Daily Gleaner*, October 4, 1964
8. *Ibid.*
9. F. Henriques: *Family and Colour in Jamaica*, London, Eyre & Spottiswoode, 1953, pp. 33–63; Madeline Kerr: *Personality and Conflict in Jamaica*, London, Collins, 1963, pp. 93–104
10. West Indies Population Census (Jamaica) 1960, Kingston, Jamaica. (Bulletin No. 20, Provisional, Dept. of Statistics)
11. *Ibid.*
12. *Ibid.*
13. *Ibid.*
14. O. C. Francis: *The People of Modern Jamaica*, Kingston, Jamaica, Dept. of Statistics, 1963
15. J. H. Parry and P. M. Sherlock: *A Short History of the British West Indies*, London, Macmillan, 1960; L. J. Ragatz: *The Fall of the Planter Class in the British Caribbean* 1763–1833 (1928, esp. chapter on 'Caribbean Society')
16. John Hearne: 'The European Heritage and Asian Influence', *Our Heritage*, University of the West Indies, Extra-Mural Public Affairs pamphlet, 1963
17. M. G. Smith, F. R. Augier, Rex Nettleford: *Report on the Ras Tafari in Kingston*, University of the West Indies, ISER, 1960
18. Frank Hill: Lecture entitled 'Racial Integration in Jamaica' delivered at UWI, February 10, 1963
19. F. Henriques: *op. cit.*
20. *Daily Gleaner*, May 6, 1964 (Editorial)
21. *Daily Gleaner*, June 24, 1964 (Letter to the Editor)
22. *Daily Gleaner*, September 10, 1964 (Letter to the Editor)
23. *Daily Gleaner*, September 22, 1964 (Letter to the Editor)

24. Shirley Maynier-Burke: 'The Jamaican Civil Rights Dilemma', *Daily Gleaner*, October 2, 1964
25. Rex Nettleford: 'The African Connexion', *Our Heritage*, UWI Extra-Mural Public Affairs pamphlet, 1963

African Redemption

1. Sam Brown: *Treatise on the Rastafari Movement* 1963, Oral History Collection, Radio Education Unit (REU), UWI
2. *Ibid.* Basic doctrines common to all Rastafarians are: 1. Ras Tafari (i.e. Haile Selassie I) is the Living God. 2. Ethiopia is the black man's home. 3. Repatriation is the way of redemption for black men. It has been foretold, and will occur shortly. 4. The ways of the white man are evil, especially for the black. See *The Rastafari Movement in Kingston, Jamaica*, Chapter IV. Sam Brown's *Treatise* lists the following tenets: 1. We strongly object to sharp implements used in the desecration of the figure of man, e.g. trimming and shaving, tattooing of skin, cutting of flesh. 2. We are basically vegetarians, making scant use of certain animal flesh yet outlawing the use of swine's flesh in any form, shell fishes, scaleless fishes, snails. 3. We worship and observe no other God but Ras Tafari outlawing all other forms of pagan worship yet respecting all believers. 4. We love and respect the brotherhood of mankind yet our first love is to the sons of Ham. 5. We disapprove and abhor utterly, hate, jealousy, envy, deceit, guile, treachery, etc. 6. We do not agree with the pleasure of present-day society and its modern evils. 7. We are avowed to create a world order of one brotherhood. 8. Our duty is to extend the hands of charity to any brother-in-distress firstly for he is of the Ras Tafari order, secondly to any human, animals, plants, etc. likewise. 9. We do adhere to the ancient laws of Ethiopia. 10. Thou shalt give no thought to the aid, titles and possessions that the enemy in his fear may seek to bestow on you, resolution to your purpose in love of Ras Tafari.'
3. Peter Worsley: *The Trumpet Shall Sound*, p. 223
4. Orlando Patterson: 'Ras Tafari: Cult of Outcasts' *New Society*, Vol. IV, No. 3, November 12, 1964, pp. 15–17
5. Vittorio Lanternari: *The Religions of the Oppressed* (A Study of Modern Messianic Cults) Alfred A. Knopf, New York, 1965, p. 136
6. G. E. Simpson: 'Political Cultism in West Kingston, Jamaica', *Social & Econ. Studies*, UWI, Vol. V, No. 2, June, 1955, pp. 133–149: 'Jamaica Revivalist Cults', *Social and Econ. Studies*, Vol. 5, 1956

7. M. G. Smith, F. R. Augier, Rex Nettleford: *The Ras Tafari Movement in Kingston, Jamaica*, ISER, UCWI, Mona, Jamaica, 1960

8. *Ibid.*

9. O. Patterson: *op. cit.*

10. Quoted by Worsley: *op. cit.*

11. Sam Brown: *op. cit.*

12. V. Lanternari: *op. cit.*

13. Notes from Draft of University Report, 1960

14. G. V. Doxey: *Survey of the Jamaican Economy*, 1969

15. R. B. Davison: 'Life and Labour in Trench Town, Kingston Jamaica in September, 1967' – a commentary on the Dept. of Statistics survey on housing conditions in Trench Town. Unpublished paper, p. 5

16. *Ibid.*

17. O. Patterson: *op. cit.*

18. *Daily Gleaner*, August 30, 1960

19. *Daily Gleaner*, August 3–6, 8–13, 15–17, 1960

20. *Daily Gleaner*, August 16, 1960. Cartoon by Leandro

21. *Sunday Gleaner*, October 12, 1969 (Editorial)

22. M. G. Smith *et al.*: *op. cit.*

23. *Daily Gleaner*, October 20, 1960 (Letter from Monsignor Wilson)

24. *Daily Gleaner*, October 25, 1960 (Letter from M. G. Smith)

25. *Daily Gleaner*, October 15, 1960. Front-page report of Statement by 'the Rt. Rev. Monsignor Gladstone Wilson, Doctor of Philosophy, Doctor of Sacred Theology, Doctor of Canon Law, Master of Arts (Soc.), Bachelor of Civil Law'. The Jamaican Monsignor was reported as saying that the University study was 'unworthy of scholars' and in danger of creating false hopes among the Rastafarians

26. *Daily Gleaner*, August 17, 1960 (Editorial)

27. *Daily Gleaner*, August 20, 1960. Letter from M. G. Smith to Editor inviting Monsignor Wilson to be specific in his criticism of the UWI study

28. *Sunday Gleaner*, August 21, 1960 (Feature by Political Reporter)

29. Raymond Prince: Paper on 'The Ras Tafari in Jamaica – a study of group beliefs and social stress'. Dr. Prince served as a PAHO/WHO Mental Health Consultant in Jamaica. May 1969

30. e.g. 'The Rastafari Brethren in Jamaica' by Sheila Kitzinger in *Comparative Studies in Society and History*, Vol. IX, No. 1, October 1966. 'Ras Tafari: The Cult of Outcasts' by Orlando Patterson in *New Society*, see reference above. *The Children of Sisyphus*, the highly acclaimed novel by Orlando Patterson, London, New Authors Ltd., 1964. *Jamaica, a Search for Identity* by Katrin Norris, London, 1962, and several Masters and doctoral

studies unpublished but for which this author has supplied information based on the 1960 Report. Also see note 29 for the article by Dr. Raymond Prince.

31. *Daily Gleaner*, August 21, 1968 (Feature by Political Reporter)
32. *Daily Gleaner*, August 3, 1960 (Statement by Premier Norman Manley)
33. *Daily Gleaner*, August 17, 1960
34. *Daily Gleaner*, August 22, 1960 (Editorials)
35. *Daily Gleaner*, August 30, 1960 (Letter from Z. Munroe-Scarlett 'Administrator, Afro-West Indian Welfare League')
36. *Daily Gleaner*, April 23, 1963 (Letter from Sam Brown)
37. Bongo Dizzy: 'Voice of the Interpreter' 1963
38. *Ibid.*
39. Speech by Dr. Okpara, Institute of Jamaica, October, 1962, Oral History Collection, Radio Education Unit (REU) UWI
40. Bongo Dizzy: *op. cit.*
41. *Sunday Gleaner*, October 19, 1969 (Editorial)
42. *Daily Gleaner*, April 20, 1966 (Editorial)
43. *Daily Gleaner*, April 22, 1966 (Front-page reports)
44. *Ibid.*
45. *Public Opinion*, April 29, 1966
46. Jay Monroe: 'Rasta Day Come' in *Sunday Gleaner*, April 24, 1966
47. *Daily Gleaner*, May 7, 1966. Also of June 14, 1966, when in a debate at the University the Senator, Mr. Wilton Hill, linked the discarding of the present monarchial arrangements to the discovery of a Jamaican identity.
48. Letter from W. Bennett, General Manager, Jamaica Broadcasting Corporation, April, 1969
49. *Daily Gleaner*, September 30 and October 12 and 17, 1969
50. M. G. Smith *et al.*: *op. cit.*, Appendix I
51. *Daily Gleaner*, July 15, 1968
52. Speech by Ras Shadrac 1963 – spokesman of Church Triumphant, Jah Rastafari Oral History Collection, REU, UWI
53. Speech by Bro. Mortimo Planno 1963 – member of 1961 Back to Africa Mission, recorded version REU, UWI. Also Speech by Okpara (*op. cit.*) to Rastafarians at the Institute of Jamaica in late 1962. He said 'but for the black man America as we know it today would not have existed. We built the big cities of Britain with our brawns, our arms, our strength. We built the New World and the Old . . .' Okpara went on to urge that similar effort be put into building Africa
54. *Sunday Gleaner*, August 21, 1960 (Feature by Political Reporter). Also *Daily Gleaner*, August 19, 1960. Article 'Back to Africa Is Nonsense' by Clinton Parchment; *Daily Gleaner*, August 26,

Letter from C. Stewart; also Speech by Okpara to Rastafarians 'There are opportunities in Africa now for those who have skills ... Get a list of those who have skills ... We start in a small way, not to have 10,000 people at once ... Let's start with ten, tweny, first class people'

55. Louise Bennett: Poem 'Back to Africa' in *Jamaica Labrish*, Sangster, Kingston, 1966, p. 234
56. *Sunday Gleaner*, August 21, 1960
57. *Daily Gleaner*, September 30, 1969 (Front-page report), also October 13, 1969
58. Statement by Premier: *Daily Gleaner*, August 19, 1960, p. 19
59. *Report of Mission to Africa*, Majority Report, pp. 1–13; Minority Report, pp. 15–23, Govt. Printer, Kingston, 1961
60. *Interim Report of Working Party on Migration to Africa*, paras. 52–3, 1961
61. *Ibid.*, esp. paras. 61 (v), 19, 22, 28, 40, 48
62. *Ibid.*, para. 58
63. *Summary Report of Technical Mission to Africa*, 1962 (unpublished)
64. *Daily Gleaner*, March 27, 1965
65. *Daily Gleaner*, May 16, 1969 (Letter to the Editor from Sam Brown)
66. *Daily Gleaner*, December 15, 1965
67. Membership Card – Rastafari Brethren Repatriation Association
68. G. E. Simpson: 'Jamaican Revivalist Cults', *Social and Econ. Studies*, UCWI, Vol. 5, No. 4, December, 1956
69. M. G. Smith *et al.*: *op. cit.*, Chapter IV
70. *Public Opinion*, April 27, 1963 (Editorial)
71. *Daily Gleaner*, April 13, 1963
72. *Public Opinion*, September 14, 1963
73. *Ibid.*, also *cf.* Speech by Ras Shadrac claiming that ganja prevented Rastafarians from being violent when hungry
74. *Public Opinion*, September 14, 1963
75. Statement by Minister of Home Affairs, to House of Representatives on April 16, 1963. See also *Daily Gleaner*, April 17, 1963
76. Eulogy by Rev. E. H. Greaves of Mount Carey Baptist Church, St. James, in *Daily Gleaner*, April 16, 1963
77. Sir Alexander Bustamante: Statement 'This Menace to Our Future', *Daily Gleaner*, October 19, 1960
78. Statement by Alexander Bustamante, Prime Minister: *Daily Gleaner*, April 17, 1963
79. *Daily Gleaner*, April 17, 1963 (Editorial)
80. John Maxwell: 'Peace and Love' in *Public Opinion*, April 27, 1963
81. *Daily Gleaner*, April 23, 1963 (Letter to the Editor from Sam Brown)

82. Paper 'Extracts on Ganja': Farquharson Institute of Public Affairs, 13 East Street, Kingston, March 12, 1969
83. R. v. George Green: Court of Appeal, Supreme Court Criminal Appeal No. 15/19. See also *Daily Gleaner*, June 28, 1969
84. Note from Mr. Justice Parnell to Jamaica Bar Association. See *Daily Gleaner*, August 6, 1969
85. *Daily Gleaner*, April 17, 1960
86. Reports on Preliminary Hearing: *Daily Gleaner*, May 3–12, 1960 Reports on Circuit Court Trial: *Daily Gleaner*, October 5–30, 1960
87. *Daily Gleaner*, June 22, 1960
88. *Ibid.* (Editorial)
89. *Daily Gleaner*, July 3, 1960
90. *Daily Gleaner*, July 18, 1960
91. *Hansard*, July 27, 1960
92. *Daily Gleaner*, June 28, 1960
93. *Daily Gleaner*, June 22, 1960
94. *Daily Gleaner*, October 30, 1960
95. *Daily Gleaner*, October 28, 1960
96. *Ibid.*
97. *Daily Gleaner*, January 28, 1968 (Letter from Ras Tafari Brethren Repatriation Association)
98. Statement by the Jamaica Council for Human Rights in *Daily Gleaner*, July 15, 1968. The raids were carried out according to the Statement on January 23, May 5 and June 3 of 1968
99. M. G. Smith *et al.*: *op. cit.*, Chapter IV
100. G. V. Doxey: *op. cit.* Also *New World* pamphlet 'Unemployment . . .', 1967.
101. *Economic Survey of Jamaica 1968*, Central Planning Unit, Kingston, Jamaica
102. G. V. Doxey, *op. cit.*
103. *Daily Gleaner*, October 24, 1969
104. George Cumper: 'The Analysis of Unemployment in Jamaica 1960 (unpublished paper)
105. *Ibid.*
106. *Daily Gleaner*, March 18, 1965 (Headline: 'Islandwide Birth-control Drive Launched')
107. *The Star*, February 8, 1968
108. *e.g.* Speech by Editor of the *Daily Gleaner*. See Report, March 19, 1969
109. *Youth Move*, Vol. 1, No. 1
110. M. G. Smith *et al.*: *op. cit.*
111. Interviews for Broadcast compiled by Robert Hill and Dermot Hussey, 1967, Oral History Collection, REU, UWI
112. *Ibid.*

113. G. White: 'Rudie, Oh Rudie' in *Caribbean Quarterly*, Vol. 13, No. 3
114. See Ref. 99 above
115. *Ibid.*
116. G. White: *op. cit.*, also Jamaica Information Service Radio broadcasts 'Arts Corner 1968' and Gordon Rohlehr's 'Sounds and Pressures' in *Moko*, June 1969
117. Peter Worsley: *op. cit.*, p. 226
118. John Patmos (or Sylvia Wynter-Carew) in 'Off the Cuff', *Daily Gleaner*, April 30, 1963
119. *Ibid.*
120. Claudius Henry: Pamphlet printed by Golding's Printery, East Street, Kingston
121. Claudius Henry, 'Violence in Jamaica', April 28, 1969, and 'I am Black', October 20, 1968 (cyclostyled pamphlets)
122. Edith Clarke: *My Mother Who Fathered Me*, 1957, London, Allen & Unwin, p. 77
123. Peter Worsley: *op. cit.*, p. 238
124. Sam Brown: *Treatise on the Rastafarian Movement*, Oral History Collection, REU, UWI
125. *Daily Gleaner*, October 16, 1969 (Editorial)
126. *Ibid.*

Jamaican Black Power

1. *Daily Gleaner*, April 10, 1969 (Report of Speech by Mrs. Esme Grant, Parliamentary Secretary, Ministry of Education); *Hansard*, May 28, 1969 (Budget Speech by Talbert Forrest, M.P. – JLP, St. Mary Western)
2. Speech by Esme Grant, Parliamentary Secretary, Ministry of Education. Report in *Daily Gleaner*, April 10, 1969
3. *Daily Gleaner*, October 22, 1968 (Letter to the Editor)
4. *Daily Gleaner*, November 26, 1968 (Letter to the Editor)
5. Speech by H. L. Shearer, Prime Minister of Jamaica at Highgate, St. Mary
6. *Guardian Weekly*, June 12, 1969 (Article 'Hurricane on the Horizon', by Clyde Sanger)
7. *The Star*, October 16, 1968
8. Amy Jacques Garvey: *Black Power in America* (Marcus Garvey's Impact on Jamaica and Africa), Kingston, Jamaica, 1968
9. Marcus Garvey, Jr.: *Sunday Gleaner*, December 1, 1968; *Daily Gleaner*, March 31, 1969, in Letters
10. *The Star*, August 30, 1969
11. *The Star*, October 22, 1968

12. *Sunday Gleaner*, August 31, 1969
13. See *Public Opinion*, particularly in period immediately following Independence
14. *Public Opinion*, August 29, 1969 (Text of Speech by G. E. Mills)
15. *The Star*, August 29, 1969 (Editorial)
16. M. G. Smith: 'A Framework for Caribbean Studies', Jamaica, Extra-Mural Dept., UCWI; 'Slavery and Emancipation in Two Societies', *Social and Economic Studies*, Vol. 3, Nos. 3 and 4, Jamaica UCWI, 1954
    Elsa Goveia: *A Study on the Historiography of the British West Indies*, Mexico, 1956; *Slave Society in the British Leeward Islands at the end of the Eighteenth Century*, Yale University Press, 1965
17. *New World Quarterly* – a journal of Caribbean Affairs and Opinion, designed to 'transform the mode of living and thinking' of the Caribbean people
18. *Guardian Weekly*, *op. cit.*
19. *Abeng*, Vol. 1, No. 13, April 26, 1969
20. T. Munroe: 'Black Power as a Political Strategy in Jamaica', a Lecture
21. Ramiro Guerra y Sanchez: *Sugar and Society in the Caribbean*, Yale University Press, 1964, p. 86
22. *Bongo Man*, Journal of African Youth, No. 1, December, 1968, p. 27, and No. 2, January–February, 1969, p. 8
    N.B. This is a cyclostyled predecessor of *Abeng* and emerged from the spate of protest pamphlets which followed on the events of October 16, 1968
23. 'Intensified White Power in Jamaica', cyclostyled broadsheet (anonymous)
24. *Economic Survey of Jamaica*, 1968 (Central Planning Unit, Jamaica)
25. *Daily Gleaner*, June 7, 1969
26. Editorial in *New World* Pamphlet No. 4, December, 1967, and Article following entitled *The Sugar Industry – Our Life or Death*, by Havelock Brewster
27. *Daily Gleaner*, August 29, 1969 (Letter to the Editor); see also *New World* Pamphlet, *op. cit.*; *Daily Gleaner*, January to August, 1969, *passim*, esp. (Report 'Desperate State of the Sugar Industry', June 11); Feature article, 'Decline in the Sugar Crop', by Farm Reporter in *Sunday Gleaner*, June 22; Feature article, 'Sugar – Two Major Crises rubbing cheek by jowl' by Farm Reporter, *Sunday Gleaner*, August 31
28. R. Guerra y Sanchez, *op. cit.*, p. 97
29. *Daily Gleaner*, September 2, 1969, 'Candidly Yours' – Column by Thomas Wright which is the pen-name of a well-known Jamaican journalist and radio-television commentator of Caucasian stock

30. Annual Reports Jamaica Tourist Board, also Article 'Jamaica . . . 1973?' in *International Business*, May, 1969, by Frank E. Block
31. *Abeng,* ol. 1, No. 5, March 1, 1969
32. *cf. Abeng*, Vol. 1, No. 6, March 8, 1969, and *Moko,* No. 4 (Article) 'Bauxite: Guinea will own her own' by Norman Girvan in which he says 'Guinea's new bauxite deal . . . shows that countries like ours can attract capital and skills from outside to develop their bauxite resources without giving these away to the large international corporations'
33. Sterling Brubaker: *Aluminium Industry*, Johns Hopkins Press, 1967, pp. 156–7
34. *Ibid.*, p. 245
35. For a stimulating study of Power see *The Active Society* (A Theory of Social and Political Processes) by Amitai Etzioni, Collier-Macmillan, London, The Free Press, N.Y., 1968, esp. Chaps. 13, 14
36. See *e.g. No More Apologizing*, Speech made on visit to Montego Bay in 1921. Reported in *Daily Gleaner*, April 4, 1921, reproduced in full in *Bongo Man*, No. 1, December, 1968. See also *Philosophy* and *Opinions*, Part 1
37. Walter Rodney, 'Why Black Power in the West Indies', *Bongo Man*, Vol. 2, pp. 3–13
38. Letter to the Editor, *Daily Gleaner*, June 7, 1969
39. Letter to the Editor, *Daily Gleaner*, June 16, 1969
40. Tom Mboya (Article): 'Back to Africa Desire Unrealistic', *Sunday Gleaner*, August 10, 1969
41. *Ibid.*
42. W. Rodney: 'African History in the Service of the Black Evolu tion', *Bongo Man*, No. 1, p. 4
43. T. Mboya: *op. cit.*
44. K. O. Dike: 'African History and Self Government', *West Africa*, March 14, 1953
45. Lloyd Best: 'Black Power and the Afro-American in Trinidad and Tobago', *Sunday Gleaner*, April 6, 1969
46. *Ibid.*
47. Report of the Prime Minister's speech headlined 'We Must Have Changes In Our Society', *Daily Gleaner*, July 19, 1969, also speeches in 1969 Budget Debate by Minister of Finance and Planning and Leader of the Opposition.
48. Eric Williams: *Capitalism and Slavery*, Andre Deutsch, London.
49. Vernon L. Arnett: 'Jamaica – Dictatorship or Democracy', *Moko*, No. 4.
50. Quoted in Lecture, 'Black Power as a Political Strategy in Jamaica' *op. cit.*
51. F. Fanon,: *The Wretched of the Earth*, McGibbon & Kee, London, 1965

52. Amy J. Garvey: *op. cit.*
53. *Bongo Man*, No. 2, p. 16
54. *Hansard*, Prime Minister's speech to Parliament, October 17, 1969
55. K. C. Burke: 'No Constitutional Guarantee or Rule of Law Breached', *Daily Gleaner*, December 7, 1968
56. *Daily Gleaner*, October 18, 1969
57. *The Star*, October 22, 1968
58. See Letters to the Editor, *Daily Gleaner*, October, 1968–April 1969
59. Letter to the Editor, *Daily Gleaner*, June 7, 1969
60. *The Star*, September 3, 1969
61. 'Statement on Black Power by the Conference of the Roman Catholic Bishops of the Antilles.' See Report, *Daily Gleaner*, September 7, 1969
62. See *Daily Gleaner*, November 24, 1967. Report 'House agrees unanimously to seek revision of present arrangements with bauxite companies' (to obtain maximum benefit for Jamaica); *Abeng*, Vol. 1, No. 7, May 24, 1969
63. *Daily Gleaner*, August 6, 1969 (Editorial)
64. *Hansard*, Speech in Budget Debate by Leader of the Opposition, June 4. See also Report, *Daily Gleaner*, June 5, 1969
65. *Public Opinion*, August 29, 1969
66. *Daily Gleaner*, September 3, 1969 (Editorial obituary of N. W. Manley)
67. Jay Monroe: 'Stock-taking on the Revolution', *Sunday Gleaner* May 18, 1965
68. *Abeng*, Vol. 1, No. 32, September 6, 1969: also *Moko*, No. 3, for commentary by James Milette on retirement speech of N. W. Manley from politics. Milette noted the old leader's attempt to 'vindicate the role' of the PNP in Jamaican development in a 'long and rambling speech . . . Much more startling though for a politician of his age and outlook was his ungrudging approbation of the sentiment of Black Power and his realisation of the historical circumstances of its development.' See also Note 49 above in reference to V. L. Arnett's view on the matter. But the recognition of 'economic denial' has also been raised in three *Gleaner* editorials on Development, April 17, 18, 19, 1969. 'Many developing countries have realised the necessity of curbing foreign participation and giving local initiative a chance, observed the third editorial
69. N. W. Manley: Speeches at annual PNP Conference, Kingston, November 1968, and at 75th birthday dinner, Kingston, July 4, 1968
70. Acceptance Speech by M. M. Manley on being elected to leadership of PNP Conference, February, 1969; also see *Public Opinion*, June 6, 1969

71. *Abeng*, Vol. 1, No. 32, September 6, 1969
72. *Daily Gleaner*, September 18, 1967
73. *Hansard*, Budget Speech by Hon. Edward Seaga, Minister of Finance and Planning, May 8, 1969
74. *Abeng*, Vol. 1, No. 32, September 6, 1969

The Melody of Europe, the Rhythm of Africa

1. M. G. Smith: 'West Indian Culture' in *Caribbean Quarterly*, Vol. 7, No. 3, also *The Plural Society in the West Indies*, University of California Press, 1965
2. *Ibid.*
3. E. B. Tyler: *Primitive Culture*, Vol. 1, New York, Harpers, 1958
4. Mervyn Morris: 'The Expatriate' (unpublished poem)
5. The majority of Jamaican leaders have since the 1950s been enunciating the multi-racial ethic usually at times of social crisis, on trips abroad, or in speeches exhorting co-ordinated social action. The motto 'Out of Many One People' was deliberately selected to express the ethic. Many Jamaicans, other than the committed Rastafarians, Black Power and Afro-Jamaican groups have expressed their doubts about the reality of the ethic in present-day Jamaica. 'Whatever people might say to the contrary, Jamaica is not a racially integrated society . . .' (Letter to Editor, *Daily Gleaner*, November 5, 1968; also 'I think those who wish to serve Jamaica can serve it best by hastening the passing of our much vaunted 'harmonious multi-racial society" the main function of which has been the destruction of the black man's soul' (Letter to Editor, *D.G.*, November 5, 1968). Other Jamaicans write about the 'campaign of hostility against fair-skinned Negro Jamaicans' (Letter, February 2, 1969) and against the assertion by black Jamaicans that Jamaica should be a 'black society' rather than a multi-racial one (Letter, *D.G.*, December 28, 1968)
6. Rex Nettleford: 'National Identity and Attitudes to Race', also West Indies Population Census (Jamaica) 1960, Kingston Jamaica Bulletin No. 20 Provisional (Department of Statistics)
   O. C. Francis: *The People of Modern Jamaica* (Kingston, Jamaica, Department of Statistics, 1963)
7. M. G. Smith: Lecture 'National Identity and Behaviour Patterns', 1965, Radio Education Unit, UWI, Kingston, Jamaica. M. G. Smith's pluralist interpretation of West Indian society has provoked a healthy debate between those who employ the pluralist model for analysis and those who see Jamaican and West Indian society as merely 'stratified'. See also *American Anthropologist*, Vol. 63,

No. 1 (Review by R. T. Smith of Social and Cultural Pluralism in the Caribbean); *Annals of the New York Academy of Science* 83 (Article on 'Social Stratification and Cultural Pluralism' by Lloyd Brathwaite); *Social and Economic Studies*, Vol. 15, No. 1, March 1966 (Article by H. I. McKenzie on 'The Plural Society Debate; some comments on a recent contribution')

8. Eric Williams: *British Historians and the West Indies*, PNM Publishing Company, Port of Spain, Trinidad, 1964, p. 134

9. B. Semmel: *Jamaican Blood and Victorian Conscience*, Cambridge, 1963

10. Eric Williams: *op. cit.*, p. 147 ff.

11. Elsa V. Goveia: *A Study on the Historiography of the West Indies to the end of the Nineteenth Century*, Mexico, 1956, p. 156

12. J. A. Froude: *The English in the West Indies or the Bow of Ulysses*, London, 1888
Elsa Goveia: *op. cit.*, p. 152 ff.
Eric Williams: *op. cit.*, p. 130–146
J. J. Thomas: *West Indies Fables* (with introduction by C. L. R. James, biographical note by Donald Wood), New Beacon Books Ltd., Port of Spain, Trinidad, 1969. This is a reprint of the 1889 publication by Unwin. J. J. Thomas was a coloured Trinidadian teacher who also published a *Creole Grammar* in 1869. H. P. Jacobs in a review of the new publication describes Thomas as a 'man of very considerable attainments and wide reading – certainly one of the most significant figures amongst New World Negroes of his day, whose vision extended to the awakening of Africa and the concept of co-operation amongst all of African descent.' (See *Daily Gleaner*, November 13, 1969)

13. Elsa Goveia: *op. cit.*, p. 155

14. Debate House of Assembly (Jamaica) 2nd Reading of Bill to abolish Legislature, November 16, 1865

15. Debate House of Assembly (Jamaica) final reading of Bill to abolish Legislature, November 21, 1865

16. *Public Opinion*, Vol. 1, 1937, *passim*

17. Rex Nettleford: 'Jamaican Black Power or Some Notes from the Horn' (above, p. 113)

18. L. Edward Brathwaite: Caribbean Critics in *New World Quarterly*, Vol. 5, Nos. 1–2, 1969, pp. 5–11

19. Louis James and Cameron King: 'The Poetry of Derek Walcott' in *Islands in Between* (Essays on West Indian literature), Oxford University Press, 1968, pp. 89–90

20. L. E. Brathwaite: *op. cit.*

21. *Ibid.*

22. Beryl Loftman Bailey: *Jamaican Creole Syntax, A Transformational Approach*, Cambridge University Press, 1966, p. 145

23. *e.g.* Thomas Wright in *Daily Gleaner*, November 4, 1969. 'For goodness' sake, let's stop talking about the "Jamaican language" unless, of course, we want to add yet another myth to the many we are so self-consciously and so pathetically producing' and elsewhere in his article 'we have inherited English a language which . . . has the advantage of being spoken in most modern industrial countries . . .'

24. Roger Mais, Vic Reid, Andrew Salkey, Orlando Patterson, Sylvia Wynter (prose), Barry Reckord, Sam Hillary, Trevor Rhone (plays), Louise Bennett, Dennis Scott, Edward Brathwaite *et al.* (poetry)

25. Gilberto Freyre: *The Masters and the Slaves*, Alfred A. Knopf, New York, 1946

26. L. E. Brathwaite: *op. cit.*

27. Elsa Goveia: *Slave Society in the British Leeward Islands at the end of the Eighteenth Century*, Yale University Press, 1965 (This serves as an excellent case study for Caribbean plantation slavery)

28. Kenneth Ramchand: Lecture to Jamaica Pen Club on McKay

29. Quoted in *Independence Anthology of Jamaican Literature*, Kingston, Jamaica, 1962. Introduced by Peter Abrahams

30. Speech by Leslie Ashenheim, April, 1966, deprecating the 'castration of minorities, the prostitution of the Senate and the bastardization of the Cabinet'

31. *Daily Gleaner*, November 13–26, 1969 (Reports of Attorney General's speech in House, Statements, Letters, Editorials)

32. *Ibid.*

33. Elsa Goveia: *op. cit.* as in Reference 27

34. Quoted in *Jamaican Heritage*, Govt. of Jamaica, 1969, p. 44

35. *Jamaica Journal*, Institute of Jamaica, Vol. 1, No. 1, 1968

36. Wendell Bell: *Jamaican Leaders' Political Attitudes in a New Nation*, University of California Press, 1964, pp. 37–49

37. Elsa Goveia: *op. cit.* as in Ref. 11 (p. 173)

38. Charles Wagley: 'Plantation America – A Culture Sphere' in *Caribbean Studies: A Symposium*, ed. by Vera Rubin, University of Washington Press, 1960

39. Orlando Patterson: *The Sociology of Slavery*, McGibbon & Kee, 1967

40. Charles Wagley: *op. cit.*, p. 7

41. *Ibid.*

42. *Ibid.*

43. O. C. Francis: *op. cit.*

44. John Mordecai: '*The West Indies: The Federal Negotiations*', Allen & Unwin, London, 1968

45. Rex Nettleford: 'African Redemption . . .' (above, p. 39)

46. See *Daily Gleaner*, Saturday, March 23, 1968, announcing Jamaica's acceptance of the Caribbean Free Trade Agreement in terms of resolution passed at the Commonwealth Heads of Government Conference held in Barbados in October, 1967
47. Elsa Goveia: *op. cit.* as in Ref. 27 (p. 177)
48. Wendell Bell: *op. cit.*
49. Same as Ref. 34
50. Budget Speech by Michael Manley, Leader of the Opposition, Jamaica House of Representatives; *Daily Gleaner*, June 5, 1969
51. Mervyn Morris: *op. cit.*
52. See Kenneth Ramchand: 'Aborigines, Their Role in West Indian Literature', *Jamaica Journal*, Vol. 3, No. 4, December 1969. Ramchand insists that though Edgar Mitelholzer and H. G. DeLisser wrote about Amerindians in their novels it is not until Harris's *Palace of the Peacock* in 1960 that the 'historical Indian' was made to 'come alive' in a way that 'no other West Indian novelist or historian has been bold enough to imagine'. The far-reaching implications for conventional approaches to West Indian historiography, sociological analysis and cultural delineation are boldly suggested in Wilson Harris's Writer-in-Residence lectures delivered at the UWI Mona Campus in late January, 1970 (*q.v.*)
53. Sylvia Wynter: 'Bernado de Balbuena: Epic Poet and Abbot of Jamaica 1562–1627', Part 2, in *Jamaica Journal*, Vol. 3, No. 4, December, 1969, pp. 21–22. The relevant passage reads in part: 'The Maroon legend which lays claim to both African and Arawak antecedents is true not in its detailed and fallible fact; but in its core. The question as to how much of *racial* fusion there really was, is irrelevant; what is important is that the myth itself, which embodies 'the self consciousness and memory of mankind' has sprung from the deeds of both peoples; . . .'

Postscript

1. The nineteen fifties also witnessed controversy over beauty contests. See Essay above on 'National Identity and Attitudes to Race', footnote, p. 26. See also article 'Different Types Beauty Contest – The Answer – Afro-Jamaican Suggestion Not Ideal', by Clifton Segree, *Star*, May 30, 1967
2. *Daily Gleaner*, August 10, 1967. Front-page report, 'Omission of Jean Rerrie from final six criticised, Changes in Judging Miss Jamaica Contests Urged at Conference'
3. *Ibid.*
4. *Daily Gleaner*, August 18, 1967 (Letter from L. P. Davidson)
5. *Daily Gleaner*, August 22, 1967 (Letter from Sefton Johnson)

6. *Daily Gleaner*, August 24, 1967 (Letter from Ken Maxwell)
7. *Daily Gleaner*, September 7, 1967 (Letter from John Andrade)
8. Thomas Wright: *Daily Gleaner*, August 24, 1967, 'Candidly Yours'
9. *Sunday Gleaner*, August 6, 1967 (Column by Political Reporter)
10. *Sunday Gleaner*, March 17, 1968 (Editorial, 'Race and Ideas')
11. *Ibid.* Also see *Daily Gleaner*, Editorial, March 13, 1968, which reads in part: 'We do not understand why the Jamaica Olympic Association has taken so long to come to the obvious conclusion that Jamaica which is committed to multi-racialism and to basic human dignity could not turn its back on these principles and compete at Mexico with a South African team entered in these circumstances. It is not just a matter of sport: it is a question of the national interest. In the international world Jamaica has already stated that its national interest includes total committal to the current struggle around the world for the universal recognition that all men are created equal regardless of the colour of their skins'. The position is a typically liberal one and does not depend on Jamaica's perception as herself as a 'black' country for it to be held by Jamaicans in general
12. Compare the speech which Jean Genet gives Felicity in his controversial play 'The Blacks' (produced in Jamaica at the Creative Arts Theatre, UWI, February, 1970). The contradictions and irony of the new black aesthetics are here cleverly expressed:
    FELICITY (to the White Queen): 'Whatever is gentle and kind and good and tender will be black. Milk will be black, sugar, rice, the sky, doves, hope, will be black. So will the opera to which we shall go, blacks that we are, in black Rolls Royces to hail black kings, to hear brass bands beneath chandeliers of black crystal . . .'
13. See Article 'Learning from the Russians' by Leonard Schapiro in *Encounter*, October, 1969, p. 63 ff.
14. See Budget Debate, 1969, House of Representatives, Jamaica
15. Report of annual PNP Conference in *Daily Gleaner*, October 27, 1969, 'Economic Nationalism is PNP Policy'
16. *e.g. Caribbean Business News*, December, 1969, Lead Article 'Jamaica's Economy Showing Flaw'; *Observer Review* (UK) of 23 November, 1969, Article 'The Two Jamaicas (A challenging personal report on the dangerous problems of a tourist's paradise)' by Colin McGlashan
    The Jamaican government is sensitive about such criticisms. At the beginning of the 1970s the Government pointedly declared the achievements of the period since independence and particularly since January, 1969. The Jamaican Prime Minister, well known for his 'Get the Facts' sessions all over the countryside, refuted

'Rumours . . . that the country was making no economic progress'.
See *Sunday Gleaner*, February 1, 1970

17. Arthur Schlesinger, Jr., Article 'The Lowering Hemisphere' in *The Atlantic*, January, 1970, p. 77 ff.

18. See *The American Dilemma*, by J. J. Servan-Schreiber, Atheneum, N.Y., 1969, p. 179 ff.

    NOTE: the matter of an elitist University education is also a very important factor in current discussions about the reform and modernization of the University of the West Indies

19. Both Jamaican political parties have expressed a commitment to mass education. The government of the day has announced its intention to make education serve the masses rather than an exclusive elite. Hence the comprehensive schools, technical high schools and junior secondary institutions. These are intended to supersede the old grammar schools hitherto oriented to a classical form of education. Government's plan to 'abandon' the traditional secondary (i.e. grammar schools) altogether has met with mixed feelings. An evening newspaper's editorial summed up the matter as follows: 'The major error of both PNP and JLP governments has been to force unsuitable children through these schools, instead of just providing more schools for those who could benefit from them. Such egalitarianism just resulted in a serious lowering of standards. Comprehensive schools must be provided and fewer and better secondary (i.e. grammar schools) for those requiring a professional or liberal education'. (*The Star*, February 10, 1970)

20. *Daily Gleaner*, September 8, 1969. Report of Speech by Edward Seaga, Minister of Finance and Planning

21. *e.g.* the 1970 National Exhibition of Paintings had a very large collection of works by Rastafarians. See Essay above on 'African Redemption . . .'

INDEX

254